# THERE IS NO SUCH THING
# AS A TYPICAL LIBRARIAN

# THERE IS NO SUCH THING
# AS A TYPICAL LIBRARIAN

Steven John Antonuccio

East of the Mountains and West of the Sun

RHYOLITE PRESS LLC
Colorado Springs, Colorado

✺

Published in the United States of America by Rhyolite Press  LLC
P.O. Box 60144
Colorado Springs, Colorado 80960
www.rhyolitepress.com

Antonuccio, Steven John

## THERE IS NO SUCH THING
## AS A TYPICAL LIBRARIAN

1st edition: April, 2019

Library of Congress Control Number: 2019935888

ISBN 978-1-943829-19-4

✺

PRINTED IN THE UNITED STATES OF AMERICA

Cover design, book design/layout by Donald R. Kallaus
Author photo, © 2019, Donald R. Kallaus

"A library outranks any other one thing a community can do to benefit its people. It is a never failing spring in the desert."

—Andrew Carnegie

**About the Cover:**

The main entrance of the Colorado Springs Carnegie Library located at 21 W. Kiowa Street. On land donated by the founder of Colorado Springs, William J. Palmer, and construction funding by the Andrew Carnegie Library Fund, this structure was completed in 1905. This crown jewel of the Pikes Peak Library District is but one of 18 Carnegie Libraries still in operation in the state of Colorado. Built of granite, marble, sandstone and brick in the Neo-classical style, it not only houses space for volumes of books, but also an auditorium, a reference room, and Special Collections; maps, photographs, manuscripts and periodicals. The south facing portion of the structure is semi-circular and fully glazed for an extraordinary view of Pikes Peak. It is listed on the National Register of Historic Places. A visit to this beautiful library is an absolute must.

Cover photograph by Don Kallaus

# CONTENTS

*Foreword*                                                                                    xi

*Acknowledgments*                                                                    xv

## STORIES

A Third of My Time In Libraries                                                      1

Library Science: The Last Refuge of an English Major          5

Dandelion Wine                                                                             9

A Poster Child for Assimilation                                                  13

A Righteous Man                                                                        29

Bodyguard Unseen                                                                     35

A Family Portrait of Strangers                                                  41

Rocky Mountain High                                                                43

Party University                                                                          47

A Smile and a Shoeshine                                                          51

Little London                                                                              55

A Quaker General                                                                      57

The Best Boss I Ever Had                                                         63

Watching the Detective                                                            67

My Own Channel                                                                       77

Back to School                                                                          81

The Storytellers of Colorado Springs                                       85

The Bluebloods of the Pikes Peak Region                              87

Mike's Peak                                                                              93

Bunnicula Lives                                                                         97

Harvest of Love                                                                       101

Scenes of War                                                                         109

The Alexander Brothers                                                          117

Everybody Welcome     125

The Cowboy Way     133

The Man Who Saved the Bell     139

The Finest Educator in Colorado     143

Name Dropping:
Some of the Notable People I Worked With     147

Kristallnacht: The Night of Broken Glass     151

The Gentle Archivist     157

*Photo Section* (family)     159

*Photo Section* (non-family)     166

A Detective Story     173

The Greater Barrier     177

Veterans Day     179

Pay It Forward     181

The Fairy God Mother of the Arts     185

The Shivers Foundation     188

Cal Otto     193

Lieutenant General Albert Patton Clark     197

The Photographers     205

Falling in Love with Mabel Barbee Lee     209

Her Furious Angels     213

The Importance of Volunteers     217

Leaving Colorado     221

Falling in Love with Pueblo     209

The Library Next Door     233

The Book People     237

My Dog Ate My Library Book     241

Type 2 Diabetes                                            245

A Confederacy of Dunces                                    247

A Revolution in the Public Library Customer Service        251

The Booksecutioner                                         255

Dogpatch, Colorado                                         259

Eliminate the Primitive Devices                            263

My Kids Are Smarter Than Me                                267

Less Than A Dog's Life                                     269

My Trip to Spain with Naiely                               273

Why I Love Libraries                                       283

Where have You Gone Andrew Carnegie?                       287


*Video Links*                                              291

*Bibliography*                                             297

*Index*                                                    299

# FOREWORD

Steve piqued my interest when he said he was writing a book about being a librarian. At first, I couldn't imagine what that would read like, but I trusted Steve to do a good job nonetheless. And, he didn't disappoint me. This book is mini-autobiography of a video producer-turned-librarian. I loved the book!

As I was explaining to folks about what I was reading, I would always end with "it is just a good read!" Translated: "Don't trust my description to give the book justice, you just have to read it." Needless to say, those I have talked to can hardly wait until this piece of work is published. They also won't be disappointed.

Let's start with the title: *There Is No Such Thing as a Typical Librarian: 30 Years Working In Public and Academic Libraries.* Who wants to read about a librarian, you ask? Don't let the title fool you. Steve is an excellent writer who has had great luck in the jobs/professions he chose. Not too many people can say that they loved all the jobs they've held. And, not many people can successfully meld a story about those jobs into an autobiography that grabs the attention of the reader. To my surprise, I couldn't put the book down and couldn't stop talking about the book to others, which has piqued their interest as well.

Steve starts with his personal family history that covers several generations on both his maternal and paternal sides. On his father's side came Sicilian immigrants and on this mother's side came Spanish immigrants. Both families were all hard-working, immigrant folks who ended up in California. It was definitely clear that Steve grew up with a Cleaver-style home life; and Steve's pride in his lineage is evident in this book as is his pride in working in libraries.

This book is a potpourri of family history, mini-history of Colorado Springs, mini-biographies of notables in Colorado Springs such as Fannie Mae Duncan, nightclub owner of the African American Cotton Club; the Alexander brothers of the Alexander Film Company in Colorado Springs; the Venetucci's and their Pumpkin Patch. Add to all of these were Steve's recollections of video documentaries on Spencer Penrose, Charles Tutt, veterans, astronauts, cowboys, and the list goes on.

How did this happen so effectively? Steve's background as a video producer, particularly for the Pikes Peak Library District, stood prominent in this book. He produced many video portraits of people and events for PPLD's cable channel; some were award winners. That, coupled with the fact that Steve has turned out to be a great storyteller with such a skill in the ease of writing, explains it all. He takes the readers through emotions, such as outright laughter, tears, pride, et cetera in the privacy of their own setting. I can't tell you the times my eyes welled up in tears nor the times I burst out in laughter scaring my dog, Sophe Sae. In fact, I still am laughing about the story of the Chihuahua and the Pitbull. I also enjoyed the titles of each of Steve's chapters allowing me a moment to second guess what would be said in that chapter.

Steve's writing style makes the book. He has an uncanny ability of linking his experiences or descriptions of other's experiences to books he read, songs he heard, and/or movies he saw. Those connections are icing on the cake for the reader. Steve's love of Ray Bradbury's books and Ray, himself, is so poignant and is reflected throughout the book. I was so moved reading Steve's response to Bradbury's passing as well as the passing of Sol

Zlochower, Steve's mentor and a bigger-than life person whom I also had the pleasure of knowing. Add to this is the story behind the plaque in Canar, Spain, dedicated to Steve's great-grandmother.

When Steve starts writing about his experiences as a branch manager in the Pueblo City-County Library District in the poorest neighborhood, it drives why public libraries are so important to our communities. Again, these stories told by a true storyteller are touching and very effective. They absolutely warmed my heart in terms of why we are dedicated to serving our communities, no matter how you define community.

One of the real pluses to this book is that Steve leaves the reader with video links on YouTube to many of the videos mentioned throughout the book. That is my next project—checking out those YouTube videos.

Who should read this book? Anyone and everyone. This book is recommended for Colorado history buffs, people living in the communities of Colorado Springs and Pueblo, librarians and library staff anywhere, any lover of libraries to include "The Book People," MLIS students and faculty, anyone in the 540 Billionaires Club, and anyone who just wants "a good read." . . . It is just that, a good read.

—Dr. Camila A. Alire
   Dean Emerita, University of New Mexico & Colorado State University
   2009-2010 President, American Library Association

# ACKNOWLEGEMENTS

"Facts are the Enemy of the Truth"
—Don Quixote

Miguel De Cervantes penned this statement for Don Quixote in his classic novel in 1605. Truer words have never been said, and I have done my best to tell the truth in this autobiography about my experiences working in a public library. However, some of the facts may be the enemy of the truth as I experienced it. The names of some of the people were changed for obvious reasons. My words are 100% the truth from my heart and perhaps 95% the actual facts.

The majority of the people I write about are no longer with us. It was a privilege to have met these amazing people and to share with them a short moment in time. I only hope that I am doing them justice by telling their life stories.

The way I have structured this book is that you can find a link to most of the programs and documentaries I mention on Youtube. A chapter by chapter index to Youtube is at the end of the book. I am also interested in your feedback and you can reach me at my personal email at anton1492@ gmail.com.

I dedicate this book to:

- My two daughters, Rachel and Laura whose great intelligence was inherited from their mother and who are both self-suffi-cient, hard-working lawyers. I love them with all my heart, and I could not be prouder of who they are as adults.

- My parents, Oliver and Soledad "Sally" Antonuccio and my three siblings, David, Mark, and Lisa, since we had the great fortune to share the same wonderful childhood.
- My "significant other" Naiely Smyer and the child we share and love, Max our German Shepherd mix dog. When I met Naiely seven years ago, she brought Max into our relationship. I often tell her that as long as Max is alive, I will be faithful to her. I could never risk that special relationship I have with Max—and Naiely. As of this writing, Max is still alive and well and I have kept my word . . . and that is the facts and the truth.
- I would also like to thank my editor Sharyn Markus and her help with the final book. She is a retired English teacher, and it is always helpful to have an English teacher look over your shoulder and make sure your grammar and sentence structure is correct.
- I would also like to thank another retired English teacher Kay Esmiol. Kay helped Fannie Mae Duncan write her autobiogra-phy and she is a good friend who made a critical suggestion on how to open this book. You can't have enough English teachers looking over your shoulder when you write a book,
- I would also like to thank Stephen Adams with the *Friends of the Colorado Springs Library* for creating the index.
- And finally I would like to thank my publisher, Don Kallaus of Rhyolite Press, who was the first one to read my book and who always believed in this project.

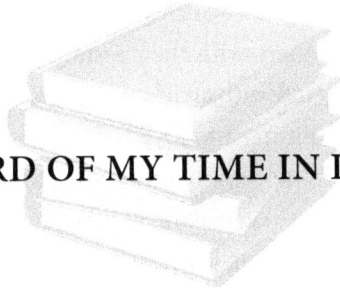

# A THIRD OF MY TIME IN LIBRARIES

"In the west, he spent a third of his time in the pool halls, a third of his time in juvenile hall, and a third in the public library."

—*On the Road* by Jack Kerouac as he describes the childhood of Dean Moriarty

The last year I spent working in libraries was as the manager of the Pueblo West Branch Library for the Pueblo City-County Library District. I was asked to return to work, after I retired in 2014, to help train a new manager for a full year contract. Although an experienced manager in other endeavors, Susan Wolf had just gotten her MLS degree and I spent the year training her how to manage the Pueblo West Branch. It was a challenging year and we worked hard together to solve several of our issues dealing with our teen customers.

After 3 p.m. each weekday, The Pueblo West Library was a petri dish for the study of juvenile behavior. It was a beautiful 25,000 square foot modern branch, with great meeting room space, study rooms, and a separate children's library with a story room and an outdoor patio. It is a seven-million-dollar branch that serves the community of Pueblo West and was part of the Pueblo City-County Library District. It was a great place to work, and we had some of the best customers in this affluent rural community. When we opened to the public at 9 a.m. our patrons included mostly retired senior citizens who loved to engage our staff in pleasant conversation. They were always polite and gracious and gladly shared stories from their past working life and diverse human experiences. In the morning, homeschoolers used our meeting rooms, and their kids were generally extremely polite. They were well behaved, and they said, "Yes, Sir," "No, Sir," and "Thank you for helping me." They were such a pleasure to work with. Around 10:30 a.m. when our Storytime began, young mothers with their toddlers came in to teach their kids the joy of reading. They left with armfuls of picture books, and their cute little kids were always entertaining and loved coming to the library. They got so excited when they found the right book. If you came to the Pueblo West branch in the morning, it was like looking at a Norman Rockwell picture of seniors, young families, and lifelong learners enjoying the many resources of this wonderful public library.

Then, the clock struck 3 p.m., I felt the staff's growing apprehension. Right next door to the library was a charter school that included kids from sixth through twelfth grades. At 3:09 a wave of adolescent humanity descended upon the library at one time. Through our windows, we watched them jay-walking across busy Joe Martinez Boulevard. Some of them ran to get inside of our library. Not to learn, not to read, not to study, but to commandeer our computers and get on Facebook or to play video games or to hog our study rooms and scribble graffiti on the walls, socialize, and fight, or to ride their skateboards and scooters in the library. I viewed it as a personal conspiracy to make me feel ten years older! From 3 p.m. to around 6 p.m., the library transformed into a juvenile detention facility, very similar to the atmosphere in the 1950's film *Blackboard Jungle*. Starting at 5 p.m. they were picked up by their parents coming home from work, or they finally walked home for din-ner. Although it tested my staff and my patience, I loved seeing young people in our library. I told my staff and reminded myself. "At least they are coming here; many libraries have trouble getting teens through the door."

Although we didn't have that problem of getting teens in the library, we just needed to find a way to channel that energy. In the year I spent at Pueblo West Library, I probably averaged a suspension a month. I made 30 phone calls to the police or 911 and two incident reports a week. An incident report was filled out every time something was stolen or vandalized or when the police were called for an emergency. Eighty percent of those incidents were related to our teens. By the time I left my job at Pueblo West, we had turned the situation around. We hired a magnificent teen librarian, Rachel Salazar, who created teen activities every week day from 3 p.m. to 5 p.m. Rachel averaged 30 teens a day for our activities. Twenty-five-year-old Rachel looked seventeen, and her youthful appearance and non-judgmental attitude allowed her to relate to our teens easily. She had lived in Pueblo West since she was a little girl, and her parents brought her to the library for Storytime. The good news was Rachel was very successful at getting the teens to participate in our programs; however, they were still adolescents who brought their drama and angst to our library. As the saying goes, be careful what you wish for, because it might just come true. Because of Rachel's success, our teen participation tripled in a few months, but adult patrons complained about the noise in the afternoon and that there were too many teens in the library. I told them we were happy the kids were in the library, and we were doing our best to provide them with programs. I also suggested to the adults, if they had a flexible schedule, to get to the library early and to leave before 3 p.m. or come by after 6 p.m. when it got a little quieter.

My experience dealing with teenagers and their problems at my branch library was the ultimate in personal Karma. As a seventeen year-old junior at Cherry Creek High School in Denver, I hung out with my friends in the school library during the lunch hour. It was a place to socialize, to flirt, and to just-be noisy teenagers. We played paper football at the table, passed notes, and made plans to drive to Cherry Creek Reservoir after school to drink beer or to smoke pot and to watch the so-called "submarine races." The poor librarian always looked beleaguered as we messed around in her library with no interest in studying. One day she approached me and told me I was suspended from the library for a week. She said I was making too much noise, and she needed to teach me a lesson.

Forty-five years later, when parents visited me to try to get their child reinstated, I always told them that same story, that I had been suspended from my high school library. "It is not the end of the world for your child to be suspended from the library. Look at me. I was suspended from my high school library and now I'm the branch manager."

When one of my employees was retiring, she cleared out her desk and found some printed photographs taken from the library security camera ten years earlier. It showed teenagers riding on skateboards and scooters and generally being rowdy in our library. She pointed out that nothing had changed in ten years; we just had new teenagers, and these kids in this picture are now 25-year-old responsible adults, who could be employed as cops, soldiers, teachers, and they could even be young parents bringing their kids to Storytime.

Time goes on, and teenagers become adults. In my case this teenager became a manager of a branch library and a walking monument to Karma. I now realize I deserved all the grief I had to deal with, in terms of rowdy teen behavior, at the Pueblo West Branch Library! If my high school librarian is reading this, I'm sure she is laughing at me with glee and even with a little bit of spite in her heart.

# LIBRARY SCIENCE:
## THE LAST REFUGE OF AN ENGLISH MAJOR

Nobody plans to be a librarian when they are a kid. It is not a profession most children pretend to be when they are playing with their friends in the backyard. They play cowboys and Indians, or cops and robbers or soldier or astronaut or professional athletes. By the time a child starts grade school, they usually have some answer to what they want to be when they grow up. A football player, a nurse, a doctor, a fireman, a soldier. No one ever gives the answer librarian. For me, I wanted to be a running back in the NFL. Fortunately for me and the NFL, that dream never happened.

Library Science is the last refuge of English Majors. At a library staff meeting, if you throw a rock, you will most likely hit an English major. Once an English major realizes no one is going to pay them to write the great American novel, they usually need to find a job that will pay their bills. If they have a family, they need to find a job that has good benefits and will allow them the flexibility to spend time with their kids. Jobs with defined pensions are rare, and most library jobs are city or county government jobs with pensions and decent benefits.

I've spent almost my entire working career in libraries. Almost 35 years working in academic and public libraries. Like most young people, I didn't consider it as profession when I graduated from the University of Colorado in 1977 with a degree in Communications with a radio/tv/film emphasis.

I wanted to be a filmmaker. I was very lucky, for most of my career, I was able to combine my training as a librarian and a documentary filmmaker. I met and worked with some amazing people and I have never been bored in my job, with the exception of my time spent sitting in meetings. Working with the public is always a challenge, but as I always told my staff, we have the best customer service job of any profession. We are not the Department of Motor Vehicles, where people spend more money than they can afford, and they are forced to wait in long lines. We serve people who 99% of the time are very polite and thankful for the services we provide. We work with seniors and young parents and children who genuinely need our help. For the most part, we work in beautiful modern facilities that have climate control and comfortable staff areas, meeting rooms, and offices. We are not roofers working in 100-degree weather doing back breaking work. Although working with books and other materials requires lifting and some strength, the physical requirements of our job are not debilitating. The Pueblo West library was a 25,000 square foot facility that required me to walk several miles a day, which was actually good for me in my attempt to stay healthy and drop the extra 30 pounds I was always fighting to lose.

A library staff consists of a diverse group of people. The minimum educational requirement is a high school diploma. Most of our material handlers (shelvers) have a high school degree and some college. Our library assistants and library specialist require a bachelor's degree to get hired. The highest level of educated employee are the librarians, which normally requires a Master's in Library Science. As Doctor Science use to say on NPR, I have a Master's degree in science. Sure, it is Library Science, and I never had to learn the periodic table, but it is a real Master's degree. Most MLS programs are two years and you can accomplish it on-line without ever stepping into the classroom or visiting the home campus. I received my Master's in Library Science through an extension program at Emporia State in 1991 when I was 36 years old. The program was offered in Denver as an intensive weekend program and the first class graduated with around 100 students. Like most of the students in the program at the time, I worked full time while going to school. I took all my classes in Denver and I have yet to set foot in Emporia, Kansas.

I have known librarians that have had a variety of backgrounds and bachelor's degrees. Although most librarians have an undergraduate English degree, I have known librarians who started out as history majors, lawyers, engineers, art majors, music majors, (real) science majors, military officers, almost every undergraduate degree and background you can imagine. That is why there are **NO** typical librarians and being a librarian is a wonderful profession. The diverse backgrounds of librarians have made for an interesting group of co-workers. I knew a librarian in graduate school who had killed a grizzly bear in Alaska. She was visiting her Uncle in the wilderness of Alaska, and she had to kill a grizzly bear to protect herself and her Uncle. She had the grizzly bear's male organ preserved and would proudly show it to us during class. Most people did not go directly from undergraduate school to graduate school to get their Master's in Library Science. Many of them, like myself, got their master's degrees after working in a library for several years and realizing they needed an MLS if they wanted to make more money or pursue a job in management.

One of the more unusual situations was a fellow student in the Denver program and a good friend of mine named Dave Goetzman. Dave was in library school during the first gulf war and was allowed to continue his weekend education while fighting in the war. Dave was a naval officer who was stationed at NORAD in Cheyenne Mountain in Colorado Springs. It is unusual to have a naval officer in Colorado, but every service was represented in Cheyenne Mountain and Dave and his family lived in Colorado Springs. He wanted to leave the Navy, so he could stay in one place and raise his two sons and that is why he was in graduate school to become a librarian. About a year into the program the first gulf war started, and Saddam Hussein decided at that time to try to expand the war by launching SCUD missiles at Israel. If you remember the early CNN coverage of the war, the SCUD missiles were a serious threat to Israel and they were a terror weapon that did reach the civilian population of Israel.

Dave, who was half Jewish, spent his working days, Monday through Friday, in Cheyenne Mountain monitoring the SCUD launches into Israel. When he monitored a missile launched from Iraq, he got on a secure phone with Israel, and gave the Israeli army the important information on the flight path and location of the launch vehicles. He told me that he thought the brass at Cheyenne Mountain made him specifically the contact with Israel, because of his Jewish heritage. He was certain his superior officers thought it would help with their rapport with this important ally.

As the SCUD missiles fell into Israel almost daily, Dave told me that the Israeli Army came very close to invading Iraq to destroy the SCUD missile launchers. Had they entered the war, other Arab countries might have allied with Iraq in their war effort. He used his best diplomacy to get Israel to trust the United States to destroy the SCUD missile launchers. He would then help The United States Air Force to direct their smart bombs at the launch targets he identified on his radar.

The first Gulf War lasted around six months. From August 1990 to February 1991. Dave never missed a class during the war. He would work his shift Monday through Friday, fighting the Gulf War at his computer in Cheyenne mountain and then drive up to class on Friday evening through Sunday morning. It was an excellent example of how a soldier could fight a modern war and not have to change their normal life schedule. Dave Goetzman, a library student in Colorado, was part of that successful effort to help Israel defend their country and the United States to win the first Gulf War. As a result of his successful efforts, he probably saved thousands of lives, he received a combat medal for his efforts.

As I said before, there is no such thing as a typical librarian. We all have eclectic backgrounds and bring our own individual experiences to the job. It is a profession that truly draws from all backgrounds. All through my career, I've always told people that getting my Master's in Library Science was one of the best decision I've ever made, and believe me, I have made my share of bad decisions.

# DANDELION WINE

When I reflect on my youth and the people I admired the most, I realize that I was meant to be a librarian. I didn't consider it as a profession at the time, but I fell in love with reading in the seventh grade at Patrick Henry Junior High School in Sunnyvale, California. It was the last half of the Sixties, and I lived in Santa Clara Valley, an area that eventually became Silicon Valley. At that time there were orchards and farmland between the asphalt freeways. In fact, my grandfather, Eugenio Calvo, had been a farmer in Mountain View for most of his adult life. He grew tomatoes and string beans and still owned several acres of farmland on San Antonio Road. Today, Mountain View is the headquarters for Google, and you can't find a single acre of farmland in the valley since the land is too valuable.

Both my parents were teachers, who met at San Jose State Teachers' College after World War II. My dad was in college on the G.I. bill and was five years older than my mother. During his freshman year, my dad saw this beautiful young woman standing in line waiting to register for an art class. He impulsively stood behind her to take the same class, hoping that he would have a chance to meet her. That woman, Soledad "Sally" Calvo, eventually became his wife and my mother. When they started their family, like most women in the 1950's, my mother quit her teaching job to raise her children. Needing more money than a teacher's salary could provide, my father quit his job teaching auto mechanics and went to work for General Motors in San Francisco. They eventually bought a modest three-bedroom home in Santa Clara and raised their four children.

My eighth-grade English teacher, Miss Mason, who was a young woman in her twenties at the time, inspired me to read. She introduced me to the science fiction author Ray Bradbury, and I immediately fell in love with his books. I had read *Martian Chronicles, The Illustrated Man, Fahrenheit 451*, and *The Golden Apple of the Sun* before I discovered the book that changed my life, *Dandelion Wine*. It was a semi-autobiographical book on Ray Bradbury's early life in Waukegan, Illinois, or what he called "Greentown" in his fictional tale. The protagonist was a 12-year-old boy named Douglas Spaulding, whose life was based on the young Ray Bradbury.

I was fortunate to be reading *Dandelion Wine* when I was around the same age as the protagonist. Douglas and I experienced together many of the angsts and wonders of life together. Early in the book he experienced a personal awakening. For the first time in his life, Doug realized he was actually alive, and that he had the free will and the imagination to create his own destiny. It wasn't a sexual awakening; it was more of a self-awakening to the miracle of life and how rare it was to be alive. The book was a series of life experiences about a boy growing up in the 1920's. Reading that book was a religious experience for me. Just like Douglas, I had my whole life ahead of me; and I realized what a wonderful gift it was to be alive. Looking back on my past 63 years I have few regrets. I have made my mistakes, and I am as flawed as any person. However, I have always appreciated my moment in time and the many opportunities and benefits I have had in my life. By the time I entered the ninth grade, I had read every book that Ray Bradbury had written at that time. As a science fiction fan, I expanded my reading to Asimov, Heinlein, Vonnegut, and Arthur C. Clarke. While I loved the hard science fiction, I never really got into the fantasy genre or any of the works written by Tolkien.

Although I don't recall how I ended up with Ray Bradbury's mailing address in Los Angeles, I assume a teacher might have given it to me, I had a way to personally contact him. I decided to write him and tell him how much I loved his books and specifically how *Dandelion Wine* had such an impact on my short life. To my amazement he wrote me back and told me that he appreciated having a young fan like me. I don't know how often a 13-year-old boy has contact with his hero, but connecting with Ray Bradbury, even if it was just a letter in his own hand, was an amazing moment for me. I cherished that letter and continued to read everything he wrote. Ray Bradbury was always a proponent of libraries. He wrote *Fahrenheit 451* in the basement of UCLA's Lawrence Clark Powell Library on a manual type-writer. *Fahrenheit 451* told the story of the importance of reading and how history could be changed by a fascist government who destroyed books. Since Ray grew up during the time Nazis burned books in Germany, he knew how it really could happen. *Fahrenheit 451* is the definitive cautionary tale on the importance of libraries and academic freedom and free access to books.

In *Dandelion Wine* Bradbury wrote one chapter entitled "The Time Machine." It was about an older man who had lived most his life in the 19th century and told stories about his own experiences with the many historic events he had seen in the 1800's. He was a living time machine. I was lucky to be in the "time machine" business since I produced "video portraits" for the Pikes Peak Library District. I was recording the local history of the Pikes Peak region through video interviews with several area residents. It was an incredible job that combined my interest in documentaries and local history.

At the 1990 American Library Association (ALA) conference in Chicago, I finally met Ray Bradbury. I had just turned 35 years old, and I was produc-ing video portraits for the Pikes Peak Library District. The ALA invited me to do a program for a couple hundred people at the conference, and I gladly showed examples of my documentary work. Ray Bradbury also presented a program at that same conference. He was in his early seventies and was returning home to Illinois. I introduced myself and told him how important his book *Dandelion Wine* was to me. I told him I had written to him when I was younger and that he had replied. He was probably just being polite, but he said he remembered me. It was a great moment in my adult life.

I don't read many books multiple times, but I do read *Dandelion Wine* every summer. Like a fine wine, *Dandelion Wine* just gets better with time. As of this writing, I have lived through 63 summers and I appreciate every day. I enjoy new experiences and appreciate both the pain and the joy of my life. It has not always been easy, but my connection to Douglas Spaulding and to Ray Bradbury has been my inspiration for every moment in my life.

# A POSTER CHILD FOR ASSIMILATION

I have always been curious about people and their life experiences. I wanted to know what made them who they are, and what obstacles they had to overcome in their lives. My mother was one of the most disciplined people I have ever met. Much more disciplined than I am. In a very short time, she went from being a poor little Spanish-speaking farm girl to a refined college-educated woman without a detectable accent. I've always said my mother was a poster child for assimilation. When she was born in 1926 in Mountain View, California, if you were a first generation American, you did everything possible to shed your family heritage and assimilate as a United States citizen. Although her first language was Spanish, she never spoke it at home when I was a child. She spoke Spanish to her parents, but she lived during a time when people looked down upon you if you were clearly immigrants. It has gotten much better since then, but in some ways, things haven't changed that much—sadly.

My mother was a very beautiful woman. In her high school picture, she looked like Rita Hayworth, another woman of Spanish heritage. My Mother's parents' story was a remarkable journey of immigrants, with minimal formal education, who worked very hard and succeeded in a country that viewed them as working-class peasants.

Although a fascinating tale, I don't think my maternal grandparents' story was unique in terms of the courage displayed by other immigrants of their generation and hardworking immigrants today. The United States is a remarkable country that rewards hard work and still provides immigrants with great opportunities. I have also worked hard, but I don't have the drive my grandparents or my parents had.

My grandfather, Eugenio Calvo, was born in the small village of Sotillo De Las Palomas, in the province of Toledo, Spain. His journey to the United States was an amazing tale of courage and toughness. My early memories were of this dirt farmer who visited our home to plant tomatoes and string beans in our backyard. His thick Spanish accent reminded me of Ricky Ricardo. By the time I was born in 1955, my grandfather had already achieved his success in life. He was born in 1898, and at 57 years old he was retired with a small fortune. When he sold his ten acres in Mountain View in 1968 for approximately one million dollars, he created a sizeable nest egg for our family. My grandparents were very generous and shared their good fortune with their children. They also loved the outdoors and spent most of their retirement at their second home in Burney, California. They loved to fish and to be with their grandchildren and to take us fishing as well. During the long drives to northern California, I asked my grandfather many questions about his youth. He shared with me many stories about leaving Spain, working in Hawaii as an indentured servant, and eventually relocating to the United States.

I have a photo of my ten-year-old grandfather and his family, shot around 1907 in Sotillo De Las Palomas. He is surrounded by his siblings and his mother, aunt, and grandmother. It was the last photo of his childhood. A time when his grandmother and parents smothered him with love. He was a bit of a mischievous child. Having a good arm, he was very accurate throwing rocks. The Catholic church in the center of town was his favorite target. He loved hurling rocks at the church's bell tower and ringing the bell. The priest always dashed out of the church and chased him home, where he hid in his grandmother's arms. He was an indulged and spoiled child who suddenly had to become a man at the tender age of 12. The abrupt end of his childhood was a bitter memory for him.

Most Spanish children had heard stories of adventure in the new world since Columbus sailed to America. The colonization of Mexico, Central and South America started out as dreams in the heads of Spanish children who eventually left their home country for adventures. My grandfather was no different. When the Hawaiian sugar cane companies handed out leaflets for free passage to Hawaii in many small towns in Spain, with an opportunity for United States citizenship, many poor Spanish peasant families took advantage of this opportunity. It was an agreement between the United States and the American owned sugar cane companies to recruit poor European peasants to work in the cane fields. The United States was threatened by the large percentage of Japanese immigrants that were coming to Hawaii and they offered a pathway to citizenship to these poor Europeans in order to change the demographics of the islands. In other words, they wanted more white Europeans from Spain and Portugal to populate this strategic United States territory.

My grandfather's uncle and aunt decided to travel to the port of Gibraltar to take a steamship around the horn of South America to the then United States territory of Hawaii and the island of Maui. They worked in the sugar cane fields for three years to pay off their passage and the opportunity to live in paradise. My 12-year-old grandfather was equally intrigued and begged his parents to let him travel to Hawaii with his aunt and uncle. He boldly predicted he would make his fortune and return to Spain with his riches to help his parents. He was the oldest of their five children, and his parents were finally convinced to let him immigrate to Hawaii.

The day he left Spain was the end of his childhood. On the two-month journey to Hawaii, 20 children died of influenza, and the harsh condition of working in the sugar cane fields took its toll on his aunt and uncle. When he was only 14 years old, his aunt and uncle abandoned him in Hawaii. Since he was still a child, he worked in a sugar cane field as a water boy, carrying buckets of water to the workers in the field. It was back-breaking work for a young boy, and he hated his experience in Hawaii. He never understood how people could consider Hawaii a paradise; Hawaii was a nightmare for this boy, who was on his own and abandoned by his family.

As Nietzsche said, "What doesn't destroy you, makes you stronger." That was the case with my grandfather. His early hardship turned my grandfather into one tough SOB, who, as a result, was very hard on his wife and family. My mother was terrified of him and his quick temper. He had told her when she was younger, that if she ever cried, he would beat her and give her a reason to cry. She stopped her tears her whole life; I never saw my mother cry about anything. My mother was an art teacher and an artist, and one of my favorite oil paintings was a self-portrait of her as a little girl. She put a tear in one of her eyes and explained that her oil painting was the only way she was finally able to cry.

By the time I knew my grandfather, he had softened and changed a great deal. He was very loving to his grandchildren and his wife. The pressure of just surviving and taking care of his family was gone because of his financial success. I loved my grandparents, and I have nothing but wonderful memories of my experiences with them. My grandfather cutting my hair and giving my brothers and I crew cuts. My grandmother keeping a low drawer in her kitchen filled with candy, so we could grab a hand full of peanut M&M's whenever we wanted. Her warm hug and gentle smile.

In 1913, when my grandfather was 15 years old, he left Hawaii and rode on a steamship to San Francisco, completely on his own. He was homeless and unemployable because of his youth. Why hire a 15-year-old teen, when there were plenty of out-of-work adults who could do the job? He told me he was starving in San Francisco and was begging for any food he could get. He was finally hired to dig ditches for half a day for 30 cents. On that amount, he could survive for at least a month since a loaf of bread was only a penny: and he could buy a loaf of bread a day. As he looked for work at some of the area farms, he trudged out of the city. At my dad's funeral, my Uncle Victor told a story about his father when he was desperate and seeking work during his first months surviving on his own in California. When he was on the road and looking for work, was so despondent and lonely that he contemplated suicide. He was going to jump off a bridge and kill himself. At that moment, he looked over the bridge and saw a nest with a mother bird feeding her babies. It reminded him that his own parents were still alive in Spain, and how much it would hurt them if they found out he had committed suicide. At that moment, he decided not to kill himself, but to keep going and to continue to look for work. There were about 100 people at my father's funeral, and half of the people, including myself and my kids, would not have existed had my grandfather made the decision to take his life. It was a real example of *It's a Wonderful Life*, if he had actually taken his life. It was a poignant moment that made me very aware how rare life is and how one bad decision could affect so many people.

Shortly after his brush with suicidal thoughts, he met a childless Japanese-American couple who hired him to do a day's work on their farm. He slept in their barn that night and was so anxious to prove himself, he rose early and finished the work before the couple woke up. They were impressed by his work ethic and kept him on as a hired hand. That couple saved his life, and he lived with them for the next few years, until he was old enough to be on his own. Although they wanted to adopt him as their own son, he told them he couldn't let them do it since his parents were still alive in Spain. At the age of 18 he was on the road again. Now an adult with a man's body, he found work in the rich agricultural farms and orchards in the Bay Area. My grandfather had the equivalent of a fifth-grade education in Spain. Although he had very little formal education, he was a highly intelligent man with a strong back. He taught himself how to read and to write English, and his knowledge of farming and his ability to speak both English and Spanish made him a very employable adult. Part of the agreement for laborers to leave Spain was a path to United States citizenship. My grandfather became a naturalized American citizen who was extremely proud of his new country.

At some of the big farms in the region, the landowners held picking competitions to reward the workers who were the most productive. My grandfather Eugenio was like an athlete when he worked in the fields. He was relentless in his speed and accuracy picking vegetables. In one competition, when he was around 20 years old, he won the top prize of $800 for his speed and volume of his work. After the growing season was over, he took his first vacation since he had left Spain, and he bought a Briscoe automobile and headed south to Mexico. Although he didn't go into detail about his trip, I'm sure he spent a couple of months drinking and partying across the border. He returned with tattoos up and down each of his arms. They were of American eagles and other patriotic symbols of his new country. He told my cousin that he wanted to show the world that he was a proud American. Shortly after his return to the United States, he worked mostly as a foreman, who communicated with both the farm owners and the mostly Mexican laborers who crossed the border as seasonal workers in California. Since he was making decent money, he was ready to settle down and to start his own family. He lived in a boarding house run by a Spanish couple who had made the same journey from Spain to Hawaii and then to Santa Clara, California. This couple had no children of their own, so they took in three orphaned foster children, who also came from Spain. One of those kids was a sixteen-year-old girl named Emilia Encarnation Lozano from the mountain village of Cañar, Spain. Emilia became his wife and my grandmother.

My grandmother had her own amazing story to tell of her journey to the United States. She was a three-year-old toddler in 1907 when she traveled with her parents, Manuel and Soledad Lozano, and a younger brother also named Manuel to Hilo, on the big island of Hawaii. Just like my grandfather, they took a steamship from Gibraltar to Hawaii to work as indentured servants in the sugar cane fields. They eventually had two more sons and settled in Santa Clara, California, to pursue the American dream. Unfortunately, that dream turned into tragedy.

Emilia (Emily) Lozano saw her share of hardship in her life, just like my grandfather. My grandfather Eugenio was completely taken with this sixteen-year-old beautiful, young Spanish girl with the same background and experiences. For her, it was a twenty-two-year old man from her home country whom she fell in love with, and he offered her a chance to escape the hardships of her life as a foster child. Her foster parents treated her more as a servant than as their own child. They were paid by Santa Clara County to take care of her and her two younger brothers; but it was a financial arrangement, and they used the three orphans as child labor.

When my grandmother was 11 years old, her mother died giving birth to her fifth child and son Antonio. The doctors warned my great-grandmother that having another child could kill her, but she went through with the birth of her son and literally sacrificed her life in order to have that child. My grandmother had to assume the role of mother to her four younger brothers. Her father Manuel Lozano was devastated by his wife's death and could barely function. Raising five children was too much for her father, so he gave up their youngest and my great Uncle Tito Tony for adoption. Antonio was adopted by a childless couple, the Sanchez family, who were very loving and caring. It wasn't until he was a young man, that he even knew they weren't his biological parents. A year after he gave up his son to adoption, Manuel was hit by a train and killed. On a foggy day, he rode his bicycle to work and stopped to wait for a train to cross the railroad tracks. After the train passed, he climbed back on his bike and crossed the track; but another train approached on an adjacent track, and he accidently rode his bike into the train's path and was killed instantly.

I can't imagine how devastated and overwhelmed my grandmother must have been. Instantly, this twelve-year-old Spanish girl had become the head of her family. She was responsible for her three younger brothers' lives, and she tried her best to make it work. The county placed her family in a foster home with two of her younger brothers. Another brother was separated and housed in another foster home. When I think of my 12-year-old grandmother being an orphan I can't complain about any of the small hardships in my life. I'm not ashamed to admit it, my second favorite book is *Anne of Green Gables*. When I saw the latest television version on Netflix, I was thinking of my orphaned grandmother the whole time, and I was crying like a baby.

My grandmother, whom my siblings and I called Nani, was the most loving person I ever knew in my life. Despite her difficult circumstances, she was never a bitter person. She was the only one who calmed my grandfather's temper when he had his violent outbursts. She was only 16 when she met my grandfather and 17 when they were married. Ten months later she gave birth to her first son, whom she named after her father, Manuel. My grandmother said that the old Spanish women in her community, counted the months to confirm the legitimacy of the birth. These two immigrants from Spain, who did not have parents or family to help them, created their own family and an amazing legacy in Mountain View, California.

My mother Soledad (Sally) Calvo spoke only Spanish until she entered public school. Being the child of Spanish immigrants her path to assimilation started when she entered school where no Spanish was spoken in her classroom. Since my mother was a shy girl, the teachers initially thought she might be mentally challenged, but it was the cultural and language barriers which prevented her from responding in school. Even at a young age, my mother was extremely intelligent and had great self-discipline and self-control. It took her only a year to become proficient in English; by the second grade, she was a straight A student. She hated the fact that she was different from other American children. She completely transformed herself into a mainstream American with no detectable accent. My grandfather was never a mainstream American; he was an immigrant farm worker, whose only opportunity in America was through his strong back and hard work in the fields. Both my grandparents, who had very little formal education, were extremely bright people, who taught themselves how to read and to write English; and they both became naturalized United States citizens.

Like most immigrants, they struggled early on with their new family. My grandfather started out as a sharecropper for a variety of farms in Santa Clara Valley. At one point, they lived on the Stanford farm in Palo Alto. One famous family story was about President Herbert Hoover coming back home to visit in Palo Alto. He stopped his chauffeured car to ask my six-year-old Uncle Manuel if he could buy some fresh-picked strawberries. Seeing it was the president of the United States, my grandfather proudly gave the American president a crate of strawberries and insisted they were a gift. A few years later, when the depression hit, my grandfather always regretted giving Hoover the strawberries.

"I should have never given Hoover those strawberries. Look how he ruined this country."

The Depression was hard on all Americans, but particularly hard for immigrants who had nothing to begin with. With food prices dropping, my maternal grandparents worked as sharecroppers for almost nothing and lived on the extra food they raised. They lived in horrible conditions, and my mother took in the horrors of her life with great conviction of how she would control her own future. When she was thirteen, she saw the classic film *Gone With the Wind*. When Scarlett O'Hara was starving and made the pledge that "as God is my witness, I will never go hungry again," my mother made that pledge with her. To her credit, once the Depression was behind her, she kept that pledge; and our family never went a day worrying about where our next meal would come from. I benefited from her pledge with Scarlett and lived a very comfortable childhood.

World War II also changed my mother's family and was the impetus for their financial success. Since my grandfather had two adult sons, he was able to acquire a deferment for his twenty year-old son, Manuel, to help him work on the farm. With the war waging in Europe, food was in demand; and the California agricultural industry was booming. Manuel was a muscular, young man whom his father worked like a horse. He depended on his son and his ability to work long hours. His second oldest son, Victor, volunteered for the Army Air Corps to become a pilot. Victor was an extremely bright young man and was valedictorian of his class at Mountain View High school. Growing up, Victor befriended Jose Antonio Villareal and they were friends for most of their childhood. After graduation, Jose joined the Navy and following the war became a writer and an English professor. His novel *Pocho*, published in 1970, is about his life growing up in Santa Clara Valley and is considered a classic of Chicano literature. Victor joined the Army Air Corps; since he tested well academically, even without a college degree, he trained to be an officer and a pilot at the age of nineteen. The Army Air Corps desperately needed pilots, and he trained to become a B-24 co-pilot and was sent to Italy with the 15th Air Force. His experiences in the war were right out of the book *Catch 22.* By the time he arrived in Italy, he was a 20-year-old co-pilot who then flew 35 combat missions over Europe. He was part of the famous Ploesti air raids and he never lost a crew member during his dangerous missions. Although he did not like to talk about the war, he told me they came back from one mission and counted almost 200 shrapnel holes in their plane. After the war, he graduated from Stanford University on the G.I. Bill. He later entered into Democratic politics and served as the mayor of Mountain View. He eventually was elected a California assemblyman and spent twenty years in California state politics, retiring as a board member of the Public Utilities Commission. He also had his own lumber business and was a successful small businessman and entrepreneur.

Although my grandfather found financial success during the war, it was a horrible time for my grandparents' best friends and farming neighbors, the Nakamura family. They were Japanese-American farmers who grew raspberries in the area. Their kids were the same age as my mother and her siblings; and they grew up together as friends. Since it was a Japanese family who took in my grandfather when he was a boy, he always respected and admired the Japanese-American farmers and the Nakamura family.

When President Franklin Delano Roosevelt signed Executive Order 9066, the Nakamura family had just a few days to dispose of their possessions. They gave their piano to my grandparents to keep while they were interned. My mother told me stories about seeing bonfires started by Japanese-American families burning their possessions; many of them burned their personal items rather than letting the scavengers take advantage of them to make a quick buck. The Nakamura family were sent to the Heart Mountain internment camp in Wyoming. When their 11-year-old son Kenney, my uncle Gene's best friend, died in an internment camp from meningitis, Mrs. Nellie Nakamura sent a telegram to my grandmother to let her know about this tragedy. The telegram was sent while my Uncle Victor was still a B-24 pilot in Italy. When my grandmother was handed the telegram, she was certain that it was about her son Victor being killed or missing in action. When she read the telegram and quickly realized it was not about her son, she fell to her knees in tears of joy. She always felt guilty about how she reacted to the news of the death of her friend's son. The Nakamura family was released from Heart Mountain on Jan. 19, 1944, with permission to travel east to Minneapolis, where they lived for two years before returning to Santa Clara Valley, They resumed their friendship with the Calvo family and my Aunt Trini was a bridesmaid at their daughter Margaret's wedding and Margaret was a bridesmaid at my Aunt Trini's wedding. Mrs. Nellie Nakamura lived to be 107 years old and died at her home in Los Altos, California.

World War II also changed the fortunes of my grandfather. It turned out he was a very good capitalist who had entrepreneurial instincts. Since

Europe and Asia were consumed with war, vegetable prices increased world-wide; and my grandfather lived in the center of some of the most fertile farm land in the world. Before Santa Clara County became Silicon Valley, it was rich farmland with many fruit orchards and vegetable farms that benefited from almost a year-round growing season. The mild weather and consistent rain fall created a farming oasis.

With the war raging, most of young men from that area joined the armed forces: and with the Japanese-American farmers sent to internment camp, farm labor was scarce. My grandfather became dependent on Mexican seasonal workers with temporary visas to do most of the work harvesting. The opportunity for my grandfather and my Uncle Manuel to make money through farming was only limited by their vision and their time. Since they didn't have the money to buy land, they leased as much farmland as they could. Many of the farms were owned by banks, and my grandfather negotiated advantageous deals to grow tomatoes and string beans all through the valley. Since they spoke fluent Spanish, they were desirable people to work for, since most of the seasonal workers came from Mexico and spoke only Spanish. The men brought their wives and children from Mexico; and they became an extended family for my mother and her siblings. My grandmother was always very generous with the workers; and since she spoke fluent Spanish, she enjoyed socializing with the workers and "adopting" their families and children. Each year when they migrated to the valley to pick the harvest, it was like a family reunion for the workers and my grandparents. My grandfather quickly abandoned his socialist views and eventually saved enough money of his own to buy a farm on San Antonio Road in the middle of Mountain View. In just a few years they went from the poorest of the Depression era families to very successful entrepreneurs.

During her high school years, they lived in a tumbled down shack which my mother and her sister derogatorily referred to as "nightmare alley." Although my grandfather was doing better financially, he was reluctant to spend the money he was saving on a nice home. "Why would I want to move into a nice home?" he asked his family. "I would have to take my work boots off at the door."

His family finally convinced him to buy a nice home; and in 1946, when my mother was a senior in high school, they built a beautiful new 2,000 square-foot, four-bedroom home with indoor plumbing on their property on San Antonio Road. It was a remarkable change for my mother and my aunt Trini, That house was the also the center of the greatest family memories of my youth. The family Christmas holidays with my siblings and cousins were my fondest memories. Since my grandparents owned an entire city block on San Antonio Road, with plenty of land to run on and two houses and an old barn, my cousins and I had unlimited hiding spots and places to play and to run.

After the war ended, Uncle Victor returned home to help with the growing family businesses. He married my Aunt Nellie (Manuela) shortly after he came home, and she was instrumental in helping him get over the PTSD he experienced from witnessing the horrors of war. The Bay Area was a prime location for the returning G.I.s to raise a family, and the population exploded. Companies like Lockheed Martin and IBM attracted high-tech engineers, whose baby-boom children eventually helped create Silicon Valley. Every day it seemed like another orchard was dug up, and the richest farmland in the world was purchased and developed into much-needed housing and schools for the growing baby boomer generation. He was now a successful entrepreneur, who opened several businesses on his property on San Antonio Road. They leased their land for a bank, a car wash that became the very successful Lozano car wash chain owned by my grandmother's brother Manuel, a gas station, and a restaurant. They built their own strip mall, and my Uncle Victor opened a liquor store as well as a sporting goods store. With his wartime experiences behind him, Victor focused on his businesses with tireless energy.

My immigrant grandparents had no more than a fifth-grade education. They left their home country as children and moved to a foreign land where they had to assimilate and to learn the language. Because of their hard work and smart entrepreneurial business skills, their lives had completely turned around by the late 1940s. They had the financial resources to help their children continue their education after high school and to live comfortably in the land of opportunity. My Mother and her siblings all attended college, including Uncle Victor and Uncle Gene, who graduated from Stanford

University. The only exception was Manuel; at first my grandfather did not want to pay for his oldest son's college education. Manuel had worked like a slave for his father in the fields from the moment he could walk. My mom said he was built like a boxer after years of back-breaking work. Since they were partners in the farming business, my grandfather didn't see why his son needed a college degree. My Grandfather finally relented, and my Uncle Manuel left Mountain View to get a degree in agriculture at the University of California at Davis. After he graduated from college, he took a vacation to Spain where he met his future wife Benita and brought her back to the United States. He bought an orchard in Gilroy and remained a farmer for the rest of his life.

It is very difficult for people to fundamentally change who they are at any time in their life, but my mother had the discipline to change who she was on two occasions after she became an adult. When my mother was a child she loved art and drawing. They didn't have the money for a pencil or paper, so she would draw in the dirt with a stick. She developed her talent and eventually went on to become an art teacher. After she was married she put her art aspiration on hold to raise a family. She was very shy and never felt comfortable showing her art, so I never saw any of her work when I was a young child. My brother Mark had her artistic gift and he was also very shy about showing anyone his work. When my mother saw that my brother was mimicking her, and he also had a lack of self-confidence with his artistic skills, she decided she needed to set a better example. After her first two kids went off to college, she started painting again and submitting her artwork to several local art shows and she won awards and was recognized for her artistic skills. She was setting an example for my brother, who learned to be more confident about showing his work and the result was that he has spent a career in the newspaper business as a cartoonist and graphic artist. Mark has worked as a graphic artist for the Las Vegas Journal Review for the past 20 years.

The other time she transformed herself was something I found out after she died. My sister told me that my mother confided in her that she had a difficult time being demonstrative with her affection to her own children. I always knew my mother loved me, but it was my father who showed us outward affection and would wrestle with us and give us the physical hugs and attention we needed. When my first daughter Rachel was born, Mother told my sister that Rachel, her first grandchild, taught her how to be demonstrative and affectionate. At 50 years old, she changed who she was and learned how to be physically affectionate to my daughter. She would repeatedly tell my daughter she loved her and would hug her and hold her, something she could never do with her own children. With each grand-child she continued to learn how to be even more affectionate and loving. If I didn't need another reason to admire Mother, what I learned about her after her death gave me an even deeper understanding who she was and how courageous she was and how she had the self-discipline to change herself for the better.

When I completed this chapter, I sent it to my 86 year-old Uncle Gene Calvo to fact check. Since he was my mother's younger brother, he knew first-hand the facts of our family history. He was invaluable in terms of confirming or questioning some of the information I wrote in this chapter. One of the things he felt was important to say about his childhood was that it was a wonderful time to grow up and how much he enjoyed it. Although my grandfather was very strict with his kids, he and my grandmother pro-vided their children with plenty of love and family support and a great place to grow up. Mountain View in the thirties had a population of around 3500 people. It was a rural area with farms and orchards and plenty of land for a young man to explore with friends and family. He said the Spanish immigrants lived in a large tight-knit community in Mountain View and they supported each other. My uncle has lived in the bay area his whole life, except for the time he spent in Europe with the United States Army in the fifties. He has seen the area grow into Silicon Valley and he has a genuine concern with young people today who spend their time looking at their phones or playing video games indoors. Although his parents didn't have money for any luxuries, his childhood was filled with healthy physical activity growing up in a town with a mild climate and some of the richest farm land in the world. All the children worked hard on the farm and they never had to worry about going hungry. There was plenty of fresh vegetable, fruits, chickens, and pigs, and my grandfather would make an annual deer hunting trip in the winter to Northern California. He would always bring home fresh deer meat for the family to enjoy. There is not a single acre of farmland or an orchard remaining in Santa Clara Valley, the land is too valuable for agriculture. My Uncle Gene has nothing but fond memories when Mountain View was a small town and he felt it was a privilege to have grown up during the time he did.

# A RIGHTEOUS MAN

My father Oliver was a righteous man. A devout Catholic, he was dedicated to his family and his country. I can't think of a time or moment my father put his own needs ahead of his family's. A member of the greatest generation, he was a man I could never be or duplicate his character. If you followed my father around for his whole life with a camera, I'm sure, like in the great Albert Brooks' movie *Defending Your Life*, there would be a few scenes that showed him being selfish or disrespectful. But, it would be very few, and just like the character played by Meryl Streep, my dad would be passed on to the next level with only a one-day trial.

We have all known righteous people in our lives. People who are willing to put their selfish interests behind what is the honorable thing to do. Although I have known many good people in my life, and I consider myself a good person, those people whom I feel meet the virtuous standard have included only my father and my maternal grandmother, "Nani."

A person is measured by their actions when no one is looking. One of my cousins told me a story about my dad during a very difficult Christmas for their family. His mother, my dad's sister, was going through some challenging times with her husband. They had ten kids, and Christmas time found them with little hope or happiness. My father paid the family a surprise visit with a car full of presents. He knew that he could provide them with a little happiness, and he was more than willing to be generous to the people he loved. I first heard this story 50 years after it happened. My father had never mentioned it to our family. When my cousin told me the story at my father's funeral, I knew it was an example that defined who he was. He just performed kind acts; he didn't brag about his generosity, and no one was necessarily looking when he implemented these acts of generosity. He helped his extended family because his heart told him to do so.

Although my father showed nothing but kindness and love to me, I struggled with his almost perfection as a teenager and young adult, knowing that it was impossible for me to be the man that he was. Escaping with alcohol and pot and doing stupid behavior when I was drunk or high as a teenager, I found it very difficult to live in his shadow. When I saw the movie *East of Eden* for the first time and then read the novel at age 17, I recognized my father in the righteous character of Adam Trask. Although Adam Trask was a little more self-righteous than righteous.

Both my parents had a difficult childhood. My mother lived in fear of her father, during a time their family lived in poverty. He was angry and afraid of not being able to support his five children, and the stress made him extremely strict with his kids. She spent most of her childhood avoiding her father's wrath. My father was the oldest son in an Italian-American family living in San Francisco during the Depression. My grandfather was frequently unemployed, and my father had to work at a very early age to help the family. He attended Balboa High School and worked at a gas station after school to help with the family's expenses. He did not have much time for a childhood, since they needed him to work. Although a gifted athlete, he was always working after school and couldn't participate in sports. Those shared hardships turned both my parents into Ward and June Cleaver in terms of how they raised their kids. For many people, "Leave it to Beaver" was a fantasy that didn't represent their childhood. For me and my siblings, it was exactly how my childhood was. My mother was trained as an art teacher at San Jose State and left her job to raise her family. She was always home to help us with our homework and made sure we were successful students. My father, who was frequently on the road as a regional service rep for Pontiac, was always home on weekends and was a gentle soul who was remarkably patient with his children.

Oliver was always good with his hands and worked as an automobile mechanic through high school. Before World War II broke out, he trained as a machinist, and toiled making parts for the defense industry. He lived at home and helped take care of his parents and five younger siblings. It was his mother's dream for him to be a priest. If her oldest son in this Italian American family joined the priesthood, it would be his mother's ticket to heaven and admiration among her friends and family. If my grandparents could have afforded losing his income after he graduated from high school, he would have attended a seminary immediately. However, they needed him to work as a machinist. As their family finances stabilized, my grandmother hoped he would become a priest. If it wasn't for Hitler and Mussolini and the start of World War II, I would not be alive. Certainly, my father would have become a priest if he didn't participate in World War II. Even though my father was working in a protected defense industry, shortly after Pearl Harbor, he volunteered. for the Army Air Corps. It was his dream to be a fighter pilot. He passed the testing and survived the initial training. Then, the flight instructors discovered he was color blind. It was a discovery that might have saved his life since fighter pilots in World War II had a high mortality rate. Instead, he trained as ground crew working on the P-51 fighters as a staff-sergeant.

After his training, he left on a ship to Burma, India, to support the Tenth Air Force. He told me when he arrived in India, they held his paycheck for the first few weeks, since the overwhelming poverty was a shock to the young American airmen. Even though they had lived through a depression in the United States, they weren't prepared to see children dying from starvation in the streets. It didn't matter that they held his paycheck from him, because he always sent his pay home to his mother and father to help with his family's economic struggles.

His mother still dreamt that when her son came back from the war, he would go to seminary to become a priest. It was difficult for my father to stand up to his mother, since he was so devoted to her. Going to war and leaving home for three years, gave my dad a chance to grow up and to think about his future. He left the Army Air Corp with only one simple dream: to meet the love of his life and to become a good husband and a father. When he came home, he told his mother his plans to raise a family and that he no longer wanted to become a priest. She reluctantly gave him her blessing, but she still held out hope. She also did her best to sabotage any potential relationship he might have.

The G.I. Bill transformed this country in many ways. Growing up in an immigrant family, my father had no ambitions to go to college. When he first graduated from high school he tried to acquire a good blue-collar job as a machinist or a mechanic, which that was his best hope. When Oliver returned after the war his younger brother, Tony, talked him into taking advantage of the G.I. Bill, and he enrolled at San Jose State Teacher's College. Since he was good with his hands, his plan was to teach industrial arts or auto mechanics. My dad Oliver has always been a physically strong man. At 5' 10" he was considered a giant compared to his 5'2" father and 4'10" mother. Since his job in the Army Air Corp required him to lift heavy artillery, he was in great physical shape after the Army, and he looked like an Adonis cut from stone. During his time at San Jose State, he lived at the YMCA and decided to box as an amateur, In 2005 my Father died at the age of 83 from Parkinson's disease. I often wondered if his short boxing career and head trauma didn't contribute to his disease. He also spent his life working with cars, and his exposure to carbon monoxide also may have contributed.

When Oliver entered San Jose State, he was a 26-year-old freshman and was anxious to meet someone who would become his future wife. How my parents met was a story I heard from my mother many times. It might sound like stalking today, but it was completely innocent behavior from my father.

My mother was a very beautiful woman. When people saw her high school photo, they thought she looked like the actress Rita Hayworth. My parents met while signing up for their fall classes. At that time, my mother was also a 19 year-old freshmen at San Jose State. Oliver noticed a woman with beautiful long, light brown hair. My mother was signing up for an art class. He instantly decided to take the same class. On their first day of class, he sat right next to her. He told her she had beautiful hair and asked her if she would like to go out. She declined politely and asked him to leave her alone.

Being ever so persistent, my dad asked her out every time he attended class. She thought he was a little creepy, but realized over time that he was sweet and harmless and that he was a decent man who had a great deal of respect for women. She finally agreed to go on a date but insisted that they go out only as friends. By the end of their date, my dad had proposed. She quickly said, "No." But, she continued to see him as a friend. As their friendship grew, they took their time to start an innocent romance. He continued to ask her almost daily to marry him and she continued to decline.

Mother told the story of the first time she met my father's mother. As you could imagine, there was a little tension. When my dad brought her to my grandmother's home, she ignored the startled young girl and looked at her son angrily. She demanded, "Oliver, I need to talk to you." They adjourned to an adjoining room in their small 1,000 square-foot home, and she started to yell at her son. "Oliver, don't you ever bring your girlfriend to my house before you see me first. You should first see your mother and then pick up your girlfriend and bring her over here." It was like a scene from the play *Marty*. Mother immediately knew what she was getting into by dating my father. My mother had reason to be concerned. Oliver was a mama's boy, and his mother remained involved in his life until the day she died.

In 1952 they were married and honeymooned at Yosemite National Park. According to my brother, my dad had told him that they were both virgins when they married. My dad was 30 years old and my mother was 25.

To my mother's credit she didn't marry a man like her father. She married an honorable man, who was patient and loving to a woman who had a tough time with her father and his temper and harshness. Mother spent most of her life trying to get over the emotional abuse she endured from her father. To her credit, she put her energy and love into her children and our education. Since our parents had been teachers, she was our personal tutor through our school years. We had no choice but to succeed in school and to attend college. My parents would not let us fail.

# BODYGUARD UNSEEN

My mother knew all of the dark secrets in our family. She was a bit of a gossip; and after she lived with her mother-in-law, my grandmother, in our home for a brief time, she found out all the family secrets on my dad's side of the family. She eventually shared those secrets with me during my many visits to her nursing home. Apparently, I am also a bit of a gossip, as well, since I am fascinated by our family history, both the good and the bad.

One of the strangest family stories that I was told is that we were descended from pirates who eventually fled to Sicily to hide out, and that we were direct descendants of the notorious Blackbeard the Pirate. It was such an absurd and oddly specific story that had been passed down for several generations, that I didn't see how it could possibly be true. Blackbeard the Pirate, whose real name was Edward Teach, was born around 1680 in England. How could we possibly be related to Blackbeard? About three years ago I had my DNA tested and it came out pretty much how I thought. It showed that I was 70% of European descent, mostly from the Iberian Peninsula and Italy. What surprised me was that my DNA also showed that I was 5% from the British Isles. That would explain the family lore about being related to Blackbeard. Perhaps I am the great-great-great-great-great-great grandson of Blackbeard the Pirate.

When my cousin was a little girl she was doing a report on Thanksgiving and she was learning about the various Native American tribes that inhabited North America before we became a country. She was visiting my grandmother and she thought it would be a good opportunity to ask her about our family heritage. "Grandma, do we have any Native American heritage in our family?" My grandmother answered her without skipping a beat and said. "Yes, our family is a member of the Black Hand tribe."

There is no other way to say this: my paternal step-great grandfather was a pimp. He was involved in organized crime in Oakland, California, during Prohibition and The Depression, and he owned a bordello and a speak easy bar in the 1920s and 1930s.

What makes this worse is that I have always been an outspoken critic of any film or television show that stereotypes Italian-Americans as mobsters. My dad and his father were two of the most honest, spiritual, and hardworking men anyone could ever meet. Yet, that family history relating to organized crime is true unfortunately; and there is no escaping it. In his novel *East of Eden* John Steinbeck examines in detail the biblical reference "Thou mayest triumph over sin." This important biblical distinction means we are men and women with free will, and we have control over what choices we make in our own life, whether it be good or evil. In her song "God Bless the Child," Billie Holiday sings, "God bless the child that's got his own." In other words, God bless the child that has his own life and determines his own fate. My father is an example of this, he took control of his life and chose a life of sacrifice and goodness. However, choosing goodness was not the decision of other members of my family.

The D'Aquila family were from Lercara Friddi, the same Sicilian town that Frank Sinatra's father was from. It is about 45 miles southeast of Palermo and around 20 miles from the famous Sicilian town of Corleone. Lercara Friddi is known for its Sulphur mines, and I'm certain my family descended from peasants who provided the labor for the mines. Great-grandfather Vincenzo D'Aquila and great-grandmother Oliva were married in Sicily, and their oldest son Vincent was born in Lercara Friddi. They immigrated to Queens, New York at the turn of the century to escape the poverty in Sicily, just like many Italian immigrants at that time. My grandmother was born in Brooklyn, and the family tried to make a life in their new home.

My great-grandparents divorced, and my great-grandmother married another Sicilian immigrant named Gaetano. Oliva took her five-year-old daughter, Anna, my grandmother, and moved with her new husband to San Francisco. Gaetano and Oliva eventually had two sons of their own. Gaetano was involved in organized crime and prostitution and bootlegging during prohibition in Oakland, California. During the turn of the 19th century, it was a different time in the San Francisco Bay Area. Bordellos and other vices were not technically legal but were ignored by corrupt law enforcement and popular with the many male sailors who visited this international port city. My great uncle Vincent stayed with his father in Brooklyn; and my grandmother and her brother Vincent maintained a long-distance sibling relationship through the mail. Although they lived on different coasts, they remained very close, all of their lives. My great-grandmother Oliva died around the time I was born. My mother had known her for a brief time and my great-grandmother and her entourage were at my parents' wedding. My mother said she was this tiny Sicilian woman with diamonds on her fingers and covered in furs, but she had a huge presence and was the matriarch and queen bee of my dad's family. She made all the decisions in her family and was the type of person to get in the middle of everyone's lives.

My grandmother's brother, Vincent D'Aquila, had a very interesting life and wrote a book, *Bodyguard Unseen*, about his experiences as an Italian soldier during World War I. The book was published in 1931 and was very similar to *All Quiet on the Western Front* since it was also an anti-war novel. His war experiences were told recently in a 2014 international BBC docudrama, *14 Stories of the Great War.*

Even though he was a naturalized citizen of the United States, since he was born in Sicily, the Italian government decided to recruit ex-patriots living in New York to join the Italian army to fight the Germans in northern Italy. This was before the United States had become involved in the war, and the Italian government also hoped by recruiting Americans, it would encourage the United States to join the war effort against the Germans.

His autobiography describes in detail his slow realization that he was sent to the front as a private to become cannon fodder. An excellent writer, Vincent was initially saved from the front lines because he knew how to use a typewriter. The headquarters needed a courier who could type and could transport messages to the front. It kept him out of the battle at first, but still brought him up close to the horrors of the front and trench warfare. At one point he went insane from his exposure to the war, and he had a vision that Christ came to him and told him to throw down his weapon. He knew if he threw down his weapon, Christ would protect him and would keep him alive; thus, the title of the book. Jesus Christ was his bodyguard unseen, as long as he rejected killing his fellow man. He instructed his fellow soldiers to throw down their weapons also; and declared Jesus Christ would protect them.

As you might imagine, he was an extreme distraction among the front-line soldiers, and the Italian Army did not know how to handle Vincent. They were afraid to make an example of him and to shoot him as a coward, since he was also an American citizen and they were hoping the Americans would enter the war on their side. They did not want to shoot an American and to have it become a distraction and an international incident. Their only option was to pull him off the front lines and to send him to an insane asylum.

In the asylum the doctors hoped to prove that he was faking his insanity, so they could send him back to the front. They finally released him and sent him to stay in a rest and rehabilitation center for weary soldiers on the Italian Riviera. He stayed there enjoying the sun and recreation until the end of the war, dating the daughter of an Italian general. His story is a fascinating book, but in many ways, he is an unreliable narrator. Was he really channeling his Catholic faith through a vision from Jesus Christ, or was he a coward who desperately wanted to escape the front lines, so he faked his insanity? In any case, he survived the war and published his anti-war autobiography. Because of the success of his book, he made a career working in the publishing industry in New York. Vincent went on to lead a life of peace and love, marrying the love of his life, Quintilia. They had two daughters, Olive and Anita, and four grandchildren. The daughters and their father Vincent, made several trips in the 1940's by train from New York to San Francisco to visit the family on the west coast. Vincent and his sister, my grandmother, stayed in touch their entire lives.

Ironically, Vincent died in his eighties in a tragic fire. While in his Queens home, his bathrobe caught fire from a space heater. He died of smoke inhalation despite his futile efforts to extinguish the fire. The end of his life was like a *Twilight Zone* episode. It was an ironic violent death in his home that came 60 years after he actively avoided a violent death on the front lines of World War I.

His book *Bodyguard Unseen* can still be found in many libraries and can be purchased on the web. I own a copy myself and always thought it would make a fascinating movie.

# A FAMILY PORTRAIT OF STRANGERS

Each Fall before Christmas my dad, who loved photography, struggled and fought with us for a half a day to take a decent Christmas card photo of our family. We took this picture for at least 12 holidays, and it always looked like a bunch of strangers were assembled randomly in the photo. My older brother David and my younger brother Mark are blondes. I was the dark child, with dark brown hair and eyes, I didn't look anything like my two brothers. I looked more liked Dustin Hoffman or Al Pacino; and my younger brother Mark looked like Vanilla Ice or Woody Harrelson. With her bright red hair and freckles, my younger sister Lisa also didn't match any of my siblings. She looked like she could have been cast as Little Orphan Annie.

My dad, who always loved a good joke, told people that I looked like the mailman; my brothers looked like the milkman; and my sister resembled the gas meter man. As kids, we rarely ate at restaurants, but we did go out to eat for breakfast every Sunday after church. When the waitress presented the bill, Dad always joked that we needed separate checks, since we obviously weren't related. In this age of DNA testing—not that I was ever worried—but I can honestly say my brothers and I had the same parents; and the DNA is proof that we are related.

However, my sister had actually been adopted, and it was difficult for her to feel like she belonged. My mother had RH-negative blood; and she was limited in terms of how many children she could have because of the RH factor. Each time she birthed a child, it was more difficult for that child to survive. At that time in the 1950s, physicians gave blood transfusion to help the child survive because the mother's blood was incompatible. Mark had several complete blood transfusion and barely survived infancy. Since my parents wanted a little girl and since Mother could not have any more children, they adopted my sister.

We are all different personalities; but we lived up to all the behavioral theories of birth order. David, my older brother, was always the responsible one. He attended Stanford University and majored in psychology. He was offered a full-ride scholarship to the University of Oregon, where he graduated with a Ph. D. Eventually, he became a psychologist and worked at the V.A. hospital in Reno, Nevada, as well as taught at the medical school for the University of Nevada in Reno. An artist like my mother, my younger brother was a very skilled cartoonist who has worked in the newspaper business for the past 30 years. He has survived in this very competitive and shrinking business as a graphic artist and page designer and has worked for the *Las Vegas Journal Review* for the past 20 years. My sister married young and did not attend college. She has worked as a bookkeeper for most of her career.

I am very close with my brothers, and we spent many years together dealing with our parents' health issues. Both my parents had the misfortune of being diagnosed with Parkinson's disease. Dad spent the last five years of his life as an invalid, and Mother spent the last eight years of her life in a nursing home. They worked hard all their lives and saved their money responsibly, as many children of the Depression did. They could afford the long-term care they needed; and David, who was their power of attorney, guided their finances and estate with sensitivity and purpose. Ward and June were great planners and well prepared for any eventuality.

# ROCKY MOUNTAIN HIGH

In 1971 my family moved to Denver, Colorado. I had lived in California until I was 16 years old. My father worked for the Pontiac Motor Division as a regional service rep out of San Francisco. Shortly after he married my mom in 1952, he realized he couldn't raise a family on a teacher's salary. He found an excellent job with General Motors that provided him a decent income with great benefits and a new company car every year. Since he worked for Pontiac, he occasionally brought home a new car to test drive. I vividly remember when he brought home the custom GTO called *The Judge*. We were very lucky in terms of not having to move in my youth because of his job. I was born in Santa Cruz and shortly after my birth, my Dad accepted the job with Pontiac; and we moved to the east bay in Hayward, California. When I was around six-year-old we moved to a newly built home in Santa Clara, in what would become Silicon Valley. I lived just a few miles from Cupertino, California, where Steve Jobs, who was my same age, was born and raised. Dad spent 16 years working out of the same office, we were all disappointed when we found out he would be transferred to Denver. This meant I had to move after I completed my sophomore year at Peterson High School in Sunnyvale, California.

The transition to a new school was difficult for me. Since my pool of finding new friends was other newcomers or outcasts, I hung out with a more alienated crowd and drank and smoked pot to escape from my teen angst. I wasn't a bad kid. I kept up my grades to over a 3.5 GPA; but in the early 1970s, the youth culture was an extension of the 60s revolution. I grew Elvis Presley side burns and long, thick brown hair. Every year the stock show was in Denver; so for two weeks, Denver returned to its cowboy roots with all the cowboys visiting the city from every corner of the state. If kids had long hair, they were advised to avoid downtown, since the cowboys had been known to pull them off the street and to cut their hair with sheep shears. We solemnly heeded that advice. Ironically, the cowboy culture eventually adopted long hair, and country singers, like Trace Adkins and Willy Nelson, have long pony tails.

Since I had enough credits to graduate from high school early in January of 1973, I spent the next six months working as a houseman at the Roadway Inn Hotel on Evans and I-25. It was an introduction to what the real work world would be like for me if I didn't get a college education. My job was part janitor, part maintenance man, and assistant to the maids by picking up all the dirty sheets in bins and carrying them down to the laundry. Also, I drove the airport limo to pick up business people flying into Denver. I stayed busy and saved my $2.25 an hour; and, like most working people, I lived for the weekends. Starting on Friday night, I partied with my friends and got drunk and high on pot. As Tom Waits explained it lyrically in his music, I was always "looking for the heart of Saturday night." I frequented 3.2 alcohol clubs, since I could buy lower alcohol beer at 18 in these discos. Like most teenaged men, I always hoped to meet the woman of my dreams. If a person drank enough - and I did back then - they could easily get drunk on 3.2 beer. The big 3.2 clubs were the *Stout Street Electric Company* downtown and *After the Gold Rush* on the west side. The discos in Denver were right out of *Saturday Night Fever* - and, of course, I owned white pants and white shoes. Occasionally, I hooked up with the women of my dreams du jour, if I was drunk enough. But, my relationships were brief and frustrating. Like most teenagers, my emotions were amplified. Nothing is quite as powerful as the angst of a lonely teenager looking for love.

Minimum-wage jobs were the best motivation for me to attend college. In August, I quit my job and took a two-week trip to California with friends. It was a trip we did on virtually no money. We stayed with relatives and slept in my car when we were on the road.

Since I knew Ray Bradbury lived in Los Angeles and I still had his home address from when I was a kid, I paid him a visit. Although at that time I didn't think about being considered a stalker, I just showed up at his doorstep. I was naïve enough to think he would remember me and would be glad to meet a fan. When I stood at his doorstep with my friend, I was so nervous that I could literally hear my heart beating. A man in his thirties answered the door and told me we had the wrong house, that Ray lived across the street. We scampered over to Ray's house, knocked on the door, and waited nervously. This time no one answered the door, and we eventually left. He was probably upstairs in his office writing. It was 17 years later that I finally got to meet him in person at the 1990 ALA conference in Chicago.

# PARTY UNIVERSITY

The University of Colorado always has had a reputation of being a party school. For several years, it ranked as the number one-party college in the country, and it was always in the top five during the Seventies. Since I attended college at CU from to 1973 to 1977, from personal experience I can tell you that the school lived up to that reputation. It was also a highly ranked academic university, and the students who graduated, including myself, still had to attend classes and to study for exams.

On a week-end, I strolled around the second floor of Arnett Hall in the Kittredge freshmen dorm where I lived. In a scene right out of Animal House, there were bongs burning in almost every room; and 18-year-old kids from all over the country were getting high and drinking beer and partying. Officially, the war in Vietnam had ended with the Paris Peace Accord in 1973, and CU was transitioning from a school filled with anti-Vietnam radicals to a school filled with kids who had left home for the first time and just wanted to party, to ski, to get high, and to have fun. At the time, there were two types of partying students:

- The first type of students partied and got high every night, and they eventually flunked out by the end of their freshmen year.
- The other type of partying students showed up to class, attempted to complete their school work during the week, and then partied on the weekend.

One friend who lived on my floor was a pre-med student who left a memorable impression. One time I was in his dorm room while he studied his biology textbook, he was also smoking a joint, drinking a beer, and listening to music on his headphones, while playing cards (Hearts) with another student. Needless to say, he flunked out by the end of his freshmen year.

During college I really didn't know what I wanted to do with my life. I was having a wonderful time, but I didn't really have any focus or goal in terms of my education. I was thinking about pre-law or journalism, but I wasn't taking it too seriously. My dad always had an 8 mm movie camera to photograph all of our family events as we grew up. My siblings and I probably had the most photographed childhood ever from that era. My father photographed every birthday, every Christmas, every trip to Disneyland. He was a bit of a hobbyist when it came to photography, but he was actually quite good at it.

It was only natural that I developed an interest in photography and 8 MM filmmaking. When I was around ten years old, I begged my father to let me borrow his 8 mm camera to shoot little neighborhood films. I shot stop- action animation of paper monsters fighting and plastic army men in battle and created small film projects for school. Although I continued making films through high school, I never really intended or thought I could make a living at it.

In my sophomore year I took a communications class. The Radio/TV/ Film curriculum really looked like something I would enjoy. The university had just hired a full-time filmmaking instructor, and they decided to create a film program under the Communication Department. I finally started taking classes in something I was specifically interested in and I thrived. I morphed from a being a **C** college student to a straight **A** student from the second semester of my sophomore year. Robert Redford, who dropped out of the University of Colorado in the fifties, had wanted to donate money to the university to start a film program. It was before he created the Sundance Film Institute, and he wanted Boulder to be his headquarters for promoting independent films. Unfortunately, we had just come out of the anti-war movement in Boulder, and the CU regents were concerned this money would go to anti-war and left-wing filmmaking. At least, this is what one of my professors told me. Even though the university declined Redford's donation, the program was still created.

In the fall semester of my junior year, I needed to complete a project for one of my film classes. I had one of the worst jobs in the world: working at a junior high school as a lunchroom monitor. Being 20 years old, I was barely older than the 13 and 14-year-old kids who were students. The pay was around $4 for each lunch hour, plus a free school lunch. I spent my hour persuading kids to act civilized and cleaned the lunch tables. I got very little respect from the kids, because I wasn't one of their teachers, but just a stranger who came to work for an hour and a half and then left. At my request, one of my friends used my Super-8 sound camera to photograph my job. It was an early reality- based documentary. A Cinema Verite comedy of me attempting to do my job. When I edited the film, it came together rather well, as a ten-minute slice of life. I entered my film into the University of Colorado Film Festival, and it won 2$^{nd}$ place and a $100 savings bond. With winning that film contest, I naively thought I could make a living in film. I would eventually find out that it wasn't quite that easy to pursue a film career in the late 1970s in Colorado.

My second film to receive some recognition was a 16 mm documentary on an 88-year-old gold miner in Idaho Springs. Michael Clarey, a World War I veteran, was a weathered older man who spent his life after the war as a prospector in Colorado. He had a remarkable vision for America and the unlimited potential for young people in this country. It was a finalist for the Student Academy Awards and helped propel my career out of college. Both of my student films can still be seen on YouTube today.

In retrospect, my four years at CU were some of the best years of my life. I finally found a career I was good at. During my junior year, I also met my future wife and the mother of my children. To my wife's credit, we both decided to stop our excessive drinking and pot smoking once we got married and started a family. At the tender age of twenty-two, my life and career were ready to begin.

# A SMILE AND A SHOESHINE

The best motivation for finding work is having to pay bills. In May 1977, I graduated with my communications degree in Radio/TV/Film; and people were beating down my door to hire me. Not! A communications degree is just slightly below an English degree in terms of employability. In August of 1977 at the young age of 22 years old, I was married. Although my wife had a decent job as an office manager for a real estate company in Boulder, the pressure was on for me to find good employment. A 22-year-old with little professional experience did not have a lot of prospects. I desperately wanted to get a job in television production, and I submitted my application to the television networks in Denver. The problem was I had zero experience at a television station, and most of the Denver television staff who worked in production had gotten their experience in smaller markets. I needed to find a job, hopefully something that would help me contribute money to my household, while still looking for work in my field.

The only jobs available to a college graduate with no experience were sales jobs; and I accepted a job with Time, Inc. selling Time-Life Books. I always loved the play *Death of a Salesman* and was fascinated with the life of a salesman. I was also fascinated with the 1969 documentary, *Salesman*, produced by the Maysles brothers. It was a Cinema Verite look at the life of a bible salesman, and the pressures of making cold-sales calls. Working at Time-Life books for three months was probably the most important job I ever had. I was not naturally outgoing, and it was difficult for me to connect with strangers. My job as a telephone solicitor, selling western series like *The Gunfighters*, forced me to get beyond my fears and helped me start a conversation with almost anyone. It served me well in my career, and it taught me how to sell myself in job interviews. It also made it easy for me as a librarian to interview people and to use my sincere interest in human nature to connect with people.

The way that phone sales worked in those days is that we would get a cold-call list from the phone book for an out-of-state city. That was part of the scam. During a time when calling long distance was a rarity, we started our pitch by saying, "I am calling long distance from Denver to tell you about this great western book series from Time-Life." If the customers bought the first book, they received the next book in the series each month. They had the option to return each book, but most customers didn't want to hassle with sending a book back in the mail, so they reluctantly paid for the next one and then the next one until they were financially obligated to the entire series.

Just like the David Mamet play *Glengarry Glen Ross,* the best leads were given to the top salesmen. The new people had to cold call from the phone book and if we were good, we might sell three to four books an hour. The experienced salesmen, who were given the better leads, sold 10 to 15 books an hour. Looking back at my work career, the worst jobs I ever had were actually the best jobs I ever had, since that negative experience motivated me to find a job I could really love.

Because of my experience selling books to strangers, I was able to get a job with a Denver industrial film production company as a salesman. JNS Communications was a very small production company, but it launched my career in film and video production. I helped sell and produce such industrial film classics as *The Safe Operation of the Telsta Aerial Lift* and

*The Annubar: An Innovative Flow Measurement Device.* We also developed a process of transferring multi-projector slideshows to film which we called *Slide Fusion.* I was unhappy with the type of film work I was doing, but I was making a living and getting better as a salesman and actually making the company more successful. I learned a great deal about sales from the owner of the company, who was as slick as they come and a very smart businessman. I approached him one day about a raise, since the company was doing well due to my sales effort. He told me he couldn't give me a raise at the time, but he could make me vice-president of JNS. I happily took the new title, and I became vice-president of a company with three staff people, including myself.

In 1979 the cable business exploded in Denver, and I volunteered to get involved at a public-access facility in the suburb of Wheatridge. I learned as much as I could about video production, and I learned how to shoot and to edit with ¾" video. In 1980 my oldest daughter Rachel was born. The pressure was on to get a better job with health insurance and retirement benefits. For the last year I worked for JNS, I checked the newspaper daily for another job in my field. It took a year, but I finally saw a job posting for a media specialist in the library for Pikes Peak Community College in Colorado Springs. It was a great job with the state of Colorado that was perfect for a family person. I finally had the experience to be qualified for the job; and, most importantly, my sales experience gave me the bravado to sell myself. Although PPCC had approximately 100 people apply for the job, I was very fortunate to be selected for the position. It was the best opportunity I've ever had, and I discovered very quickly that I loved working in a library.

# LITTLE LONDON

Boulder and Colorado Springs have only one thing in common. They are both beautiful cities at the foot of the Front Range. Boulder is known for the stunning rock formation, the Flatirons, adjacent to the town. Colorado Springs is known for being in the shadow of the 14,110 foot Pikes Peak, perhaps the most commercialized mountain in the country. Tourists arrive at the top of Pikes Peak by car on the paved road used for the famous Pikes Peak Hill Climb race. Also, people can ascend Pikes Peak by the Cog Railroad that was built in 1891. Another route to the top is the 12-mile hiking trail from Manitou Springs on Barr Trail that is also used for the annual Pikes Peak footrace marathon. It is the only fourteener that has a gift shop and a restaurant at the top, where shoppers can buy souvenirs and can eat freshly baked donuts or hot chili.

However, Boulder and Colorado Springs are the complete opposite in terms of politics. Boulder, which is also known as the Peoples Republic of Boulder, passed a growth initiative to limit the population, which resulted in horribly inflated prices for basic homes. Colorado Springs is a city that has never said no to a developer and has grown from a town of 40,000 people in 1960 to a town and county of more than 700,000 people in 2018.

Colorado Springs has always been a city that is politically conservative with several military bases, including Fort Carson Army Base, Peterson Air Force Base, North American Aerospace Defense Command (NORAD), and the United States Air Force Academy, the most visited site in Colorado. Colorado Springs is also headquarters to many conservative religious organizations, with the most prominent one being James Dobson's Focus on the Family. When I arrived in Colorado Springs in 1982, Pikes Peak Community College had just built the campus on land that was donated by Fort Carson. The campus was adjacent to the Army post and a sizable percentage of the students were returning Vietnam veterans who were attending school on the G.I. Bill. As a result, there was a great mix of students from 18 to 80 years old. I always loved working and teaching at a community college. The students were there to learn, and the teachers were required to have only master's degrees in their fields. While many of the instructors were not traditional academics, they had 20 years or more experience working in the professions they taught.

# THE QUAKER GENERAL

During the 26 years I worked in Colorado Springs I fell in the love with the rich history of the area, including the variety of people who have passed through the Pikes Peak region. From the indigenous Utes who were the original residents to the gold prospectors seeking their fortune during the Cripple Creek Gold Rush, the common characteristic of these rugged westerners was their appreciation for the natural beauty and the opportunity the Pikes Peak region offered.

No one I met or read about in terms of their impact on the history of Colorado Springs compared to the contributions of the city founder, General William Jackson Palmer. General Palmer is unparalleled in what he accomplished in his remarkable life. General Palmer, the son of Quakers, was not an imposing man. He had a slight build and carried approximately 140 pounds on his 5'7" frame. He had reddish brown hair, and even as a 28-year-old general, fighting as a cavalry officer in the Civil War, his boyish looks made him appear to be a teenager. But his courage, intelligence, entrepreneurial instincts, great vision and ability to work hard, made him equivalent to the Elon Musk of his time.

Raised a Quaker in Pennsylvania, General Palmer abhorred war and any form of violence, but his religious conviction and abolitionist beliefs allowed him to overcome his distaste of war. He joined the Union Army and he successfully became a cavalry officer who recruited his own regiment at the age of 25 in 1861. He was a righteous man and never drank or swore. His courage as a cavalry officer led to his operating as a spy in the South.

Since he worked for the railroads before becoming a soldier, he assumed an alias and pretended to represent an English company looking to build railroads in the South. Instead, he secretly tracked confederate troops' movements. General Palmer, a skilled horseman, moved quickly through the South to accomplish his spying missions. He knew he would be shot if captured; and at one point he was caught and rightfully accused of being a spy. He maintained he was a civilian, but the confederate army had their doubts and imprisoned him for four months. He awaited his fate of being shot as a spy, but his life was saved in a prisoner exchange for a prominent Richmond citizen who had been captured by the North.

Palmer returned to the battlefield, continued to fight in the war, and was part of the brigade that followed Jefferson Davis as he tried to flee the country to Mexico. Palmer captured several wagons that were part of the Jefferson Davis entourage which contained millions in gold bullion and other valuables that were used to fund the confederacy. He was awarded the Medal of Honor for his bravery, and in 1865, he mustered out of the Army as a Brigadier General.

After the Civil War, General Palmer reclaimed his first love: expanding rail service throughout the United States. He decided to go into business for himself, along with many of the Civil War veterans who found their fortunes in the western United States. When Palmer arrived in the Pikes Peak region in 1869, he fell in love with the Front Range and the area that became the city he founded: Colorado Springs. His dream was to create a railroad to run through the mountains and the front range from Denver to Albuquerque, New Mexico. He built the Denver and Rio Grande railroad as well as the Rio Grande Western Railway through the Rocky Mountains. A year earlier he had married his young wife Queen Mellen, who was originally born in the United States but loved visiting England. Queen never really adjusted to living in Colorado Springs. Having a weak heart, she never acclimated to the high altitude which affected her health. General Palmer did his best to make Colorado Springs a comfortable home for Queen. With his new fortune, he turned Colorado Springs into "Little London." He helped found Colorado College, and near his railroad he built the luxurious Antlers Hotel. He insisted that Colorado Springs be a dry city, where alcohol was prohibited. He spent a small fortune building a castle for his queen, the beautiful Glen Eyrie estate. This magnificent home, which is now used as a retreat for the Navigators religious organization, is just north of the Garden of the Gods. The Navigators have opened the castle to the public, and they give tours and host English tea parties on a regular basis. It is well worth the visit to tour the Glen Eyrie castle today.

In an effort to keep "Little London" pristine, without any smokestack industries, he built the steel mill to supply his railroad, 30 miles to the south of Colorado Springs in Pueblo. This blue-collar town can thank General Palmer for providing livable wages to many immigrants from Mexico, Italy, Ireland, and eastern Europe. They lived beneath the smokestacks and built a city of such diversity and charm that few ever want to leave Pueblo. As a result, the population is represented by several generations of Pueblo natives. For the last seven years of my career, I worked as a branch manager for the Pueblo City-County Library District, and Pueblo has become my home in retirement.

General Palmer was also responsible for bringing African-American families to Colorado Springs. Many of his personal staff were African Americans, and he financially supported African-American scholarships and education.

General Palmer's first two daughters were born in Colorado Springs, and Queen Palmer had her first heart attack while pregnant. Since it was too much for Queen to stay in the high altitude of Colorado Springs, the General agreed to let her move back to England with their two daughters while she recovered from her various health issues. It was a difficult time for General Palmer, and he traveled back and forth between England and Colorado. His various railroad businesses needed his attention as well, so he couldn't leave Colorado entirely to be with his family. Queen died in

England at 44 years old, and it devastated the General. His daughters moved back to Colorado Springs at Glenn Eyrie, and he retired from most of his businesses by the age of 60. The general spent his retirement giving away four million dollars to his employees and various charities in Colorado. It was equivalent to 100 million in 2018 dollars. He was an avid conservationist and donated money to many environmental causes.

General Palmer was physically fit from years of living in the mountains and riding across the state as a master horseman. He might have lived to be one hundred if it wasn't for a tragic accident that paralyzed him from the neck down. When horseback riding with friends near his home, one of the women who was riding in the party had difficulty with her skittish horse. Ever the gentleman, General Palmer offered the woman his gentle steed and ended up riding her jumpy horse. When he approached his home, he reached down to open the gate, while still on horseback, just like he had done a thousand times in the past. The skittish horse bucked as the General was leaning forward, and he tumbled off the horse and awkwardly hit his head, breaking his neck. Tragically, as a result of his critical injury he was paralyzed. It was a miracle he even survived the accident, but the General had the money to afford the best doctors and technology to help him with his paralysis. The General lived another two years being cared for in his wheelchair. In 1907, he invited the men of his Pennsylvania cavalry to Colorado to celebrate their annual reunion. The General paid for everything and housed his men at his Antlers Hotel. He even allowed his men to drink alcohol in Colorado Springs and ignored the laws of the dry town he founded.

When he died in 1909 at the age of 72, the entire state of Colorado flew their flags at half-mast. This pacifist Quaker general had lived an astounding life. General Palmer built railroads across the state of Colorado, but he was also a devoted family man to his three daughters and a loving husband who built a castle for his queen. He was a generous employer, who paid medical bills and set up retirement funds for his dedicated employees. He was a great man who gave the equivalent of 100 million dollars to various causes and charities in Colorado and was a conservationist who loved nature and the beautiful mountains of Colorado. He was a man who has done more for the Pikes Peak region than any other person.

In 1992, I had the privilege of taping an interview with General Palmer's great -granddaughter, Louisa Creed. She lived in England and was visiting Colorado with her husband to tour the city her great-grandfather had founded. She looked like her great grandmother Queen Palmer and had the same beautiful, big brown eyes. She was very soft-spoken with her British accent and spoke lovingly of her grandmother, General Palmer's daughter. Her grandmother had told her many stories about her father, the General, and his gentle nature, quiet courage, and his brilliant mind.

A statue of General Palmer is positioned in the middle of the intersection of East Platte and North Nevada Avenue in downtown Colorado Springs. Palmer sits on his horse facing the mountain he loved. For years, the statue has caused controversy, and many people have wanted to move it, since the traffic on Platte and Nevada have had to dart around it dangerously. Although it has been discussed at many city council meetings, the people of Colorado Springs have always voted against moving the statue. No history loving citizen of Colorado Springs would dare cause the general to lose his view of the mountain he loved.

# THE BEST BOSS I EVER HAD

Starting with my first paper route at 11 years old, I probably have had close to 40 bosses or supervisors over the course of a fifty-year working career. The range of the quality of my supervisors covers a vast array of competence and ability. Having been a boss myself, I understand how challenging it is to monitor a work force and to balance all the personalities supervisors deal with.

When I took the job at Pikes Peak Community College, the man who hired me in the library had been promoted to vice president of the college. About six months after I was hired, his position was open; and we needed to hire a new college library director. I was fortunate to be assigned to the hiring committee. It was an opportunity to pick the right person I would report to. Although very competent when it came to organization, our previous library director was a difficult and demanding person to work for; and many of our staff were afraid of him. The person we were hiring would not directly work for our previous director, so it gave our staff freedom to pick the right person whose decisions would not be second guessed by the former director.

Dr. Camila Alire had been working for Denver University as an assistant dean and professor. In 1982 Denver University decided to eliminate their library program; and, fortunately, for Pikes Peak Community College, Camila was looking for a job. Camila, is a bundle of positive energy. Five feet one inches tall with her shoes on, she is always smiling and looking for a positive way to solve any challenge. When she entered the room for the interview, even before we asked her a question, I knew she was the person we needed to hire. She reminded me of my Spanish grandmother because of her ease with people and positive outlook on life. In her early 30s at the time, she was a great listener and was extremely curious about every person she met. A Colorado native, Camila was born in the small town of Monte Vista, in the San Luis Valley near the Great Sand Dunes National Monument. The San Luis Valley is one of most interesting and isolated spots in Colorado. Originally the home of the mountain Utes, the area was settled by the Spaniards in the 1500's who assimilated with the indigenous people and forced them to adopt their Spanish language and culture. Many of the people who live in the valley today are direct descendants of those original Mountain Utes and the early Spanish explorers. Monte Vista, which means "mountain view" in English, had changed very little in the past century. Dr. Camila Alire, one of the most successful people to come out of Monte Vista, was a former high school cheerleader who was a fireball of energy and independence. She had a stellar career in libraries and eventually was elected the president of the American Library Association (ALA) from 2009 to 2010.

The reason I became a librarian is because of Camila Alire. She was a walking billboard for the profession. Although I'm sure she had her moments of frustration, it was a rare occasion to see her without a smile. She was by far the best boss I ever had. She let me have the freedom to work on any project I wanted, as long as I worked hard and helped my patrons who were the various teachers and professors at Pikes Peak Community College. As media specialist, I did a variety of video productions and operated the closed-circuit system we used to run programming for the college classes. With Camila as our library director, it was almost like Camelot. I enjoyed going to work and knew she always had my back, as long as I contributed to the department's goals.

Over the course of my career, I always tried to stay in touch with Camila and used her as a reference for many jobs. She moved on to bigger positions and had a storied career in academic libraries. In 2012, President Obama appointed her to the Council on the Humanities. If you ever had the honor to work for her or to be her friend, you will never find a more down- to-earth leader. However, she ruined me for the rest of my career. Since I left Pikes Peak Community College in 1986, I had some very good bosses, but I never worked for anyone who lived up to her standards as a leader and as a friend.

# WATCHING THE DETECTIVE

Working at Pikes Peak Community College (PPCC) was the beginning of my career as a documentary video maker. I finally had the equipment and the opportunity to create educational documentaries that challenged me and allowed me to establish my career. Of all the people I met in my life, no one influenced me more than a retired New York City detective named Sol Zlochower. Sol believed in my talent and encouraged me to do my best work. When I reflect on the friends I have had in my life, I realize that I was closest to Sol Zlochower. While I loved my father, and appreciated the opportunities he provided me, we never crossed over from a father and son relationship to a relationship where I felt comfortable enough to tell him my hopes, dreams, and disappointments. Since I married at 22 years old and never again lived in the same city as my parents, we were lucky if we got together for more than a few weeks during the year. My parents had relocated from Colorado to Texas two years before I graduated from the University of Colorado. They visited their grandchildren; but it was always a brief visit and never enough time to talk seriously with my dad about life in general. It wasn't anyone's fault; it just was the way it was, since we didn't have that many shared experiences as adults.

Over time, Sol became a second father to me. Before he died I could tell him almost anything, and he could do the same with me. It is very difficult for me to write about our friendship even today. As I look back at my life, I can count on one hand the people whom I felt completely comfortable to reveal my true self and to share my most intimate thoughts. I knew Sol for 13 years, from 1981 until his death from ALS (Lou Gehrig's disease) in 1994. Shortly after I started work as a media specialist at PPCC, I met Sol at the library. I loved my four years working in an educational library at a community college. It was the first decent job I had that allowed me to purchase a home and to support my family. Since it was a State of Colorado job, it had excellent benefits which included health care and retirement; and it also paid a livable wage. As a media specialist, I was hired to help the instructors with producing educational video productions and to assist them with whatever video needs they had in the classroom.

When I first met Sol, he was in his mid-50's; and with his solid grey hair, he looked older than he was. He taught in the criminal justice program and had been honored several times as the state-wide community college teacher of the year. Sol had blue-collar roots, and his family were Jewish refugees from both Russia and Europe who immigrated in the early 1900s to New York. He said it was just like *Fiddler on the Roof* for the Zlochower family, since they were fleeing Jewish persecution in Russia. His relatives, who remained in Russia and Europe, died during the Holocaust.

Since he was one of the star instructors at the college, it was very important for me to keep him happy. My first impression was that he was a little demanding and difficult. He had been a police detective in New York City for 20 years, and he was used to intimidating people to get what he wanted. He was teaching criminal justice when he first approached me to tape his crisis intervention class. He asked me to video tape the mock crisis intervention scenarios and then play them back in class so he could critique each taped skit with his students. It was almost like an improv class where some of his students played the criminals, and the other students portrayed the cops. The students who performed as the criminals had the most fun; they escalated the situation and made it very difficult for the students who portrayed the cops. All the time this was going on Sol assumed the role as the director. He critiqued what the students had done and would tell an appropriate story from his own experiences as a NYPD police detective and the best way to deal with a difficult situation. The class had to be held in the college theatre, since over 100 criminal justice students enrolled in his class.

I immediately understood why he was teacher of the year; he was so dynamic and based on his background, extremely qualified to teach criminal justice students. He was an entertainer and loved being a teacher. He told me later that being a teacher literally saved his life. Born into a working class Jewish family in New York City, he had joined the Navy at the end of World War II to become a pilot. The war ended before the Navy shipped him overseas. After the service, he worked as an airline clerk where he met and married his wife Gladys. He was a 25-year-old man with a young family looking for a good job with benefits when he applied to the NYC Police Department. After leaving the airline, he worked in the garment district repairing handbags when he applied to become a police officer. He told me that before he became a cop, he was a nice, shy Jewish young man who was just trying to improve his life.

His personality completely changed over the 20 years he was a police officer. He morphed into a hardened racist who trusted no one. Because of his intimate exposure to all types of crime, he was very difficult and strict with his two daughters. He worked for the New York Police Department during a time when the mob ran the city, and corruption and bribery were part of being a New York City cop. The corrupt cops pocketed a pool of money from taking various bribes and they split their profits at the end of each month from their pad of illegal payoffs.

This type of corruption was explored in the movie *Serpico*. Sol stayed away from being a narcotics detective because the temptation to take cash bribes was too much to resist. Instead, he became a homicide detective and enjoyed the challenge of trying to solve murders. By the time he left the force, he had transformed into a racist because most of his dealings with minorities were as criminals. Being one of the few Jewish policemen on the force, he always felt a little out of place. For most of his time on the force, his partner was an Italian-American man with whom he had remained close to throughout their lives. He explained that his partner had to be closer to him than even his wife and kids, since they depended on each other in life-and-death situations.

For most of Sol's career he worked in high-crime areas, including Harlem and Brooklyn; and he made over 1,000 arrests during his career. When he was 45, he retired with a gold shield but didn't really have any idea what he wanted to do. Working in dangerous and demanding situations for 20 years left him with many emotional scars and post-traumatic stress. He knew he couldn't continue to work in law enforcement, so he decided to teach. He had earned his four-year degree at night school, while he was working full time as a cop. He thought about law school, but an opportunity opened for him to teach at Western Illinois University. The university allowed him to earn his master's degree if he agreed to teach criminal justice. At Western Illinois, he discovered that teaching was his calling. He never felt that he could help anyone as a cop. The arrests were the end of his contacts with these broken people who had turned to lives of crime. Once he became a teacher, he really felt that he could actually help people and he abandoned his racist feelings.

His students loved him, and he was named teacher of the year at Western Illinois. One time he told me about a highly-recruited basketball player in his class. The student rarely showed up to class, and Sol deservedly flunked him. The basketball coach, who could normally intimidate professors into giving his athletes passing grades, angrily approached Sol. "Why did you give my athlete an F?" he screamed. Sol, who was incapable of being intimidated by anyone, calmly responded, "Because I couldn't give him a G." It was that sense of humor and sharp wit that made him a popular professor.

After ten years at Western Illinois, this New York City kid decided to live his lifelong dream of moving to the mountains, so he applied for a job at Pikes Peak Community College in Colorado Springs. Since the criminal justice program was happy to acquire such an accomplished instructor, he moved his wife and youngest daughter to Woodland Park. A man of many talents, he designed and built a beautiful home and commuted the 30 minutes from his remote mountain house to his teaching job.

One aspect I loved about working at a community college is that professors worked in their professions for a number of years before they actually taught. They didn't transfer from one academic institution to another to get their Ph. Ds and then teach. They were usually very hard-working people who earned their master's degrees after they worked in their professions for several years. That was the case with Sol; students couldn't ask for a more qualified professor who had seen every possible situation in his job as a cop.

Sol lived a dozen lives during his time as a NYC detective. He had a thousand stories to match each of his thousand arrests. One of the stories was about the unlimited physical strength of women. Early in his career, he worked vice and posed as a john. When he entered the tenth-story apartment, three female prostitutes propositioned him. Since he was working undercover, he didn't carry a gun with him; but showed the three ladies his badge and attempted to arrest them. His partner was downstairs in case Sol needed him, waiting in an unmarked car. The three ladies began to fight him and resist arrest. He tried to run out the door; but like most New York City apartments, the door had multiple locks to open it. He almost got the door open when they dragged him away toward the window. They were determined to throw him out of the window, which would have killed him instantly. At 6' and 200 pounds, Sol was physically very strong, but despite his strength he had great difficulty breaking away from the three women as they dragged him towards the open window. At the last minute he broke free and ran back to the door. This went on two or three times in a comic ballet before he was finally able to open the door and run downstairs to his partner. Sol and his partner grabbed their guns, returned to the apartment, and arrested the three women. He advised me never to underestimate the physical strength of women, particularly when they were upset and filled with adrenalin.

It didn't take long before Sol and I became friends. After a rough beginning when we first met, for whatever reason, he took a liking to me; I reminded him of his youthful self, a young man who had a family at an early age and was working hard to make a living. He also wanted to do more than just tape his criminal-justice programs; he wanted to produce documentaries. That was my goal as well: to produce educational documentaries that were also entertaining. He was teaching the correctional programs at the time and knew the people, including the director, in the Colorado Department of Corrections. Sol was a natural interviewer because of his detective background, a Mike Wallace type interviewer, who was fearless and was willing to ask the most difficult questions.

Our first hour-long, comprehensive documentary, *Outlaws of the New West*, was on the contemporary western Colorado prison system. It was a major project for the both of us and required five separate days of shooting at all the major prison facilities near Canon City. We were a two-man crew; Sol was the interviewer, and I was the camera person and editor. It was a perfect marriage of our talents. He was fearless working with and interviewing the inmates while I was skilled at working behind the scenes doing production. Back then video equipment weighed a ton; fortunately, I was young and physically fit and could carry the tripod, camera, ¾" Umatic video recorder, and lights. It was just Sol and I, and he also helped carrying some of the equipment between each location. I had never been to prison before, as a criminal or as a guest. Sol was completely at ease and walked through the prison with no fear. We mingled with the prisoners without any special protection, and the inmates were more than willing to break up their boredom by being on camera and helping us with the documentary.

The most interesting facility was the women's prison. The ladies were happy to have contact with the outside world and especially the opportunity to talk to two men. The documentary was shown statewide on the PBS affiliate in Denver several times. It received several awards in Colorado and nationally, and it was a real boost for my job. Other instructors wanted me to help them produce documentaries which kept me busy. However, I happily dropped everything to do another documentary with Sol. We became very close through the making of this first documentary and I became the son he never had, and he became the father I never had a chance to bond with as an adult.

At the time of our video project, *Scared Straight* was a well-known prison documentary that introduced juvenile offenders to the realities of prison. The Colorado Department of Corrections had a similar program called *Shape Up*. It was different in that the inmates didn't go out of their way to frighten the kids; it was more of an honest look at the horrors of prison life. Sol decided we should tape the program and produce our second documentary. The inmates involved were proud of the *Shape-Up* program and very helpful in allowing us access to their lives in prison. Our documentary *Shape-Up: An Alternative to Scared Straight* was even more successful than *Outlaws of the West*. The 30-minute documentary was shown statewide on the PBS affiliate KRMA - Denver. When it was nominated for a regional Emmy and a national cable ACE award, we both planned to travel to Las Vegas to attend the national ACE award ceremonies. Unfortunately, Sol and Gladys' 28-year-old daughter Amy, who lived with her husband in Colorado, had developed a malignant melanoma. In six short months she passed away. His surviving older daughter Maida, who lived in New York her entire career, was a computer software engineer for both AT&T and IBM. Amy's death devastated the entire family and Sol just wanted to work on more projects to stay busy.

As time went on Sol followed me from job to job. I worked for Pikes Peak Community College for four years and then was offered a job with the area cable company to produce local programming. At first it looked like a wonderful opportunity with more money and bigger budgets for production. Sol and I worked together on another project with the Department of Corrections on the high percentage of drug offenders in prison. The title of the documentary was *Jails, Institutions, or Death*. The title was taken from an inmate who talked about the horrors of drug addiction and the three possible outcomes if drug users didn't become clean. I learned a great deal about video production during my two years with the cable company, but my work schedule was difficult on my family and myself. I was working 70 hours a week trying to fill a cable channel with programming. Like *Wayne's World* we were producing public access and local origination programming. I could write an entire book on my experiences working for the cable company and the variety of people I met working with public access.

Under our city contract, I assisted with the local school districts and the public library to provide programming and access to our cable system. Because of that outreach, I had the good fortune to work with Judy Evans, the communications manager for the Pikes Peak Library District and my eventual boss. The Pikes Peak Library District was hoping to have their own cable channel for producing a variety of programs from the library. The cable company also provided some financial support through our cable agreement with the city. The director of the library, Ken Dowlin, had written the book the *Electronic Library.* Ken was well respected as an innovator who was one of the first library directors to automate his library. The Pikes Peak Library District had one of the first computerized public access catalogs in the nation he called *Maggie's Place,* since It was housed in the same place where Maggie the librarian had worked.

When they opened a job for a manager of their cable efforts, I jumped at the opportunity. It was an excellent job with retirement and medical benefits and was perfect for my young family. I spent the next 20 years with the Pikes Peak Library District, and it was my incentive to go on to graduate school to earn my Masters in Library Science through an extension program at Emporia State University.

The Pikes Peak Library District was very generous to allow me to continue producing documentaries with Sol. Since he was a well-respected professor, PPLD encouraged me to keep doing our projects together. Our last hour-long documentary was a comprehensive history on the Colorado Department of Corrections. Through interviews with long-term inmates and retired staff members, we told the history of this famous western prison. In the 1950's a theatrical film, *Canon City,* featured a famous prison break that actually took place at the prison in the 40's. We secured the rights to the film and showed various clips which featured an interview with Roy Best, the warden at the time. It was another successful project for us, and we were again nominated for several local cable awards as well as another national ACE award.

I had just completed my master's degree when Sol began to have balance problems. He lived in Woodland Park at 8,500 feet and wondered if the altitude was contributing to his balance and breathing problems. He had always been a very healthy man, who at 64, helped me with the laborious task of moving to a new home. Living in the mountains, he was physically active with chopping wood and building two homes there. He was a Renaissance man, an oil painter and master carpenter. He loved art and architecture; and if he had not become a cop, most likely he could have become a successful architect, just like his younger brother.

Since Sol knew something was wrong, he made an appointment at the Mayo clinic in Phoenix and was diagnosed with ALS in 1993. He knew it was a death sentence. Like Lou Gehrig and Stephen Hawkings, he was well aware of his eventual fate. A man who had lost his daughter to cancer and who had lived a thousand lives as a detective, he could clearly see the end. I tried to spend as much time with Sol and his wife Gladys as I could that last year. They knew they couldn't keep their home In Woodland Park, since living at that altitude was problematic. They bought a home in Sun City, Arizona, and made plans to move where his sister and brother had retired. If it was possible, we actually became closer during those last months. When a person knows his fate, he holds on tighter to the people he loves. He confided in me that he did not want to burden his wife with a long-extended illness, so he pledged to me that he would never spend a day in a nursing home.

The last time I saw Sol alive was at his home in Woodland Park. He was already feeling the effects of ALS and had to be on oxygen. I was visiting with Sol and his wife at their beautiful mountain home that he had designed and built. Amy's and his artwork covered the walls. I didn't want to leave, since I knew this was the end and the last time I would see him alive. When I drove down the mountain, I cried quietly. Sol was one of the closest people I had known in my life. We had done some of our best work together producing our five documentaries, but our friendship was the greatest result of our partnership. After he moved to Arizona, we talked on the phone every week. He stayed as positive as he could, but I knew the ALS was taking its toll.

Six months after he moved to Arizona, Sol's brother called to tell me Sol had died. In the middle of the night, he had gotten up from his bed and went back to sleep on the couch in his living room. The next morning his wife found him lying on the couch and not breathing. By the time the ambulance arrived, Sol was dead. Like he promised, he never spent a day in a nursing home or a hospital at the end. It is very difficult for me to write about this even now. We all have moments in time that we have shared with people we love. The twelve years I spent as Sol's friend are extremely precious to me. He made me a better person and challenged me with each project. He made me laugh and he made me cry.

# MY OWN CHANNEL

When I started at the Pikes Peak Library District in 1988, I was given my own channel to program. The city contract with the cable company required them to provide the library with their own cable access channel. The Library Channel 17 was an empty canvas to fill. At the time, The Library Channel was on the basic channel tier and broadcast into the homes of 70,000 cable subscribers which translated into almost 200,000 people. It potentially reached almost half of the residents of El Paso County and was an opportunity to bring a variety of local historical and library information into our patrons' homes.

I had produced thousands of programs for local cable in my two previous jobs with Pikes Peak Community College and Colorado Springs Cablevision, but this was different. This was my own channel to program and the opportunity to cultivate an audience. It was a daunting task for one person to fill a channel with quality programming. Over the next 20 years, I did my best to fill it with a variety of programs on Pikes Peak regional history and library-supported projects. It was during that time that I met some of the most amazing people. I focused my programming on video portraits. These were documentaries on the residents of Colorado Springs who were pivotal to our local history. We produced hundreds of these video portraits, and I conducted many of the interviews. It was a terrific opportunity to meet the movers and the shakers of our community.

Everyone I interviewed was gracious and appreciated our effort to capture their life in a video portrait. We combined the interview footage of the portrait with a variety of still pictures to tell the story. Just like the Ken Burns documentaries, we used a variety of stills and a front projection system that allowed us to do movement on each photo. As the technology advanced in future years, the computer-editing systems allowed us to use the same movement on the photos with digital effects.

We produced a monthly schedule that gave us a variety of flexibility. When we weren't showing original documentaries and informational programs on the channel, we ran PowerPoint visual graphics that promoted the library events for that week. After our original evening programming ended, starting around 10 p.m., we ran a satellite feed of the Classic Arts Showcase, a noncommercial feed that showed classic music, dance, and theatrical performance in a series of short five-to-ten minute videos. Funded by the Lloyd Rigler Foundation, it is an amazing mix of art performance that covered a variety of genres. Whenever we had technical problems or if it was off the air, we heard from our viewers immediately. They loved the Classic Arts Showcase, and it was a perfect match with our historical programming.

Colorado Springs and the Pikes Peak region is a beautiful area with great parks and a magnificent view of the mountains. Since General Palmer founded the city in 1871, many talented photographers who were attracted by the scenic beauty, photographed this natural wonderland over the years. The Pikes Peak Library District had a tremendous collection of historic photographs and films that covered the history of the region. It would be hard to find a more photographed community than Colorado Springs. Because of this photographic history, we were provided with a wealth of visual material for our video portraits and our award-winning history series, *Colorado Springs: The Way It Was.*

In the beginning, it was just me producing all the programming. I was the chef, the food prep, the server, and the busboy all in one. As time went on, I hired two staff members who helped me create and provide programming for the library channel. Dave Rickert was transferred to my department after my second year, and Danny Walter was added to my staff after my fifth year. We also used a variety of volunteers and had a small substitute budget to hire extra people as needed. One of our volunteers was Bob Fitzmorris, a man who had been in television since it began. He helped launch the local ABC affiliate KRDO on the air in the 1950's and worked as a director during the early days of television. Bob was always an upbeat person who told the cleanest jokes. He loved puns and always introduced himself by saying, "Hello, my name is Bob; I spell it with one "O." Other volunteers and substitute employees who helped us with our programming included Peter Blaney, Lee Graham, Mary Gilcreest, and Ralph Giordano, plus a variety of interns and students.

Many times, people in the community provided us with their own programming which aired on the channel - if it met our technology standards and was non-commercial. There are many talented individual video makers who lived in Colorado Springs and provided us with great programming. Ralph Giordano, an NYU graduate and former employee of mine at the cable company, was active in recruiting local talent and produced dozens of his own programs for our channel. University of Colorado at Colorado Springs video students provided us with some very unique student films and Ralph produced his own program featuring local films and video artists. Jim Ciletti, who with his wife Mary owns *Hooked on Books* in Colorado Springs, is also a talented filmmaker and poet. Jim provided us with an excellent short film called *Bear Dance*. It was a documentary on the centuries old Ute Native American tribal dance, where the young women selected their male dance partners. It was a beautifully shot film that I programed many times on our channel. Rick Zahradnik, a good friend who I mention in another chapter, is a local actor and was a great source of comedic films for our channel. His comedies were often brilliant and featured the very talented local acting community.

Having our own channel to operate original programs made all the difference to our efforts to reach patrons. We reached a large audience on cable, and the local history was a significant part of our programming.

Since Colorado Springs had a large military population, we worked closely with the Veterans Day committee producing video portraits on the parade's grand marshal and other veterans. Working with our local history department and the Pioneers Museum, we did our part to teach the history of our community to the city's newcomers. With the military population turning over every three to four years, we always had a fresh audience who wanted to learn about the history of their new community.

During my 20 years at the Pikes Peak Library District I worked under some excellent Library Directors and Communication Managers who were my direct supervisors. It seemed like the management of the library changed every four years and I had to always sell the new leadership on why they should continue to fund us. I started briefly under Ken Dowlin, who left after my first month with the library. Then it was New York native Bernie Margolis, Pat Losinski (who was wonderful library director and stayed for six years), Jose Aponte, and finally Paula Miller. Paula had a gentle nature and was always supportive of our work.

In 2004 Jose Aponte conceived an award winning video project entitled *De Donde Eres?* which included over 30 interviews with prominent Hispanic individuals and families in Southern Colorado. It explored their diverse Hispanic heritage and what the word Hispanic means in terms of culture and country of origin. Two edited versions of De Donde Eres? are available to watch on YouTube.

During the twenty plus years our directors changed, associate director Sydne Caler would step in to provide excellent consistent leadership as the interim director. Recently John Spears was hired as the new library director and CEO and John has shown strong leadership in his first two years. I also worked under some wonderful Communication Directors including Judy Evans, Sheila Ferguson and Dee Sabol.

# BACK TO SCHOOL

In 1989 I thought I was dying. I started having difficulty swallowing. It got to the point that I was able to eat only soft foods. I lost 40 pounds in about three months. Losing weight was the only good byproduct of my health issues. I reached my ideal weight and looked healthy. As we tried to figure out what was wrong with me, my doctor commented how good I looked from losing 40 pounds. To quote Billy Crystal's Fernando I told him, "It is not how good you feel, but how good you look, and I looked marvelous." The best way to describe my health issue is I felt like there was a stick in my throat all my time. It also interfered with my breathing, and there were a couple times I felt like I was slowly suffocating. For anyone who has dealt with health issues—and that is probably everyone who is reading this—it is an attention getter and causes thoughts about mortality. No one is guaranteed even a day. The doctor's scoped my throat and found some scar tissue that might have been the problem; they extracted a sample and tested it for throat cancer. Fortunately, the cancer test was benign, but they were unsure of the cause of the scar tissue. My doctor speculated it could have been caused from acid reflux, or it could have been a chemical irritation I may have gotten during a dental cleaning. In any case, it took almost two years before I slowly felt normal again, and I could swallow properly.

While in the middle of this health crisis, I decided to attend graduate school. The Pikes Peak Library District had offered scholarship money for any staff member who wanted to earn a Master's in Library Science. After the closure of the Denver University Library School in 1982, there had not been a library school in Colorado for almost seven years. Emporia State in Kansas took advantage of this opportunity and opened an extension program in Colorado. The program was designed for people who were working and needed a flexible schedule to get their degrees. Almost 130 people, including myself, signed up for this accredited Master's in Library Science program that took approximately 2 ½ years to complete.

The classes were taught one at a time for a three-week period. We attended class Friday evenings, all day Saturdays and Sunday mornings for three weeks in a row. We had the next week off and started again the following week with a new class. We also appreciated additional breaks during the summer and holidays. Our students represented employees from almost every public and academic library in the state. Most of us were in our thirties at the time, and the camaraderie among the students was the best part of the program. Several of the students from Colorado Springs rented a room in a fellow student's Denver home. Living in that home was like a weekend retreat, and it was in some ways like going back to college, since I started drinking again.

In order to deal with my chronic pain while swallowing, I was prescribed opiate pain pills which did help; and I started taking three of these pills each day. It didn't take long for me to become addicted. As I recovered, I slowly weaned myself from three to two pills to one and down to ½ a pill per day. In order to help me get off these pills, I used alcohol as a substitute. I bought a small bottle of rum for the weekend classes and drank enough to get me through the three days of school. Some of my fellow students met at a bar on Friday before class, and I guzzled a few beers and had a slight buzz for Friday's class. On Saturdays and Sundays, I sipped from my bottle of rum. It was not the not the most responsible approach to dealing with my pain, but I made sure I never got drunk enough to be a danger to myself or anyone else, just enough to numb the pain. I hate to say it, but I had a 3.9 grade-point average when I graduated, and I essentially progressed through graduate school slightly drunk. Once I got through the two years of chronic pain, I stopped drinking. I can happily say I don't drink anymore, except an occasional glass of wine.

Despite my alcohol consumption, I did learn a great deal through the Emporia State program. I tell everyone: library school is not law school, but students still need to pay attention in class. Both my daughters graduated from law schools, and I'm certain they had to complete ten times the work I did to get their law degrees. Most MLS programs require a great deal of reading and writing, but there was also plenty of repetition in a number of my classes. In 1991, word processing and personal computers were just starting to take off. With all the writing we had to do, having access to a word processor made my life easier. By the time we graduated, our class size had decreased to around 90 people. I advise anyone who is working in a library to eventually pursue an MLS degree – if they want to make more money and have an opportunity to do specialized work or become managers. Prior experience working in libraries before you get your degree also makes for better librarians. Many librarians began their career as shelvers; and they have seen how a library works on every level. The best decision I ever made was getting my Master's Degree in Library Science. Anyone who wants a career in libraries should eventually acquire a graduate degree in library science, but please don't do what I did, I recommend that you try and go through the program sober.

# THE STORYTELLERS OF COLORADO SPRINGS

If someone were to identify the two most important storytellers and authors from Colorado Springs, it would have to be Frank Waters and Marshall Sprague. Frank Waters, who was born in Colorado Springs in 1902, was probably the most influential and renowned Colorado author. He was part Cheyenne Native American and that had a significant influence on his writing. As a novelist, he was the contemporary of John Steinbeck and Ernest Hemmingway and wrote about the unique American experience. His most famous novels *The People of the Valley* and *The Man Who Killed the Deer* celebrated the native American experience in the Southwest. I had the privilege to meet and to videotape Frank Waters at a program sponsored by the Pioneers Museum in 1992. He was 90 years old at the time as he reminisced about his childhood. His first historical biography, *Midas of the Rockies*, was published in 1937 and was the definitive biography on Cripple Creek millionaire Winfield Scott Stratton. Frank Waters died in 1995, and the Frank Waters Foundation continues to benefit the arts with literary retreats near the Sangre De Christo Mountains in the San Luis Valley he loved.

Marshall Sprague, who was born in 1909 in Newark, Ohio, moved to Colorado Springs after he contracted tuberculosis in 1941. He had been married for only two years to Edna Jane, known to her friends as E.J., when they both moved to Colorado for his health. The Pikes Peak region was known for its great climate and dry air, and thousands of people with tuberculous relocated to Colorado Springs in the early part of the 20<sup>th</sup> century to "take the cure." The cure at the time, before antibiotics, required isolation and rest for several years and moderate exercise in a dry mountain climate.

Marshall Sprague had been a journalist for the *New York Times*, as well as working as a journalist in Paris and China. While recuperating in Colorado Springs, he started writing non-fiction historical novels. His 1953 book *Money Mountain* was the definitive history of the Cripple Creek gold rush. A year prior to his death in 1994, I had sat down with our special collections manager Ree Mobley to videotape Marshall and Edna Jane. They were a delightful couple who made us feel at home. We produced a 30-minute documentary on his life and work in Colorado. The title of the documentary was *The Life and Good Times of Marshall Sprague*. Marshall Sprague loved jazz music and still played clarinet with a local group of jazz enthusiasts. Without a doubt, Marshall Sprague is still the premier journalist and non-fiction author of the Pikes Peak region.

# THE BLUEBLOODS OF THE PIKES PEAK REGION

Although General William Jackson Palmer founded Colorado Springs, it was the wealth and the guidance of Spencer Penrose that brought the city into the 20<sup>th</sup> century. The two men were vastly different in personality and style, but they had one thing in common: their genuine love for the Pikes Peak region and the city of Colorado Springs that was their home. Spencer Penrose, who heralded from a prominent Philadelphia family, was the black sheep of this very successful clan of physicians, businessmen, and politicians. Graduating last in his class from Harvard University, he was a lady's man who loved to box and was quick to use his fist. His family was embarrassed by his antics and helped finance his desire to leave Philadelphia to go out west to find his fortune. His brashness was an asset in the Wild West, and he relocated to the Pikes Peak region at the invitation of his childhood friend Charles Leaming Tutt, Sr. They became partners in the real estate business and invested in a gold mine in Cripple Creek. That was the beginning of Spencer Penrose's great fortune that would eventually be put into an influential charitable trust, The El Pomar Foundation. Although Spencer's fortune was mostly generated by his copper mines in Utah, it is his famous five-star luxury Broadmoor Hotel he is mostly widely known for.

The Broadmoor Hotel, built in 1909, has a rich tradition. When Charles Leaming Tutt, Sr. died at the early age of 45, his only child and son, Charles Leaming Tutt, Jr. was just 19 years old. Mr. Penrose felt an obligation to guide the fortunes of his late partner's son and he made him secretary of the Broadmoor Hotel. Penrose had a close relationship with Charles and Charles' three sons until Spencer's death in 1939. When Mr. Penrose was the age of 41, the handsome bachelor and playboy finally settled down and married the beautiful widow, Julie Veniers. It was Julie's influence over Spencer that convinced him to create the El Pomar Foundation. His tremendous fortune at the time of his death, including his most famous asset, the Broadmoor Hotel, was placed in a trust for the foundation. The El Pomar Foundation was created to fund non-profit Colorado organizations. Since the foundation was created in 1939, the board of directors has given over $100,000,000 to local Colorado non-profits,

Over the years, several members of the Tutt family have guided the foundation; and in their very capable hands it has grown to a $500,000,000 charity that gives away $20,000,000 annually. After Spencer's death, Julie Penrose promoted Charles Leaming Tutt to be president of the Broadmoor Hotel in 1939; and he also became president of the El Pomar Foundation upon Julie's death in 1954.

Very few people who were living in Colorado, at the time I produced the documentary in 1988, had known Spencer Penrose personally. When we opened the studio in 1988, I met Charles Leaming Tutt, III. He was on the board of the friends of the Pikes Peak Library District. In his seventies at the time, he was a very kind gentleman who wanted to preserve the family's history while the three brothers were still alive to record it. Charlie Tutt, III, a Princeton graduate, was the only brother to have left Colorado Springs to pursue a career as mechanical engineer for General Motors. His younger brother Russell Thayer Tutt and William Thayer Tutt stayed in Colorado Springs and worked for the El Pomar Foundation and the Broadmoor Hotel for their entire careers. They all had enjoyed a close relationship with Spencer Penrose and had many personal stories they could tell about this great leader of Colorado Springs.

Knowing I was working with the royalty of Colorado Springs and the first family of the Broadmoor Hotel, I was a little intimidated when I started the project. My first project was a 30-minute interview and documentary on Ben Wendelken. Mr. Wendelken was a man of humble roots whose mother owned a boarding house in Colorado Springs. As a young man, Ben worked as a laborer on the Broadmoor Hotel when it was built in 1909. A brilliant student, he attended Colorado College and eventually became an attorney. He first met Spencer Penrose when he was suing him in court and was his legal adversary. Ben did such an exemplary job in the courtroom that Mr. Penrose decided after the trial to hire him as one of his attorneys. After Penrose died, Ben worked with his widow Julie to create the El Pomar Foundation. He remained as the attorney for the El Pomar Foundation until his death in 1991. The 30-minute documentary on Ben was a success, and his good nature and Jimmie Stewart- like humility came through during the interview.

My next project was the sixty-minute documentary on the three Tutt brothers. I entitled it "The Tutt Legacy." Charlie Tutt was most helpful on guiding me through this project. Although a blue blood who came from a wealthy family, Charlie was in reality a grease monkey who loved to tinker with cars and spent a career with General Motors. He reminded me of my blue-collar Father, who also loved working with cars and my father had also spent his career with General Motors. Even though we had very different backgrounds, Charlie and I connected. The three Tutt brothers had wonderful stories about working with Mr. Penrose and being around the Broadmoor Hotel for their careers. Thayer Tutt related how the Depression affected this luxury hotel; and at times during the early 1930's, they registered only a dozen guests on a single day. Mr. Penrose used his vast wealth to keep the doors open and his staff employed. He loved the hotel so much that he never thought about closing it.

It was Charlie's foresight to conduct the interviews; three years after the documentaries were completed, all the Tutt brothers and Ben Wendelken had died. Since the time I produced the documentary, the El Pomar

Foundation has sold the hotel. Their offices are still on the Broadmoor grounds, and they also operate the Penrose House Conference Center. The Penrose House Conference Center is located in the original Spanish-style home of Julie and Spencer Penrose, just blocks away from the hotel. The home is available for no charge to any non-profit organization in Colorado to hold meetings and events. When I was still working, both the Pikes Peak Library District and the Pueblo City-County Library District, both organizations had used the Penrose House Conference Center for planning retreats. There is not a more beautiful spot in Colorado to hold a planning event. The center has several meeting rooms and millions of dollars of historic art work on the walls. And, secret shelves behind movable walls that shelved hundreds of bottles of alcohol during Prohibition. Deer and other wildlife run freely on the grounds.

Through the making of the documentary, Charles Tutt and I became friends. He was very pleased with the final production and knew the value it had for regional history. To my surprise he invited me as his guest to one of the most exclusive clubs in Colorado, The Cooking Club. The famous and less famous like myself were invited to this traditional event where we participated by cooking steaks and lobsters and served the food to the members. The twenty guests sat down for the dinner and celebrated the tradition that Mr. Penrose started. Everyone dressed up in chefs' clothing, and we posed for a picture in front of the house where the event took place near the Broadmoor Hotel. To say I was intimidated by the stature of the guests was an understatement. Fortunately, Charlie sensed my uneasiness and made me feel comfortable and welcomed. This is how the other half lived; it was lifestyles of the rich and famous. Two prominent individuals at the event were one of the Coors brothers and a famous Italian born figure-skating coach, Carlo Fassi. Carlo had coached American figure skater and gold medalist Peggy Fleming.

After everyone had a few drinks and we all loosened up, I quickly realized that the rich and famous were not much different from the rest of us. They told crude jokes that I remember to this day, and I happily joined in the laughter. Coach Fassi told a joke I still remember. He told the story of two World War II generals who were allies. One German general and one

Italian general who were sharing information about how they led their men into battle. The German general said that he always wore a red jacket in battle, in case he was shot and started bleeding. His red blood would match his jacket, and his men wouldn't notice he was hurt and would keep fighting. The Italian general thought it was a brilliant idea, so he went back to his tailor and asked him to make him "brown pants" for his next battle. I have always been grateful to Charles Leaming Tutt, III for involving me in this wonderful project and inviting me to the Cooking Club.

I can't say enough about the El Pomar Foundation and their generosity to public libraries across the state. The Tutt family is still very connected to El Pomar and the current vice-chairman is Russell Thayer Tutt Jr. who is the son of Russell Tutt Sr. As vice-chairman and chief investment officer, Russell Thayer Tutt Jr. has skillfully guided the investments of the El Pomar foundation for the past 30 years. They have given millions of dollars to the Pikes Peak Library District, and our Colorado Springs downtown library is named after Spencer Penrose. Mr. Penrose was a tough and focused man who made his fortune from hard work and never-apologize determination. With the influence of his wife Julie Penrose, together they created the El Pomar Foundation. Through their personal wealth and charitable legacy, this most generous couple continues to help hundreds of non-profits in Colorado.

# MIKE'S PEAK

One of my favorite documentaries, was also one of the most difficult ones for me to produce personally and was entitled *Mike's Peak*. It was a documentary on the life of Mike Hopkins, a former athlete who worked in construction as an adult. In an unfortunate accident, he fell from a roof of a building and hit his head. The serious brain injury should have left him completely paralyzed. With the help of his family, and particularly his brother Steve, he regained the ability to walk with two metal crutches. I met Mike at a local gym I frequented and I watched him climb on the Stairmaster machine almost every day. He held onto the handles on each side to give him balance as he moved his legs furiously up and down at a high rate of speed. To look at him stationary or sitting down, he looked like an incredible physical specimen with strong arms and tree-trunk muscular legs. His brain injury was responsible for his lack of balance and inability to speak clearly, making it difficult for him to communicate and even walk without some support.

Through my visits to the gym during my lunch hour, we became acquainted. Although I had to listen closely and often asked him to repeat what he was saying, over time I understood him as he told me about his life. He often gave me handouts that he wrote on a computer and printed out. It explained what had happened to him, what his goal was in his life, and he included some religious quotes. He was determined to ascend Pikes Peak in one day. He wanted to hike from the base of Pikes Peak at the beginning of Barr Trail at 7,500 feet, over 12 miles to the 14,114-feet summit. Pikes Peak, which is also known as America's mountain, had inspired Katherine Lee Bates to write *American the Beautiful*. Before I met Mike, I had climbed the trail up Pikes Peak at least six times. My best time for hiking this 12-mile ascent was six hours. It was a relatively easy trail to walk and did not require any technical climbing, but the last three miles above timberline were quite difficult. Most hikers averaged a mile an hour. Also, hikers had to deal with frequent afternoon thunderstorms which could turn deadly. I have known personally one local photographer who died from a lightning strike on Pikes Peak. The key to reducing the lightning risk was to start the hike early in the morning and to ascend the top of the mountain by 2 p.m. before the thunder storms rolled in.

Mike knew I produced documentaries for a living, and he asked me if I could videotape his attempt to climb the mountain in one day. Being ever so polite, I replied that I would think about it. However, I knew it could turn into a suicide mission; if we didn't make it to the top of Pikes Peak, we would have to carry him down the mountain, which would be a nightmare. When he picked his first date, I was delighted to find out it was on my wedding anniversary. I politely informed him I couldn't do it and I had the best excuse: my anniversary. Since he desperately wanted me to tape his attempt, he changed the date of the hike to the following week to accommodate my schedule. This meant I had no excuse and I had to go!

I owned a small, light-weight Sony Handicam with a couple extra batteries, which made it easy to videotape the hike. I didn't bring a tripod or any extra equipment, so I could also assist with the physical demands of helping him with the hike. Our crew was a small group of eight men and women, including Mike's brother Steve, who had helped him through his difficult rehab. Knowing the journey would take at least 12 hours with our best effort, we arrived at the trailhead at 3:50 a.m. His 70-year-old father who did not hike, but urged us on and also planned to meet us at the top with an eight-passenger van to drive us down. His father, a World War II veteran, had been disabled from polio as a child and walked with a limp. He lied about his disability when he joined the Navy and pretended he had just twisted his ankle during basic training. He spent the next three years in the Navy and managed to serve his country in wartime, despite his disability. So, Mike had a strong role model to inspire him.

Mike's brother, Steve Hopkins, who was a contractor by trade, created the poles needed to assist Mike up the mountain. They were parallel bars on either side of him, so he could balance himself as he walked. One person walked in the front with Mike In the middle, and one person in the back. Mike propelled his very strong legs forward, but he couldn't keep his balance without the poles. When there wasn't any room for the poles or when the trail was too steep, he grabbed onto the person in front of him. The person in back lifted him up by the wide belt around his waist. Even the strongest person couldn't last more than ten or fifteen minutes guiding the polls in front or in back of him. With the seven helpers, we climbed with three teams and one extra person to fill in as needed. During the journey, I interviewed Mike about his life and what climbing Pikes Peak meant to him. At 10:45 a.m. we reached Barr Camp, which at 10,000 feet was only half way up the trail to Pikes Peak, and we still had the most difficult six miles to finish.

At that point I was certain we would never make it to the top. Mike had confessed that he did not get any sleep the night before because of his nervous anticipation. He was operating on fumes, and I was positive we would carry him down the trail, which would probably mean at least an additional day on the mountain. As we approached timberline and three miles to go, I was a little more optimistic that we would make it to the top. Although three miles to climb meant at least another five hours hiking with Mike, if all went well, it looked like we would ascend the top by 7 p.m. an hour before the sun set. As we rested at timberline, I asked Mike why he decided to make his climb. "Because I'm brain injured," he joked and then he explained, "The reason I'm doing this stupid thing is to inspire other people. Everyone has challenges in their life, it is just mine are more obvious. I want to inspire people to keep on trying in life."

Sure enough, as if on cue, an afternoon thunderstorm hit the top of the mountain and surrounded us. Fearless Mike wanted to walk in the thunderstorm. During a thunderstorm above timberline on a mountain, climbers have no protection. The lighting strikes and thunderclaps were below and above us. We were inside a cloud that produced terrifying electricity. I huddled by a rock and hoped Mike had a little credit with God. In 15 minutes the storm passed and we were back on the trail to help get Mike to the top.

At 12,000 feet, there isn't much oxygen, and movement slows, particularly after an exhausting climb helping Mike up the mountain. During the last two miles, we no longer carried the poles on the winding and steeper trail. At this point there was no other option; we had to get him to the top. I volunteered to take the ass end of the climb. I held onto Mike's wide belt and pushed him up the mountain as he grabbed onto the belt of his brother in front. He kept his strong legs moving forward. It was like carrying a refrigerator up a staircase. For the last mile, I refused to give up my position and just pushed forward, knowing I was the lucky one who wasn't brain injured. I had no excuse not to give every ounce of my remaining strength. When the trail leveled out for the last 100 yards of the climb, I grabbed my camera; and with the last minute of battery life shot Mike walking with his arm around his brother reaching the 14,115-foot summit of Pikes Peak. It was 6:45 P.M., and the 12-mile journey to the top had lasted 14 hours.

Mike's Father was waiting for us, and it was a tearful celebration at the top. The entire crew posed for a picture at the summit, and we all were overwhelmed and exhausted by our team accomplishment.

The documentary went together very easily, and I narrated it in the first person and talked honestly about my experiences. It won several statewide cable awards and a shorter version can be seen on YouTube under the title "Mike's Peak." Mike convinced me to climb again the next two years. Although there were different teams, we succeeded each time. It was inspirational each time, but it never compared to the emotions we all felt the first time we made it to the top in one day.

# BUNNICULA LIVES

Why would someone steal from a library? Patrons can acquire anything they want in the collection for free, as long as they have library cards. However, theft has always been a problem at a public library. Most libraries have security gates as a deterrent, but gate alarms are a pain to check every time a patron sets one off. In the vast majority of the cases, when the gate alarm goes off, it is an innocent mistake by the patron, who didn't check out one item properly. There are those rare cases when deliberate attempts to steal something do occur.

At Pueblo West Library, we had candy machines that were the bane of my existence. A child with skinny arms could stretch his hand up the inside of the machine to steal candy from the bottom row. I wasted many hours with the candy machine company trying to come up with a solution. Leaving the bottom row empty would have solved our candy theft problem. The sales representative told me that the occasional pastry or candy that was stolen from the bottom row was an acceptable loss. Acceptable for them, but not for me. Security cameras filmed the machine area, and I was the one assigned to catch the kids, to write an incident report, and to suspend them.

During my year at Pueblo West, I suspended three kids for stealing candy. These were affluent kids who most likely had $20 in their pockets when they stole a $1.00 pastry. It was just the thrill and challenge that motivated them to steal.

The most popular items to steal from our collection were video games and DVDs. The more sophisticated thieves removed the security labels from the DVD or shoved them in a backpack and found a way to climb over or around the sides of our security gates. The DVDs ended up in pawn shops that paid a $1.00 per DVD. Like any retail store, having security is a way of life. Sometimes I was fortunate to have a security guard, but most of the time security was left up to staff and the branch manager. A couple of times I had patrons in the bathroom when we locked up the building, only to have them set off the alarm when they tried to leave. It was innocent on the part of the patrons, who had just lost track of time.

Before I arrived at the Pueblo City-County Library District, there was a popular true story that involved our trusting former chief financial officer. During normal public hours, he left the Rawlings Library when someone exited the building at the same time with several library computers on a book cart. He didn't recognize the person, but he assumed it was an outside vendor or an employee he didn't know taking the computers to be repaired or replaced. The CFO politely opened the door for the man with the cart. The man thanked him and pushed the cart to the parking lot where he unloaded the computers into his car. He was actually a brazen thief who stole the computers. It took some time before the former CFO could tell the story and could laugh at his misguided politeness. The library's insurance policy covered the loss.

When I worked at the Pikes Peak Library District at the East Library, we had no security guards overnight. Our security system was a motion detector; and if there was any problem and it sensed some motion, it signaled a silent alarm that alerted the Colorado Springs Police Department.

One morning at 2 a.m., the motion detector set off the silent alarm. The police arrived within 15 minutes, and our security manager was called to meet them. They checked all the windows and exterior doors, but there was no apparent break in. The East library was over 30,000 square feet of real estate, so the cops decided to let two of their police dogs loose to check the building. Fifteen minutes lapsed, and the dogs hadn't returned. Assuming the dogs had cornered a criminal, they pulled their guns and searched for their dogs. Once they entered the library, they saw their dogs in the distance cornering something in the children's department. As they got closer, they realized that is wasn't a person the dogs were cornering. The dogs were hovering over a cage that held the library rabbit, Bunnicula, named after the bunny in the popular children's story. The poor, two-year-old bunny appeared to be dead. The police ordered their dogs to heel, and they opened the cage hoping the rabbit was still alive. It appeared that Bunnicula had a heart attack. Since the cops were trained in CPR, they tried their best to revive the bunny. They threw water on his face and massaged his chest with their fingers. They were delighted to see that Bunnicula was showing signs of breathing and was brought back to life.

It turned out the motion detector was set off because a swarm of miller moths were flying inside the library, and their combined motion was enough to set off the alarm. Bunnicula lived another ten years. In terms of bunny years, that was a long life. Thanks to the life-saving skills of the Colorado Springs Police Department, the children of Colorado Springs were able to enjoy holding and petting the ever- popular Bunnicula for many more years.

# HARVEST OF LOVE

When I first moved to Colorado Springs, my two girls were very young, and since we didn't have much disposable income at the time, we were always looking for inexpensive things for them to do. I quickly learned about the Venetucci pumpkin farm that allowed kids to walk in the pumpkin field to pick their own pumpkins for free. The Venetucci farm was open to the public during October, leading up to Halloween. This farm family had displayed this incredible generosity for almost 30 years, since the early 1950s. The farm was owned by a married couple, Nic and Bambi Venetucci. Nic was in his seventies at that time, and Bambi was twenty years younger. They had no children of their own, and this was their way of giving back to the community's young people.

It was quite an operation that required several volunteers to make it successful. There were set hours to visit the farm, and you would park your car in a field, walk to a nearby pumpkin patch, and pick your own pumpkins. During the week, school buses arrived in the morning with their classes. For many of these city kids, it was the first time they had ever seen a farm.

When I moved to Colorado Springs, it was a city of 350,000 people. The

Venetucci's gave away an average of 40,000 pumpkins per year. At least a third of the children in the city visited the Venetucci farm each year. I did not meet Nic and Bambi during my kids' first visit. My girls, like most children, ran through the fields and picked a pumpkin they could barely lift. We repeated this adventure every year until I started working for the Pikes Peak Library District. In 1990, one of the local school districts approached the library and recommended documenting this generous family by interviewing Nic and producing a video portrait on his life.

I jumped at the opportunity to record the family history. It was a unique story, and the Venetucci family needed to be honored for their generosity. I also wanted to tell a positive story about an Italian-American family. I had a chip on my shoulders from all the negative films that portrayed Italian Americans as criminals and mobsters. With my long ethnic name, people wondered or joked about my Mafia connections. My father also was sensitive to this portrayal, knowing how loving and gentle his father was. His mother always told an amusing story related to this type of stereotyping when he was younger. He came home from school when he was around six years old and complained to his mother that another child had told him that "all Italians are cutthroats." My grandmother immediately became upset and advised him, "Don't let other people insult you like that; you know, from your own family, that Italians are hard-working people who love their country and their families." My dad looked at my grandmother with innocent eyes and asked his mom, "What's a cut throat?" My grandmother then laughed and realized her gentle and naive son didn't even know what the insult meant.

There was nothing I could do about all these mob stories and negative portrayals of Italian Americans, but I could produce a positive documentary about this amazing and generous family. As I learned more about the Venetucci family, I realized the story of the family had more depth than any 30-minute documentary could do it justice.

Nic Venetucci married Bambi when he was 60 years old. They had a secret romance for almost 30 years before they finally married. Even though they were both children of Italian-American immigrants and devout Catholics, Nic's family rejected Bambi because she had been born blind. They kept their romance a discreet secret until his mother passed away, and Nic finally married Bambi and brought her to live with him on the farm.

Both Nic and Bambi came from coal-mining families and were first generation Americans. To escape poverty in their home country, many Italians immigrated to the United States in the early 1900s. They were mostly poor peasants with minimal formal educations who had strong backs and were willing to take any job they could find. Most Americans at that time were unwilling to work underground in the hazardous coal mines, so many immigrants took those dangerous jobs when they first arrived in the United States. At that time, the homes in America were heated by coal-burning stoves, long before natural gas became the heating source of choice.

Underground coal mines were numerous throughout Colorado, and Bambi's father worked in a coal mine near Boulder. The Venetucci family worked in a coal mine in Papetown, near Colorado Springs. The goal of most immigrant coal miners was to work hard and to bring the rest of their immigrant families to the United States. If they worked even harder and saved their money, they hoped to leave the mines and to start a small business or to buy a farm. That was the Venetucci family's dream.

When Nic was 13 years old, his family bought a farm in Security, Colorado. It was a difficult life, but they were delighted to work on their own farm making money for themselves. Working outside meant that they didn't risk their lives every time they descended into the mine. With the start of the Great Depression, food prices plummeted, and farming became an even more difficult life that required all the kids to work hard in order to survive and to keep the farm. Nic was an average student whose formal education ended after the eighth grade. He was needed on the farm at an early age to help the family raise cattle and to grow corn.

Nic's real interest was baseball. In the early 1930s, he played on numerous amateur teams in Colorado Springs. Professional baseball was the most popular sport in the United States then, and there was no bigger star than the "Bambino," Babe Ruth of the New York Yankees. Nic was a catcher with a powerful arm. He was about the same size as Yogi Berra and had natural athletic ability. Every company in the area had their own amateur hardball team. The Alexander Film Company and the coal mining companies all sported baseball teams, and Nic was a sought-after local player. His dream was to leave the farm to play professional baseball. He knew if he stayed in Colorado Springs, he lost a chance to achieve his dream.

At 19 years old, he saved his money and begged his parents to let him attend a California baseball school where the professional teams sent scouts to find prospects for their farm teams. After he completed the baseball school, to his amazement, he was signed by the New York Yankees to play on one of their farm teams. In one year he advanced from a D-farm team to an A- farm team for the Yankees . His future was very bright in professional baseball - until his father called. His older brother was killed in a well accident on the farm. The gas pump generator that brought the water from the well caught fire, killing his brother instantly from the resulting explosion. His father needed Nic back on the farm to help his grieving family and to take the place of his older brother, who had been running the farm. Without hesitation, Nic abandoned his professional baseball dream and returned to Colorado. He never looked back, and from the age of 22, until he died in his 80s, he never regretted abandoning his baseball dream to be the devoted son his family depended on.

Working 12 hours a day on his farm didn't leave much time for socializing. Other than going to St. Mary's Catholic Church on Sundays, he didn't have time to meet women and to start his own family. It was a lonely existence, but he knew his parents needed him. As Colorado Springs expanded, it turned out the city needed more water to supply the growing population's needs. During an extended drought, the situation in the city became desperate. The exclusive Broadmoor Hotel, built by Spencer Penrose in 1918, suddenly did not have enough water to keep their famous golf courses green.

The Venetucci farm was over the water-rich Widefield aquifer. The water supply on the Venetucci farm was plentiful and very valuable. The city and the Broadmoor Hotel signed a deal with the Venetuccis to pay for their water and to pump a portion of their water to the Broadmoor Hotel. Since the water was worth a small fortune, the Venetucci family slowly acquired real wealth from their water supply. Although they still farmed their land, the financial pressure that Nic felt when he abandoned his baseball career was now over.

He now was free to concentrate on the pumpkin and corn business. One day he was delivering a truck full of pumpkins to a store downtown when he noticed a group of kids staring at the bright orange pumpkins. Feeling generous, he invited the kids to select a free pumpkin off his truck and to carry it home. Other kids noticed and asked Nic if they could have a free pumpkin, He gave away half his truck load that day, and that was the impetus for the great pumpkin giveaway at the Venetucci farm. Nic expanded the pumpkin giveaway and invited local schools to visit the farm and allowed each student to pick a free pumpkin.

Bambi had her own fascinating history before she ever met Nic. Bambi Marcantonio's journey to Colorado Springs began as a child when she was sent to the Colorado School for the Deaf and Blind for her education. Born with limited sight that she lost completely by the time she was five years old, Bambi spent her early life in a close and loving immigrant Italian-American family. Her father was a coal miner who eventually left the mines and became a skilled carpenter. She was very close to her father who always told her in Italian to *dammi la mano* which translated to "give me your hand." He showed her what a bird felt like, or a frog, or a tree, and many other wonderful living things she was unable to see. When she was seven years old, her parents realized that without her sight, she couldn't learn in a traditional school.

In the 1870s the generous General William Jackson Palmer founded The Colorado School for the Deaf and Blind. Two of the early graduates were a deaf couple who were the parents of Lon Chaney, the silent film star who was also known as the man of a thousand faces. His ability to express himself visually was enhanced by his experiences communicating with his deaf parents. Bambi's parents realized her best bet for an education was for her to attend the Colorado School for the Deaf and Blind.

For Bambi, whose first language was Italian, it was a difficult adjustment to attend a boarding school one hundred miles from her home. When her parents arrived in Colorado Springs on the train with their little girl, the three of them cried openly, knowing Bambi couldn't live with them anymore. They realized that they needed to leave her at the school in order for her to develop the skills she needed to live independently as a blind woman. Bambi was an extremely bright, young woman who flourished in school. She learned Braille, and her whole world opened up once she developed the ability to read. She read as many braille books as she could find. Upon graduation from the school in 1949, she attended the University of Colorado. Because of her blindness, everything was a challenge, but she was determined to become the first blind graduate at C.U. and to eventually become a teacher.

After graduation in 1954, she applied for a teaching job at her old school in Colorado Springs. It took some time, but she was hired eventually as the first blind alumni to teach at the school; and for the next 30 years she taught young blind students how to read and to survive in the world. She was honored as the Colorado Teacher of the Year in 1983, because of her teaching ability and her unique perspective for relating to her students.

What brought Nic and Bambi together was an amusing encounter that ended up becoming a life-long romance. Bambi was in her mid-20s, and Nic was almost 20 years older in his early 40s. Nic noticed Bambi in church and wondered who this attractive, young woman was. Even though Bambi was blind, she wore glasses to avoid drawing attention to her disability. She didn't want to be known as that blind woman, since she was a very capable individual who maneuvered very well in familiar settings, like Saint Mary's Church in Colorado Springs or in her apartment.

Nic asked his sister who this attractive woman was and found out where she lived. He went to Bambi's apartment with a box of fresh vegetables and introduced himself. She invited him in for coffee, and Nic still had no idea that Bambi was blind. She walked around her familiar apartment with no problems, and they had a pleasant conversation. Nic asked if he could call her on the phone, and she gave him her phone number. When Nic called her the next day, they spoke for hours. They were two lonely people who had been waiting their whole lives to find their soulmates. Since they were both Catholics, the children of Italian immigrants whose fathers had worked in the mines, they had so much common. Bambi talked about her life as a teacher at the Deaf and Blind School and how she would love to bring her students to the farm to pick pumpkins. Nic invited Bambi to his farm, and he wanted to introduce her to his mother. At this point Bambi knew she had to tell him she was blind. "I know you didn't know this, since I wore glasses when you met me, and I was in the familiar surroundings of my apartment, but I was born blind."

When Bambi tells the story she recalls a long moment of silence on the phone, and she knew that this would most likely be her last conversation with Nic. After the initial shock, Nic started talking again. "I had no idea. You get a long pretty well. If it is O.K. with you, I would like to call you again… and I would love to have you and your students visit my farm." Bambi instantly knew this farmer was a good man. "I would love to go. We have busses at the school, and we could make it a field trip."

After a hard day on the farm, Nic called Bambi almost every night, and they both reviewed their day. When Nic had a chance, he brought a box of vegetables to her apartment, and they chatted for hours about their hopes and dreams. It was very difficult for them to have an open relationship. His family didn't see how Nic could marry a blind woman and bring her on the farm. Despite the fact she was a college-educated, independent woman, his family didn't see how she could be useful to Nic if they were to marry. Bambi felt horrible about being rejected by his family. They were so compatible in every way, and they loved each other. Reluctantly, she agreed to keep their relationship a secret.

Their clandestine romance survived for the next 30 years, until his mother died. Nic and his brother Tony were now alone on the farm. Finally, there was no obstacle to their love, and Nic asked Bambi to marry him. She was 50 years old and he was 70 when she moved into the family home on the farm. She made that house her own; and as a capable, educated woman she became his business partner, taking care of the correspondence and the bills that needed to be paid. She was an excellent cook and had a precise memory for everything in her kitchen. During the harvest, she was a big help with feeding the workers. Over the telephone, she arranged the school visits that became a massive undertaking with 50,000 visitors to the farm each October.

When I met Bambi and Nic for the documentary, Bambi wanted to keep a low profile. She didn't even want me to mention in the documentary the fact she was blind, but she was comfortable and proud to talk about her husband. She wanted the documentary to be about Nic, but Bambi's story was equally important. Fortunately for the library, she had been writing an autobiography about her experiences growing up blind and living in a loving immigrant family. She also wrote about her relationship with Nic and her many life struggles. She wrote her autobiography on a Braille typewriter and then read her Braille chapters into a cassette recorder. My wife listened to the cassette and transcribed her words on a computer. Over the period of a few months, she completed her book, *Dammi La Mano (Give me Your Hand)*. The Friends of the Pikes Peak Library District published her book, and the first 1,000 copies sold out immediately. She recorded an audio version of her book in her own words, and it is a valuable resource for Colorado Springs history.

While producing the documentary and helping Bambi publish her book, I got to know the family very well. One of the my most extraordinary experiences was sitting in Bambi and Nic Venetucci 's kitchen and enjoying a home-cooked meal. My parents were also invited, since they were visiting Colorado Springs at the time. It was amazing how Bambi moved through her kitchen with ease, knowing the location of every obstacle and the placement of every pot and pan. The Venetucci farm was famous for their sweet corn, and my family and I enjoyed a meal of spaghetti, her delicious homemade meatballs, and ears of cooked sweet corn. Nic pointed out to me, "You better not put salt or butter on my sweet corn; it is so tasty by itself, it would be a sin if you put anything on it." He was right; his sweet corn was the best corn I have ever eaten.

It was one of those rare moments that brought together many of the people I loved, sharing a meal in this remarkable couple's home. It was a moment in time that can never be repeated. As Lou Reed says in his song, It was a *Perfect Day.*

When I reflect on the many fascinating and remarkable people I have met and interviewed, most of them have now passed on. As I analyze my own life, I realize my best moments are a series of shared experiences. Those experiences remained locked in time. Once that special time has passed, they can only exist in my heart and memory. I have been fortunate to have had spent many wonderful moments with the people I love. That's all we have in the end: the moments in time shared with loved ones during this remarkable human experience,

# SCENES OF WAR

During my career at the Pikes Peak Library District producing documentaries, one person led to another in terms of a new subject for each documentary. In 1989, I produced a documentary on Dorothy Heller, the first Colorado Springs police woman. At the time, she was 90 years old, and she lived on ten acres in northern Colorado Springs. Her husband, Larry Heller, who had died a few years earlier, bought the property in the 1930s when Colorado Springs' population was 30,000. Larry was a sculptor artist and painter who worked for the Alexander Film Company as an art director and an occasional actor when needed. Childless, the Hellers lived an amazing life on their secluded property with a home and a studio and art gallery.

One of Larry and Dorothy's dear friends was a co-worker and cinematographer, Jim Bates, who was 72 years old when I first met him. When I interviewed Jim about the Heller family, he mentioned some wonderful aspects about their friendship and how talented Larry was as an artist. As I talked to Jim, I realized that an even more valuable documentary was sitting in my studio. Jim told me about his time at the Alexander Film Company in the 1930s through the 1960s and this incredible motion picture collection he had saved over the years.

The Alexander Film Company was a major film advertising company in Colorado Springs. They produced commercials or what they called advertising playlets nationally and at one time had a staff of 600 people locally. Jim started working for the Alexander Film Company right out of Colorado Springs High School in 1935 and was hired and trained as a cinematographer. His collection of films were the amazing home movies of Colorado Springs. The Alexander brothers gladly donated the resources of their company to promote the city's beauty for tourism.

They had produced several films for the Colorado Springs Chamber of Commerce on the attractions in the Pikes Peak region. In almost every decade from the 1930s to the 1960s, a new film was produced, and all of the films were time capsules of the history of the region. Jim, who was also a still photographer, was happy to donate his still photography and all of his films to the Pikes Peak Library District. However, it wasn't his film collection that I was interested in for a documentary; it was Jim's experiences as a combat photographer in World War II from the D-Day invasion to the fall of Germany that I wanted to capture. His life as a combat photographer, jumping with the pre-invasion 82$^{nd}$ airborne on D minus one and photographing the war in Europe from the front lines, was a story of an ordinary man in extraordinary circumstances.

As a young man, Jim resembled a young Tom Cruz. Around 5' 7" tall, Jim had boyish good looks with dark brown, curly hair and an athletic build, when he volunteered for the United States Army in 1943. By the time he volunteered as a 25-year-old recruit, he had already had seven years' experience as a motion picture cinematographer. Since the Army Signal Corps was looking for combat photographers with his experience, Jim was selected and trained with approximately 300 other Signal Corps technicians. The Army also trained Jim to be a soldier, since they knew that the combat photographer's job was to be at the front lines to photograph the battles. After his training, he was sent to England to prepare for the invasion. He enjoyed his time in England. Although training for the invasion, he still had time to sightsee and to meet the British civilians who embraced the

Americans and treated them like family. In England he met his future wife, Monica. They started an innocent romance and spent as much time as they could together, knowing that Jim could lose his life during the upcoming invasion and war in Europe.

As the invasion grew closer, one of the colonels with the 82nd Airborne needed a volunteer. He wanted a combat photographer to document the 82nd Airborne for their planned jump as pre-invasion troopers. Jim was happy to be that volunteer, but he had never trained as a trooper and had never made a jump. The colonel provided Jim with the proper training, and he made one successful jump before the invasion.

The invasion was set for June 6; and on June 5 around 9 p.m., Jim climbed into a plane to jump with the 82nd Airborne. Jim was weighted down by all his camera equipment and weapons and had very little mobility. Jim weighed only 140 pounds and with an additional 100 pounds in equipment, he could barely move. On June 5 when Jim jumped into France, his life almost ended during his first minute as a combat photographer. The plane carrying him flew off course, and the pilot dropped him in a flooded area the Germans had created to protect the coast from the invasion. With all the weight of his equipment, Jim sank straight down into the water; he was certain he was going to drown. As he held his last breath, a breeze caught his parachute. It saved his life as the wind pulled him to the shore. Many members of the 82nd Airborne drowned that night in the same flooded area. Lucky to be alive, Jim quickly realized that all his equipment was wet and unusable. Instead, he concentrated on being a soldier to do his part to support the invasion. On the next morning, he killed his first enemy soldier with a grenade that he threw at an enemy jeep. The German was not expecting to run into American paratroopers and thought Jim was just another German soldier as he drove by him without pointing his gun at Jim.

The next day Jim reunited with the Signal Corps and resupplied his photography equipment from a glider. He marched with the 82nd Airborne and started his role as a combat photographer as they pushed through the hedge row.

The rumor was the SS was not taking any American prisoners, that they would shoot them out of convenience rather than taking them back behind to their lines. The 82$^{nd}$ Airborne had captured some German SS soldiers, and many of the troopers were angry at them, knowing they had shot unarmed American prisoners. They lined the SS prisoners up against a wall, and one of the troopers shouted at Jim, "Take your goddamn pictures." The trooper shot the prisoners. Capturing only a few seconds of the prisoners being shot on film, Jim spent the rest of the day fearing for his life if he had been caught. That footage would have been in the hands of the Germans and could be used for propaganda. He eventually sent his film to the Signal Corps headquarters to be developed. They sent him a terse message, "Do not film prisoners being shot under any circumstances."

Jim continued to follow the 82$^{nd}$ Airborne as they moved through France. When they reached the U-boat pens at Chourberg, he entered one of the underground facilities with a couple of other soldiers. They were alone when they noticed a white flag. Almost 100 German prisoners surrendered to Jim and the other two American soldiers, not knowing Jim was practically alone. He ordered them to surrender their weapons and to walk with their hands up to the road leading to the Allied forces. He informed them they would eventually come in contact with other American troops at some point. After the initial invasion, the push through France to Paris was met with little resistance. Upon liberating Paris, Jim had a chance to rest and to enjoy the city. As Christmas approached, the soldiers thought the Germans might surrender by the end of 1944. How wrong they were!

The Malmedy massacre occurred on December 17 in Malmedy, France. The SS gunned down 81 American prisoners, and their bodies were abandoned on the frozen ground. Jim was ordered to travel to Malmedy to film the atrocities. It was a difficult assignment to see unarmed Americans brutally shot and left to die. It was the beginning of the Battle of the Bulge and the most challenging time for Jim as a combat photographer.

He was assigned to the Third Armored Division and followed General George Patton as they rushed to rescue the soldiers who were under siege at Bastogne. In the middle of the winter, in snowy conditions he hitched a ride on a tank that needed an extra gunner. As the American Sherman tank moved through the Belgium forest, the soldiers encountered a battle with a German tiger tank. The Sherman tank took a direct hit, and Jim's back was sprayed with shrapnel. He toppled to the ground through the trap door under the tank and crawled to safety. The whole time he kept shooting film. The story of the battle and the footage he shot was featured in a 2000 Steven Spielberg documentary, *Shooting War*, narrated by Tom Hanks.

Jim was placed on the hood of a jeep and driven to a field hospital. While he was on the jeep, he continued to shoot film of the battle. The doctors couldn't remove all of the shrapnel in his back at the field hospital, and some of metal remained in his back until the day he died. As he recovered in the hospital, the Battle of the Bulge was raging; and the Army needed any healthy soldier available to help in the fight. Jim wanted to return to the action; and after only two weeks, he was back on the front lines shooting the end of this famous battle.

As the unit moved across Germany, Jim's most famous footage was yet to be shot. On March 6, Jim followed the Third Armored Division as they entered Cologne, Germany for a fierce battle at the banks of the Rhine River. The American tanks were no match for the German tiger tanks throughout every battle in Europe. The Third Armored Division recently had received the new American M26 Pershing tanks that finally were equal to the best tanks in the German army. Jim's assignment during the Battle of Cologne was to shadow one of the new American tanks in hopes of capturing an actual tank battle on film. Jim shot some amazing footage during this house-to-house battle of Cologne. At the foot of the famous Cologne Cathedral, a German Panther tank planted itself in front of the church in a symbolic, almost a suicidal gesture, to protect the city and this famous cathedral.

The American tank commander hid behind a nearby building and advised Jim. "If you can get inside the building and on a balcony, you might be able to photograph a tank battle." Jim climbed up to the balcony and put on his telescopic lens. He held the camera as steady as he could as the American tank pulled up underneath him and fired several shots into the Panther tank. The Panther tank was destroyed, and the injured crew members jumped out the top of the tank. The shells continued to pound the Panther as the crew members collapsed around the tank and died from their shrapnel wounds. It was an amazing day of filming for Jim, and he was awarded the Bronze Star for his bravery under fire. The entire documentary, "Scenes of War," is on YouTube for anyone to see Jim's remarkable footage.

With the end of the war, Jim's work was not done. It was his job to film the horrors of the Nordhausen Concentration Camp. Nordhausen,, Germany was the location of a factory to build the V2 rockets that the Nazis used as terror weapons over London. Jewish and other European prison laborers built the rockets. Jim filmed the horrific aftermath of the emaciated survivors of this slave labor camp. He told me that one of the prisoners gave him a tour through the factory and described what they called the "death job." Glass insulation, needed to cool the rocket, was toxic to the touch. The prisoner who was assigned the job of crawling into the rocket to install the insulation eventually died from the cuts he received when the bits of glass entered his bloodstream. The footage Jim shot affected him so profoundly that he never wanted to see it again. He knew how important it was to document this horror, but he didn't want to see any the footage after it was processed.

His final job in Germany was to shoot a boat filled with American soldiers suffering from what was called "shell shock," but it was actually post-traumatic stress from their wartime experiences. The choir traveled up and down the banks of the Rhine River to sing to the German civilians in a gesture of healing and forgiveness. They docked in each city, and the Germans listened to their choir and sang with the soldiers trying to heal from their mental wounds.

Jim returned to England to find his British girlfriend Monica and proposed marriage. He brought Monica to the United States, and he returned to his job at the Alexander Film Company.

When Jim first saw J. Don Alexander, the owner of the company, J. Don asked, "Jim, where have you been for the past few years? I've been looking all over for you. Welcome home." Jim and J. Don tearfully embraced, and he resumed his job as a filmmaker and raised his family with Monica in Colorado Springs.

The Alexander Film Company was a major producer of theatrical commercials. The Alexander Film Company produced most of the industrial and commercial films for the American automakers. One commercial Jim worked on for Chevrolet was considered a remarkable achievement in advertising for the time. In the early 1960s Jim engineered a camera-helicopter mount that sat on a custom gyroscope to stabilize it and to protect it from the helicopter's movement and the vibration. This amazing camera mount was developed 15 years before the popular Steadicam was created. This patented camera gyroscope for aerial photography created a mini-renaissance for the Alexander Film Company. Many major motion picture companies and advertising agencies around the country hired the company to shoot aerial photography.

The literal peak of the use of this aerial cinematic achievement was a commercial for Chevrolet that was shot in Moab, Utah. It featured young model Shirley Rumsey sitting in a new 1964 Chevy convertible. What made this commercial unique was that the car and the model were perched on top of a precarious 2,000-foot sandstone pinnacle called Castle Rock, it was two times as tall as the Empire State Building. This was during the height of the Madison Avenue advertising era of the 1960s, and the commercial was a big-budget ad costing thousands of dollars to produce. A twin-rotor Boeing vertol helicopter lifted the car in sections onto Castle Rock where it was re-assembled. The fierce wind made lifting the car and shooting the commercial especially difficult, requiring five days to complete the job. The model was terrified of the precarious location and insisted that a technician, hidden underneath the car during the shooting, stay with her. In one commercial shot, the outline of the technician can be seen crouching behind the car.

During the last day of shooting, the winds became hazardous as the day progressed. Concerned about the danger of using the helicopter in the high winds, it looked like the technician and the model would have to spend the night on top of Castle Rock and wait for the winds to calm down. The technician's wife had accompanied him on the location in Utah, and she was not happy with the possibility of her husband spending the night on the rock with the model. She insisted, "There is no way my husband is going to spend the night on that rock with that slut." Fortunately, the winds subsided at dusk, and the model and the technician were brought down from the peak. The two-minute commercial was a spectacular award-winning success, premiering nationally during the popular *Bonanza* television series on Sunday nights. It was also shown on all of the popular shows of the era, including "The Jimmy Dean Show," "Route 66," and "The Price is Right."

When I was assembling the documentary on Jim Bates, the project literally almost ended with a bang. He had collected many souvenirs during his campaign across Europe, and one of his most-prized possessions was an authentic German Lugar. He brought the pistol to my studio to show me his collection, which also included a Nazi flag and a German-produced 16-mm combat film on the German U-boat effort. Before I held the Lugar in my hand, I asked him whether it was loaded. Jim told me it wasn't, and I almost pulled the trigger. Fortunately, I decided it probably wasn't a good idea to try it - even though it wasn't loaded. Jim grabbed the gun out of my hand and noticed a loaded clip was still in the gun. "I'm sorry; it is loaded." I didn't tell him I almost pulled the trigger. The lesson that should be learned from this is: never pull the trigger on an unfamiliar gun, unless you have personal knowledge it is unloaded.

*Scenes of War* won several cable awards and was shown nationally on The History Channel. We also held a local premiere for 200 people. We featured Jim's World War II still photography in our art gallery during the premiere; and his photo of Winston Churchill touring the German Reichstag at the end of the war captured an amazing piece of history. Jim personally developed a print of that photograph that I have hanging in my home office.

Six years after I finished the documentary on Jim Bates, I was contacted by film critic and writer Richard Schickel, who was hired by Steven Spielberg to write *Shooting War*. They wanted to interview Jim; but at this point in his life, his health wouldn't allow it. They decided to use the interview footage I shot, and they were able to find Jim Bates' original combat footage of The Battle of the Bulge tank battle in the National Archives.

Jim remained a good friend for the rest of his life. Since we shared the same interest in photography and film, he was very appreciative of my efforts to make this hour-long documentary on his life. I've included the following link to YouTube that shows this famous Chevy commercial that Jim Bates worked on as well as the link to the full hour-long version of *Scenes of War*.

# THE ALEXANDER BROTHERS

As I said before, one video interview always led to another. Jim Bates introduced me to the fascinating history of the Alexander Film Company, which led to my academic research paper on the two Alexander brothers and founders of that company.

Julian Don Alexander and Don Miller Alexander were born in Keokuk, Iowa. They were eight years apart in age and light years apart in terms of personality. The older brother, J. Don, was a pure salesman. He was an extrovert who was extremely outgoing and flamboyant, and he spent his life "riding on a smile and a shoeshine" to quote Arthur Miller. The younger brother, Don M., was an engineering genius, who graduated from Washington State University in Spokane with a degree in electrical engineering. He was a Rhodes Scholar who decided to partner with his brother in Spokane. Don M. was an introvert who preferred inventing new products for their company more than socializing. He never married, until he was a man in his sixties, and spent most of his life in the background, engineering the products his brother sold. In 1917 they opened their first business, The Alexander Electric Company. It was a perfect marriage of talent between the two brothers. J. Don promoted the business and brought in the customers, and Don M. used his engineering talents to satisfy the customers.

When a client asked the Alexanders if they could make a sales film, J. Don always the positive salesman, immediately said, "Yes." He really did not know how to make a movie! With the help of his technically minded brother, they figured out what they needed to do to produce their first commercial film, and they delighted the client. The Alexander Film Company was incorporated in 1919 in Spokane, Washington. The Alexander brother produced what they called "advertising playlets" for local businesses.

After the turn of the 20th century, it took only a short time for the motion picture industry to dominate Americans' entertainment habits. People stopped going to opera houses to see live entertainment and instead flocked to the motion-picture theater every Friday and Saturday nights to watch the popular silent film stars. Motion-picture films became an inexpensive form of entertainment for the masses. Silent film actors, such as Charlie Chaplin and Rudolph Valentino, became larger than life. Their images and exploits dominated American life, and they were viewed as the superstars of their era. Don M. recognized the potential of using motion-picture film to sell advertising to this ready-made mass audience. It took little time to sell the idea to Spokane businesses, and the Alexander Film Company flourished locally. It was 1924, the beginning of the Roaring 20s and the flapper era. Women recently had won the right to vote, and American business was creating new products, including mass-produced cars and household items, for women and American families.

With his local success, Don M. knew his concept of selling theatrical advertising would work in every small town in America. This was before long-distance phone lines and Federal Express overnight delivery. However, conducting this kind of a business on a national level presented many logistical problems. For example, how could a producer deliver custom theatrical advertisements to the local theaters in a timely manner? Don M., always the innovator, saw the potential of the commercial use of airplanes for expanding his business. Frustrated with the quality of biplanes of that era, the Alexander brothers manufactured their own airplane to help them with travel in their film business. Alexander Aircraft Industries was born.

"Some of the salesmen had a very large sales territory," recalled former Alexander employee Leland Feitz. " J. Don believed in flying and was the 91$^{st}$ man to be licensed as a pilot in the United States." Don M. was the engineer who designed an airplane for the sales force, and the more it was seen the more popular it became. Soon the airplane was manufactured for the general public. Don M's engineering skills translated to aeronautics. Alexander Aircraft's Eaglerock became the most reliable and popular biplane of its era. A young pilot, Charles Lindbergh, wanted to fly the Eaglerock to make his historic transatlantic flight, but his custom plane could not be manufactured in time. Lindberg instead purchased the now famous Ryan monoplane that he named the "The Spirit of St. Louis."

As their theater advertising business expanded nationally, the brothers realized that they needed to be more centrally located in order to provide service in a timely manner to their clients on both coasts. In 1923, they moved their entire operation from Spokane to Englewood, Colorado, a suburb south of Denver. In Englewood, Alexander Aircraft expanded the film company and the aircraft manufacturing plant to a multi-million dollar operation.

Early mass production of aircrafts presented unique safety challenges. On April 20, 1928, a spark from an electric fan in the paint department created the initial explosion and fire. The accident in their aircraft manufacturing plant resulted in 11 fatalities. "The deaths happened because in the room where they applied this so-called dope, which was highly flammable, the doors swung in; and when this explosion happened, the people rushed to the doors and pushed against them," said Leland Feitz," and several perished in that fire."

It was a devastating time for the Alexander Brothers who were accustomed to one success after another during the 14 years they had been in business. Following the explosion, they faced criminal manslaughter charges and the potential demise of their thriving company. The Alexander brothers were found guilty on four counts of violating the Colorado Facilities Act. They were each fined $1,000 and given suspended sentences of 90 days. The more serious manslaughter charges were dropped. During that time, the Alexanders moved their growing business to the sleepy resort town of Colorado Springs. Officials in the city made an attractive offer of free land and a beautiful scenic location for motion- picture production. In one night, 75 trucks and a crew of employees and volunteers moved the entire operation to 260 acres on North Nevada Avenue.

Despite the industrial accident, the Alexanders continued to construct their popular Eaglerock biplane in Colorado Springs along with the new Bullet monoplane, one of the earliest planes with retractable wheels. The theatrical advertising company thrived as motion-picture films became more and more popular. The 1929 stock market crash changed the aircraft company's fortunes. Even though many people were out of work during The Depression, they still spent their last penny to escape to the local movie theater and the Alexander Film Company remained a healthy enterprise. Theatrical advertising continued to be a successful way to promote struggling local businesses, allowing them to compete in a tougher market.

With the aircraft manufacturing company closing its doors, the Alexander brothers concentrated on their theatrical advertising business. J. Don, the shrewd businessman, bought out his struggling competitors. By 1933 the Alexanders were the largest producer of theatrical advertising and promotional film shorts in the world. The real secret to the Alexander Film Company's success, in addition to offering a quality product, was the emphasis on the salesman. J. Don respected his sales staff and provided them a very generous commission structure. It was the golden era for sales, and methods were not always orthodox, if not borderline unethical. Their Fortune 500 clients were wined, dined and lodged at the luxury Broadmoor Hotel; and they used the scenic beauty of Colorado Springs to sell their clients on working with them.

J. Don believed in the power of positive thinking and could make anyone feel like they were best friends. Don M. was just the opposite. A brilliant engineer who invented an early motion- picture color-film process, Don M. was an introvert who experienced difficulty relating to people. Don M. gladly allowed J. Don management of the Alexander staff. They were two very different people who needed each other to make the business successful. "J. Don always passed out turkeys at Christmas time and hams at Easter time. When the circus would come to town, J. Don would buy a wad of tickets, and it was amazing how he would know how many tickets everyone needed," Feitz remembered.

At the peak of their success in the 1940s and early 1950s, the Alexander Film Company employed 600 people in Colorado Springs and also had offices in New York, Chicago, and Los Angeles.

With the beginning of commercial television in the 1940s, networks needed a way to pay for their free programming. Copying the success of the theatrical advertising that the Alexander brothers had been producing for the past 20 years, television used the same formula of advertising playlets to pay for this new broadcast medium.

Ironically, television initiated the demise of the Alexander Film Company. People stopped going to the movie theaters, and national and local businesses turned to television with their advertising dollars. Initially, the executives of the Alexander Film Company saw television as a passing fad and were reluctant to alienate their theater clients. Eventually, they produced television commercials for their national clients; and in the early 1960s they produced big-budget and high-concept national commercials for television. "It just about ruined the company when television came along. There were about 17,000 theaters running Alexander movie ads; and after a few years when TV came along, those theaters closed. Drive-in theaters saved the company during those years. During the summer months business was pretty good," Feitz said.

As the audience for movie theaters decreased, a new boom in outdoor drive-in theaters fit the lifestyle of families and the growing baby boomers. People loaded up the family in the car, and movie-going continued to be popular thanks to this outdoor phenomenon. The Alexander Film Company soon became the primary producer of theatrical advertising for drive-in movie theaters. They expanded into animation, creating the dancing popcorn and the dancing hotdog to encourage people to buy more refreshments at the snack bar between feature films. The Alexander Film Company created the familiar commercial countdown, which indicated how many minutes remained until show time. Attendees in the 50s and 60s saw the Alexander Film Company logo at the end of each commercial.

J. Don Alexander was the heart of the company and when he died in May 1955, the Alexander Film Company started a slow decline. At 70 years old, he had built his advertising playlet company into a multi-million dollar business and one of the largest employers in Colorado Springs. He was a leading member of the Colorado Springs Chamber of Commerce and was on the board of the Colorado School for the Deaf and Blind. Always a proponent of business, J. Don was also a foremost advocate of Junior Achievement. During a private conversation with Alexander employee Leland Feitz, however, he expressed disappointment in his business success. "One thing I remember very well was the last conversation I had with J. Don, and this was only a few days before the man died. We'd been talking about his life, and I said it must have been awfully wonderful to have lived a full life and turned an idea into an organization that supported many hundred families and to have made friends all over the world. I said 'I will always envy you for what you have done' and then he said, 'Leland… we have been total failures'…and that really surprised me because I thought he was a great success…he was a multi-millionaire with a yacht and a private plane. He said, 'If we played our cards right and held on to the aircraft business, we would have had a factory that reached from here to the Air Force Academy.' He died disappointed."

Without his charismatic brother to run the company, Don M. Alexander sold the controlling interest of the Alexander Film Company to the Allied Film Company in December 1957. Keith Munroe took over as president. Don M. retired from the day-to-day business activities, but he remained active with the company as chairman of the board. Don M. lived quietly in Colorado Springs for the remainder of his life. He was involved locally with the Boy Scouts of America and provided leadership and capital for the establishment of Camp Alexander near Lake George. The company exchanged hands several times before his death in 1971, at the age of 76.

The story of the Alexander Film Company is a tribute to entrepreneurism and an original advertising idea that eventually created an $80 billion dollar a year television advertising industry.

In the past 4 years I have given over a dozen public programs on the history of the Alexander Film Company. Each time I do a program I meet former Alexander staff or friends that knew the Alexander brothers personally and I learn something new about the family. During a recent program I discovered that Don M. Alexander did get married in his sixties to the widow of his brother J Don. The three of them for years had lived in the same 12,000 square foot home on Wood avenue. After J Don died in 1955, his brother continued to live in the house with his brother's widow Gertrude, who was seven years his senior and in her seventies at that time. Gertrude was a very outgoing woman who was able to connect personally with her introverted brother-in-law. Their marriage was most likely a marriage of convenience between two older people that knew each other well and had a life-long friendship. They were also concerned about appearances since they were two unmarried people who were living in the same house, so Don M. and his former sister-in-law Gertrude made the decision to get married.

# EVERYBODY WELCOME

W hen I first met Fannie Mae Duncan in 1990, her remarkable career in Colorado Springs was already history. She had moved to Aurora, Colorado in the 1980s and she still felt some bitterness about what happened to The Cotton Club in Colorado Springs, when urban renewal razed her nightclub in 1975. She did not let it damper her spirits, and at 72-years-old she was as charming and optimistic as the day she opened her first business in the 1940s in Colorado Springs.

The Pioneers Museum in Colorado Springs decided to honor her back in 1990 with a display of items from her bar and restaurant called "The Cotton Club", it was named after the famous African American night club in Harlem. Unlike the Cotton Club in New York, her business was owned by African Americans and her customers were both black and white patrons.

It was a club that featured the best jazz, blues, and rock musicians from the late 1940's through the 1960s and she welcomed everyone in her club.

At a time when Colorado Springs practiced its own form of segregation, and black musicians were not allowed to play in the five-star hotels like the Broadmoor, Fannie Mae offered a venue for the best African American talent in the country. Although the small African American population in Colorado Springs frequented her businesses as well as the G.I.s at Fort Carson, she knew she could not succeed without white patrons visiting her club. The white students from Colorado College and other white adults were initially afraid to enter her club since it was considered a "black" nightclub. She wanted to make it clear that all people were welcome in her business, so she cleared out her front window and hung a sign that read "Everybody Welcome." Her club became a success, her wealth and influence increased, and she slowly became a very respected business woman in Colorado Springs. She was the first African-American businesswoman in Colorado Springs to accomplish such status.

I had never heard of Fannie Mae Duncan until the Pioneers museum approached me about doing an interview with her and producing a documentary on her life. When I was first introduced to Fannie Mae Duncan, it only took a few minutes before I decided she was the most charming person I have ever met in my life.

This project was a collaboration from the beginning. The head of our local history department, Ree Mobley, did the research and the interview with Fannie. I brought in my friend Mark Bell to help with the production, he was a skilled video producer who also happened to be an African American. It was a perfect team with great chemistry, and Fannie Mae's amazing life made it the most successful documentary I had ever worked on in my career. We interviewed her in our studio and at her home in Aurora, Colorado. We also copied her personal photographs to enhance the visuals in the documentary. She wore this wonderful hat in the interview, and in many ways was still locked in the time period of the 40s and 50s during the height of her success. As her story unfolded it became obvious that this amazing woman fought with great passion to be successful. She was an entrepreneur whose sales skills and endearing personality and love for all people was the key to her business success.

Fannie Mae was born Fannie Mae Bragg in the small town of Luther, Oklahoma. She moved to Colorado Springs in 1933 when she was just 15 years old. Her family had to leave Oklahoma after the death of her father in an automobile accident. The family had been sharecroppers and her mother couldn't support her seven children on her own. Frances the oldest sister was sent out to Colorado Springs to live with a cousin, and she found a job as a maid for a wealthy white family. Over a 2-year period Francis sent all of her earnings to the family. The money covered the expense of all "The Bragg's trip to Colorado Springs in the summer of 1933. Fannie Mae was a top student and her first ambition was to be a nurse. She graduated from high school in 1938 and in 1942 she began working in the Raven Club for black soldiers at Camp Carson. At that time Camp Carson was still segregated and she helped the black soldiers with writing letters to their families, as well as running the soda fountain. She was an attractive young woman and the soldiers loved her youthful energy. Before she knew it, because of her personal charm, the soda fountain was a financial success and the Raven Club was a very popular place.

She realized it was her charisma and business acumen that made the soda fountain a success and she knew if she had her own business she would be making all this money for herself. At eighteen years old she married Ed Duncan, who was ten years older than her and worked as a local handy man. It was a perfect marriage for a young woman who wanted to run her own business. The city owned a building that they rented out for a cafe. The original person who had the lease could not make the payments to the city and closed the shop. Fannie saw it as a perfect opportunity to start a business that would focus on serving black patrons. She went to the city manager at the time and explained that the black population in the Springs was growing, because of the influx of the black soldiers at Fort Carson, and there were no restaurants in town that would serve black patrons. The City Manager was concerned about her youth, but he still allowed her to lease the building on a three-month trial. By the end of the trial her little coffee shop was filled with patrons and her career as a business woman took off in Colorado Springs. In a few years she bought her own building and expanded her restaurant. She bought a two-story building in a great location downtown, but the building needed work. Since her husband Ed was a handy man, he could do all the refurbishing work himself, which saved them money. Fannie wanted to use the upstairs for a night club. She wanted to call it the "Cotton Club", after the famous New York City night club.

Unlike the cotton club in New York, this club would be owned and operated by African Americans. Her sister Ozena was a singer who had performed with Duke Ellington. She had the connections in the music business and she knew she could get a steady flow of black entertainers who were at the top of their profession. Artists like Etta James, Bo Diddly, Chuck Berry, Lionel Hampton, Duke Ellington would all come through Colorado Springs on their national tours and perform at the Cotton Club.

She knew her business could not survive with just the black patrons in Colorado Springs. She put together a plan to expand her business and targeted the white soldiers at Fort Carson and the college students at Colorado College as potential patrons. As she said in the documentary, "I didn't care if they were blue, purple, or red, the only thing that I was concerned with is that they were 21 and came into my business with money that was green."

Her biggest problem was that her musicians couldn't stay in any of the hotels in town, because the hotels were all whites only. Most of them would stay at her house or with other black families in Colorado Springs. To make things easier for her guests she purchased a 42-room mansion and moved the entire building to the only block in town that allowed blacks to live. She moved into the mansion and made it her own private hotel for the black performers and other black business people or visitors that came through town.

The 1950s was the golden era for Fannie Mae and her family and her businesses thrived for the next 20 years. Ironically, since these great musicians weren't able to play in the nicest hotels in Colorado Springs, she had a captive audience at her club. Excellent established musicians like Duke Ellington could only perform at the Cotton Club. It wasn't until integration was practiced in the 1960s that her business declined. The other businesses and hotels had finally opened up to all ethnic groups. The African American population in Colorado Springs was around 10% or 4,000 people in the 1950s, and she depended on that population to exclusively use her many businesses as well as the white population to visit her clubs to see exclusive black entertainment they could not enjoy anywhere else. She embraced integration and realized it was a small price to pay to live in a fair and integrated society.

The decline in her business was quick after integration, and by the early

1970's she struggled to keep her doors open. Compounding her problems was that her business was downtown and on one of the main access roads to the city of Colorado Springs. The white leaders in Colorado Springs secretly were concerned that people who were entering the city for the first time would first see black faces and that would scare them away. They used what was then was called urban renewal to condemn her buildings and they made her a cash payment to leave downtown. This was a bitter time for Fannie Mae and she ended up moving to the Denver suburb of Aurora where I first interviewed her. Nothing stays the same, but for a brief and shining moment it was like living in Camelot for Fannie Mae. Everything she touched turned to gold.

During the 50s she made a very unusual alliance with the white redneck sheriff by the name of Chief Irvin "Dad" Bruce in Colorado Springs. "Dad" Bruce was a good old boy from the South who policed the city of Colorado Springs like he owned it. He was a fair man, but you didn't want to anger Dad Bruce if you lived in Colorado Springs at that time. Being from a small town in the South he had grown up with African Americans that he worked with and befriended. Although they lived separately in their own little communities, he had known many African American women like Fannie and he had great affection for her. Since Fannie was a country girl from Oklahoma, they immediately hit it off. She knew she had to charm "Dad" Bruce if she were to have a successful business in his city. If a crime took place, and it was a member of the black community who was the culprit, "Dad" would go to Fannie to find out who it was. In many cases the guilty party would surrender at the police station, rather than facing the wrath of Fannie Mae. Between the two of them, they made sure that both the black and white community abided by the law and allowed everyone to live in a safe and racially peaceful community. She was like the African American Godfather or the black mayor of Colorado Springs. If you were an African American in trouble, or if you just needed a job, as long as you were honest with her, you could always go to Fannie Mae for help.

It was during the early days of integration when Chief Bruce became concerned. Many of the white businesses were upset that white men and white women were going to the Cotton Club, and they were losing business to Fannie. To compound the problem for the leaders in the white community was that whites and blacks were also mixing and dancing in her club. Chief Bruce was receiving so many complaints that he talked to Fannie directly and told her that she had to limit her business to only black customers. Knowing the United States Constitution, she told him that if she refused white customer to come into her business, she would be sued as well as lose money by refusing half her customers. He finally relented after talking to the city attorney and told her to continue letting everyone in. Over time they developed a close friendship, and like the film *In the heat of the Night* they continued to work as a black and white team, making sure the city ran smoothly for all people.

Fannie Mae never had any children of her own, but she helped raise her nephews and nieces. Her sister Selena was a singer and a single mother and was constantly on the road, so she left her son Sylvester with Fannie. Syl was like her own son and she taught him all she knew about business. She also made sure he worked hard for her and at a very early age was running errands and cleaning her buildings. Sylvester Franklin went on to college at the University of Colorado and became an executive for IBM.

When Fannie Mae was in her 50s, her younger brother had gotten a white woman from Wyoming pregnant. When she had the baby, her family insisted that she put it up for adoption, so they took the baby girl to an orphanage in Pueblo, Colorado.

When Fannie Mae found out what happened, she immediately drove down to Pueblo. She announced to the orphanage that any baby that was related to her was not going to stay an orphan, and she immediately adopted the little girl. She raised the baby Renee as her own daughter, with all the advantages of a household full of love and privilege. Renee was a bright young woman who went on to get a degree from Vassar college.

The documentary was an incredible project and was probably the most successful video I worked on during my career. We were nominated for a Heartland Emmy award and won several other national awards. The collaboration with Mark Bell worked out very well and he also did the narration on the documentary. Mark and I became good friends and we worked on many other projects. Unfortunately, Mark Bell died from complication from a blood clot, after routine knee surgery on December 29, of 2010. He was 59 years old.

We showed the documentary on television locally in Colorado Springs as well as state wide on PBS and nationally on the history channel. One of the viewers of the documentary was a local middle school teacher by the name of Kay Esmiol who happened to see it on cable one night. Kay taught English and theater at Eagleview Middle School and was looking for an original musical to produce that featured a minority lead. After seeing "Everybody Welcome" she called me for the contact information for Fannie Mae Duncan and she got a hold of her. Fannie was excited that middle school kids wanted to tell her life story in a musical and Kay's original play and musical was a local success. Fannie came to opening night and the students met Fannie after performing the play and they became like family to her. Kay and Fannie became very close and Kay, who is an excellent writer, offered to help Fannie write an autobiography. Together they collaborated on an autobiography that they called "Everybody Welcome: A Memoir of Fannie Mae Duncan and the Cotton Club." It was published in 2013 and it is a comprehensive, entertaining and poignant book on her incredible life.

I was born in 1955 and unfortunately most of the people I am writing about in this biography have passed on. It is understandable, since it was a self-selecting elderly population we produced these video portraits on. The fact is that most of the people we interviewed were over 70 years old, and since they had lived a full life, they had a fascinating story to tell. Bambi and Nic Venectucci, Jim Bates, the Tutt brothers, Fannie Mae Duncan, Sol Zlochower have all passed on, but I was fortunate enough to share a time and place with all of them.

All you have is that moment in time with these amazing people. 50 years with my father, 58 years with my mother, 10 years with Sol, 5 years with Fannie Mae Duncan, 10 years with Nic and Bambi Venetucci, 7 years with Jim Bates. Brief moments, but long enough to become close and have genuine love and respect for these good people who had an impact on my life. As I look back on my life, there are some days that I miss them all desperately.

# THE COWBOY WAY

"Stand up for yourself and others, respect your God, your country, your elders, and always tell the truth."

There are many definitions of the *The Cowboy Way*, but the above statement by an aspiring young bull rider, best sums up the philosophy of the *The Cowboy Way*. You don't have to be a real cowboy to live your life *The Cowboy Way*. My father is an example of a man whose values and virtues mirrored the cowboy lifestyle, but he never rode a horse. *The Cowboy Way* is the lifestyle followed by a great many men and women living in Colorado. The Pikes Peak Region is rich in western history and tradition. Both the Santé Fe trail and the Goodnight Loving trail ran through southern Colorado, where many a cattle drive in the 1800's took place. Since 1946 the nationally respected *Pikes Peak or Bust Rodeo* has been an annual Colorado Springs tradition. The Pikes Peak Library District has several historic films on the rodeo and parade that was shot by the Alexander Film Company in the late 40s, 50s and 60s. It is a time capsule of how downtown looked during that time period. In 1949 the Pikes Peak Range Riders was formed to support the rodeo with an annual horseback ride around Pikes Peak. The Alexander Film Company and Jim Bates produced several films on the ride in the 50s and 60s that are also part of the PPLD collection. In 1979 Colorado Springs became the headquarters for the *Pro Rodeo Hall of Fame and Museum of the American Cowboy*. It is a modern museum with a multi-media program that celebrates *The Cowboy Way* and the many rodeo athletes that have risked their lives performing in this traditional American sport. In 1992 the *Professional Bull Riders Association* moved their headquarter to Pueblo, Colorado. The city of Pueblo is also the host city of the *Colorado State Fair* since 1869, when 2,000 people gathered at the banks of the Arkansas river for a horse exhibition.

*Western Horseman* magazine, whose offices were in Colorado Springs from 1943 to 2010, celebrated the ranching lifestyle and is a literary record of our cowboy culture and history. Long time *Westen Horseman* publisher Richard "Dick" Spencer lived his entire life *The Cowboy Way*. Born in 1921 in Dallas, Texas, he served his country as a combat paratrooper throughout Europe during World War II. A journalism graduate from the University of Iowa, he moved to Colorado Springs in 1951 to work at the *Western Horse-man* magazine and eventually became publisher until his death from cancer in 1989. In 1988 he developed a friendship with then Pikes Peak Library District director Bernie Margolis and they decided to create *The Great Pikes Peak Cowboy Poetry Gathering* in 1989. Dick Spencer never lived long enough to see the first poetry gathering, but for the next five years the Pikes Peak Library District worked with his widow Vivian Spencer and hosted this event that featured the best in western music and literature. Bernie Margolis and Dick Spencer's friendship was an unusual alliance between two very different people. A Jewish kid from Queens, Bernie Margolis appreciated the western heritage of the community he served. and he saw an opportunity to embrace that heritage with a variety of library programming. A staunched defender of libraries and their value to a community, Bernie started an arts and literature renaissance in Colorado Springs by embracing and support-ing *The Imagination Celebration, The Pikes Peak Writers Conference*, and the *Great Pikes Peak Cowboy Poetry Gathering*. For me, these three events gave me hundreds of hours of original programming for my channel. With the poetry gathering, I had a front row seat to some of the finest western musi-cians and western storytellers this country had to offer. Bernie Margolis and his wife Amanda would attend every event in their western wear. Bernie, who with his full grey beard looked more like a rabbi, would promote this event with all the love in his heart. Each year Bernie would put on cowboy boots, wrangler jeans, a bolo tie, and a fancy Stetson cowboy hat. As hard as Bernie tried to look like a cowboy, I'm afraid he would still look like a rabbi wearing western clothes. However, he was fully invested in this poetry gathering, to honor his friendship with Dick Spencer.

Now I am a California boy who came of age in the 60s and 70s. My record collection included the music of Joni Mitchell, Jimi Hendrix, The Rolling Stones, Bob Dylan, and Led Zeppelin. Other than being a fan of the music of Hank Williams, I was not acquainted with traditional western and cowboy music. It didn't take me long to fall in love with the harmonizing music of *The Sons of the San Juaquin*, the yodeling brilliance of cowboy historian and western singer and master guitar player Don Edwards, and the storytelling of such great cowboy poets as Waddie Mitchell and Baxter Black. Other brilliant performers who were featured at the annual gathering included *Riders in the Sky* and western songwriter and guitarist Gary McMahon. For one week a year, this California boy put on a cowboy hat and had the privilege to work with some of the finest people you will ever meet. They lived their life in *The Cowboy Way*, and their amazing talent was only matched by their humility.

Before the library had access to a video truck, we used to carry our remote equipment in what we called the PVOM or what my staff called the PVOMIT when we struggled to carry it up stairs. PVOM was short for Portable Video Operational Module and it would make your back sore just looking at it. It was three anvil cases that weighed 200 pounds each, and we would carefully carry it from our van to the Pikes Peak Center to record these events. We would hook the three cases together and then direct the event from the basement of the Pikes Peak Center, The setup process would take at least two hours and cost us several pulled muscles trying to transport it down to the basement. After one of the events, where Cowboy Poet Waddie Mitchell was the headliner, we were struggling to carry our equipment back to the van. Waddie Mitchell noticed our difficulty hauling our equipment and he stopped to offer to help us. Before we could even answer, he was taking one corner of an anvil case and helping us carrying it to the van. He didn't leave the Pikes Peak Center, until he helped us break down all of our equipment that night. This was the headliner of that evenings performance, and here he was a 40-year-old roadie generously helping us carry this cumbersome equipment.

Without any exception, all of the western performers we worked with had the same humble attitude. I taped hundreds of programs with the *Great Pikes Peak Cowboy Gathering* and I never heard one four letter word from anyone. These performers were always G-rated and relied on their immense talent and storytelling ability to entertain a family audience. Some of the acts might have been considered corny, but no one responded in delight more than the children that were entertained by Sky shivers and his border collie dog, Miss Kitty. Sky Shivers promoted his act as western stories of his cowboy life mixed with mediocre tricks by his dog Miss Kitty. Miss Kitty would leap on his back on cue to the delight of the kids watching his presentation. They would learn wholesome tales about the west from Sky Shivers and get pure love and entertainment from Miss Kitty.

Miss Kitty had a litter of pure bred border collies and one of her puppies was adopted by fellow library employees and married couple Dave Doman and his wife Virginia Carlson. For 12 years their dog Dalton would sit at our feet during our monthly poker games at Dave's house. Dalton would wait patiently for us to drop some food from the table and was an unofficial member of our game. Dave Doman hosted the longest running poker game in the state of Colorado and possibly the country. The monthly nickel-dime-quarter game began in 1982, over 36 years ago, and Rick Duval and Dave Doman are two of the original players that are still participating in the game. Dave and Virginia have graciously hosted the game at their home for most of those 35 years. As you can imagine the participants have changed over time, and I joined the game in the early 1990's. Our current players include myself, Andy Lyon, Jim Ash, Mike Hart, as well as original members Dave Doman and Rick Duval.

I had the pleasure of befriending and working closely with two cowboy poets in Baxter Black and Gary McMahan. Baxter Black, who is the number one cowboy poet in the country, lived at that time on a ranch near Brighton, Colorado. He was a highly educated man who became a large animal veterinarian before he became a full-time performer. I had the opportunity to visit his ranch in Brighton and he had a map that represented the hundreds of cities he performed at across the nation. A pin represented each city and state and county fair he performed at over the years. The map was covered with pins and it represented his grass roots career of performing in rural America. When I first watched Baxter Black perform, I realized his style and storytelling resembled Richard Pryor. Although Baxter Blacks performances were G-Rated, he acted out each story brilliantly with character impersonations, facial expressions, and remarkable timing. Baxter Black was similar to Richard Pryor in that he was a comic storyteller, that didn't just stand on stage and tell jokes. He would fill the 1200 seat Pikes Peak Center every time he came to Colorado Springs to perform.

I got to know Gary McMahan when he came to our studio to produce a promotional tape from clips of his performances we videotaped over the years. He was a gentleman and a real cowboy who had made a living, as he tells it, with a horse or a guitar for the past 40 years. He had written over 300 western songs for such artists as Garth Brooks and he would sit by the mailbox collecting his songwriting royalties, when he wasn't performing his music and storytelling. He was also a skilled yodeler, which is a lost art that only a handful of performers can do today. I remember one of his performances when he told the story about having a Phd from MIT. He later explained that he had gotten a Post Hole Digger from Milligan Implement and Tractors. That was the kind of humor that would make you smile and was always family friendly at the gathering.

Most of the western artists who performed were represented by local talent agent Scott O'Malley. Scott O'Malley is the Broadway Danny Rose of western music agents. A farm kid from Indiana he is exceedingly honest and loyal to his clients and has always lived his life *The Cowboy Way*. He would do anything for the musical talent he represents and in return they also have given him their undying loyalty. His clients remain his friend and talent for decades. Some of the most loyal acts he represents include Waddie Mitchell, Don Edwards, the *Sons of the San Joaquin* and *Flash Cadillac*. *Flash Cadillac* is a traditional rock and roll band that was featured in the 1973 film *American Graffiti*. Scott has represented all of these remarkable talents for over 30 years. A not so well-kept secret is his *Western Jubilee Warehouse* at his offices in Colorado Springs on East Cucharras Street. It is an intimate 100-seat theater that he uses for smaller events and personal concerts for his performers. The theater is covered from floor to ceiling with western paraphernalia and is one of the finest settings to listen to an intimate concert. Scott was gracious enough to provide his location for my retirement party from PPLD in 2008. His friend and long-time photographer, Don Kallaus, has been very supportive and personally involved in helping me publish this book. Recently Scott has signed a group from Pueblo called *The Haunted Wind Chimes*. This folk and bluegrass group is as talented as any of the acts Scott represents. I have had the privilege to see them perform in a sold-out venue at the Pueblo Sangre De Christo Arts Center.

The Renaissance patron of western music and western arts, library director Bernie Margolis, left the Pikes Peak Library District in 1997 to take the prestigious job as director of the Boston Public Library. He left that job in 2008 to become the New York State Librarian. In 2010 he developed a rare form of Leukemia that he fought valiantly for eight years until his death on April 14, 2018. This Jewish kid from Queens lived his entire life *The Cowboy Way.*

# THE MAN WHO SAVED THE BELL

ill Bowers was a 96-year-old photographer for the Colorado Springs Fine Arts Center when I first met him. I needed to get some photographs from Bill for one of my documentaries and he gave me a bounty of photographs and several films he shot in Colorado Springs in the 1940's and 1950's. I realized immediately that a documentary on Bill and his amazing life needed to be done. At the time, Bill Bowers was still working and paying into social security. The Social Security Administration thought it was a scam that a 96-year-old man would still be working, so they asked him to come into the social security office in person to prove he actually existed and was still alive. Bill paraphrased Mark Twain by telling me he would start each day reading the Colorado Springs Gazette and check the obituaries, if he didn't see his name in the obits, he would go to work.

During his 80-year working life doing a variety of jobs, which included several years as an officer in the military, he had seen and done almost everything. Born in Colorado Springs in 1903 he started his Army career as an ROTC student at the University of Arizona back in the early 1920's. He was commissioned as a cavalry officer and assigned to a unit of African

American Buffalo Soldiers. At that time, only white men were allowed to be officers of the black troops. During his summer ROTC service he and his Buffalo Soldier cavalry unit would help chase Pancho Villa across the United States border into Mexico. He eventually left the Army and became a stockbroker. On the day he married his college sweetheart in 1929, the stock market crashed, and he struggled financially during the depression years with his new wife.

Bill was called back to active duty as an officer at the age of 39 in 1942 and was in the Army Air Corps until 1946. While in the Army Air Corps Bill came across the bell that was in the U.S. Arizona when it was sunk at Pearl Harbor. He was serving on the west coast at that time and was doing inventory at the Puget Sound Naval Yard in Bremerton, Washington when he came across a crate containing a ship's bell that was slated to be melted down as scrap metal. It turned out the bell had historic value since it was from the U.S. Arizona and was made of silver and copper that was mined from the state. Since Bill was a graduate of the University of Arizona, he felt the bell should be saved and he contacted the current UA president Alfred Atkinson to tell him what he had found. Alfred Atkinson asked Arizona Governor Sidney Osborn to save the bell, and he intervened and had the bell sent in 1946 to the University of Arizona where it remains today in the Old Memorial Student Union. Ringing the bell is still a cherished tradition at the University. Every third Wednesday of each month at 12:07 PM, representing the infamous date of December 7th, the bell is rung to honor the sailors who lost their lives on the U.S. Arizona on December 7th.

After Bill left the Army Air Corps he had breathing problems and it turned out his lungs were damaged and the doctor told him he had only 5 years to live. Thinking he would be living a short life, he wanted to work doing something he loved and decided to dedicate his life to photography. For the next 61 years he shot motion picture film and photography in the Pikes Peak region. His photography collection is now an important resource of the Colorado Springs Fine Arts center. His company, Knutson-Bowers was the official photographer for the Pikes Peak Hill climb. He and his partner Knutson sold their company in the 1960's and Bill went to work as the official photographer for the Colorado Springs Fine Arts Center, where he continued to work as a photographer for the next 40 years. I always enjoyed doing documentaries on photographers since they provided me with plenty of visual material to make the documentary more entertaining and artistic. Bill was a very handsome man at 96 and had a full head of gray hair. At six-feet tall he still stood very erect and was very physically fit and stayed active by walking everywhere.

When I finished the documentary, I asked him what he thought of his video portrait. He was very polite and said we did a nice job with the content and mixing in his photographs, but he thought the studio lighting during the sit-down interview made him look old. At first, I didn't know how to respond. He was 96 years old and I wanted to ask him how old did the lighting make him look, 105 or 106 perhaps? I bit my tongue and told him I thought he looked good and I appreciated a critique from a skilled photographer. It doesn't matter how old you are, especially if you were always a good-looking man your whole life, but vanity always plays a part in how we perceive ourselves. I can honestly say I'm no different than Bill when I see a picture of myself now in my sixties, I always immediately focus on my double chin and how much I look like my Dad when he was an older man. Bill remained a great friend until the day in 2003, when he was 100 years old, and he read the morning paper and saw his name listed in the obituary. It was the first day he didn't bother going to work and he is now resting in peace for eternity. To honor their special alumni for saving the bell from the U.S. Arizona, The University of Arizona rang the bell seven times in 2003, in memory of Bill Bowers.

# THE FINEST EDUCATOR IN COLORADO

Richard Marold was the director of the Cheyenne Mountain Heritage Center and the publisher of their magazine, *KIVA*, when I first met him in 1999. After talking to Richard, I discovered we had a connection: Bambi Venetucci. Richard's daughter, who was born partially blind, had been one of Bambi Venetucci's students at the Colorado School for the Deaf and Blind. Richard remained friends with Bambi after his daughter left the school, and they had stayed in touch over the years. Richard first approached me with a film he had produced on innovative Colorado educator Dr. Lloyd "Pappy" Shaw that was shot in the late 1920s, 1930s and early 1940s on 16 mm film. It was a polished collection of films that documented the innovative educational programs during that time frame at the Cheyenne Mountain School District. Richard had graduated from Cheyenne Mountain High School in the early 1950s, and he personally knew Lloyd Shaw. Richard was a very talented Chautauqua performer and was doing his own performance as Dr. Lloyd Shaw. Richard also created Chautauqua performances of Winfield Scott Stratton and Franklin Delano Roosevelt.

Dr. Lloyd Shaw was an educator, coach, and principal at the Cheyenne Mountain School from 1916 to 1951. A graduate of Colorado College, he started his teaching career at Colorado Springs High School before accepting a job with the Cheyenne Mountain School. The school served the children on the west side, the Broadmoor area, and the orphans who lived at the Myron Stratton Home. This remarkable 16-mm film, shot by Lloyd Shaw himself, showed the school when it was one of the finest public schools in the country. It could be considered one of the first charter schools in the United States, since Lloyd Shaw put his stamp on the school featuring a variety of programs and activities for his students that would still be considered innovative by today's standards. Lloyd Shaw used this film to promote his innovative school at educator conferences across the country. There was so much film footage to work with that Richard Marold created two one-hour programs. Dr. Lloyd Shaw, who loved photography and filmmaking, shot this film with a tripod and displayed some advanced cinematography skills for the time. Impressed by the quality of the original film, we did a high-quality transfer to digital video at the Alexander Film and Video Company. Richard Marold narrated both programs and provided his personal insight from his 13 years of experience as a student in Cheyenne Mountain schools.

Lloyd firmly believed that education should not be confined to classrooms. His school was in the perfect location to promote nature. At the time Colorado Springs had no more than 40,000 residents, and the Cheyenne Mountain School literally backed up to the national forest on the west side of Colorado Springs. The school's backyard opened up to the entire Rocky Mountain west. An environmentalist and a naturalist, Shaw oversaw the building of a nature conservatory at the school. The students worked in the nature center and were exposed to the variety of wildlife that lived nearby. The original Ute Indians were still living in Colorado Springs then, and they were invited to teach the students about their history and love for nature, while speaking informally in the schools circular Kiva.

Dr. Shaw believed that education needed a hands-on component, and everything the school taught had some sort of practical application to it.

He believed that sports at the school should involve both boys and girls and encouraged athletic endeavors that involved all of his students.

Students had to learn how to dance. He felt dancing was both an aesthetic and an athletic endeavor that was beneficial to students' spirit and health. Dr. Shaw was a national leader in the revival of American folk and square dancing. He traveled around the country collecting material and research on American square dancing and is credited for its preservation.

He was a nationally renowned square-dancing caller, and the Cheyenne Mountain School dance team performed across the country and won numerous awards. In the summer of 1946, he was invited to Hollywood to help with the production of the western *Duel in the Sun* starring Gregory Peck. He was hired to choreograph the square dance sequence during a western barbecue in the film and was also featured in the film as the square dance caller.

Horseback riding and other traditions of western life were encouraged. Many of the students owned their own horses and rode them to school. Dr. Shaw sponsored horseback-riding excursions through the nearby mountain trails so that his students could enjoy the natural beauty of the area. The school also sponsored an annual rodeo. Students participated in numerous field trips across Colorado to experience nature up close in the state and the national parks. Every year the senior class took a field trip to Rocky Mountain National Park. The students also participated in cross country and downhill skiing, before the popular ski areas of Colorado even existed. The school owned their own high-powered telescope that they set up at night for evening astronomy classes.

The Alexander Aircraft Company donated gliders to the school, and the students flew the gliders tethered to a moving vehicle. They also had a $5 Ford Club where students spent up to $5 to rebuild Model T Fords and turned them into off-road jalopies. They learned about auto mechanics in the process of rebuilding these cars. All of these activities were documented in his films, and there was also footage of young Lloyd Shaw enjoying these many activities with his students. The students never called him "Dr. Shaw." He was always known as "Pappy Shaw." His students were his greatest advocates and spoke in superlatives about the best education that anyone could hope for in this country. His many books and collectibles are preserved in a replica of his office, which is currently housed at the Cheyenne Heritage Center. Dr. Shaw died of a stroke in 1959; yet, the memory of his personal impact on his students and his dedication to preserving American square dancing is his living legacy. Dr. Lloyd Shaw is considered by his students and local historians as one of the finest Colorado educators of his time.

# NAME DROPPING:
## SOME OF THE NOTABLE PEOPLE I WORKED WITH

### SCOTT CARPENTER

I had the opportunity to meet and to interview two astronauts who had a connection with Colorado. Scott Carpenter, who was born in Boulder, Colorado, was one of the original Friendship Seven astronauts. When he was a boy, he had lived during the summer in the small town of Palmer Lake, just north of Colorado Springs. We were working on a history on the town of Palmer Lake when my co-producer, Jim Sawatzki, secured an interview with him. Scott agreed to talk about his memories of Palmer Lake when it was a sleepy, little tourist destination. At the time of the interview, Scott was living in Vail. He was in great shape for a man in his sixties and still looked the part of the handsome Mercury astronaut he was in his thirties. We sat down for an hour as he talked about his youth in Colorado and his love for Palmer Lake. As one of the seven Mercury Astronauts he was featured in the book and the movie *The Right Stuff*, which told their amazing story. When you first met him, you instantly recognized that he was a man of incredible character and accomplishments by the way he carried himself during the interview. He definitely had *The Right Stuff*.

## JIM IRWIN

Colonel Jim Irwin, an astronaut on Apollo 15, was one of 12 people to have walked on the moon. A deeply religious man, Jim made his home in Colorado Springs. He created the High Flight Foundation, a religious organization dedicated to promoting Christianity. Of all the people I met in my life, he was the only person who completely overwhelmed me when I shook his hand. I kept thinking, "This man had walked on the moon - and I'm shaking the hand of a man who had accomplished a most rare feat." In 1988, he gave an hour-long program for the library, as he talked about his experiences in the Air Force and as an astronaut on Apollo 15. It was on the eve of the first shuttle flight after the Challenger disaster. He spoke with great pride about his time as an astronaut and his hope and faith for our country's return to space. He was a man of great humility and had persisted with heroic effort to become an astronaut, even after being diagnosed with heart disease. After his historic flight, Jim Irwin had three serious heart attacks; yet, he pursued his life and foundation with great dedication. Three years after we produced the program, in August of 1991, he died of a heart attack.

## BUCK O'NEIL

While working in the Communication Department at the Pikes Peak Library District, we were always looking for excellent programming to cablecast. We created "live" programming from our meeting room at the East library, and it was a way we could extend our programming directly into our patrons' homes. Some of the most successful live programming included two presentations we filmed with former Negro Leagues player and professional baseball historian Buck O'Neil. He is a familiar face to anyone who enjoyed the Ken Burns documentary on baseball. Buck was in his mid-80s when he visited Colorado Springs and delivered an amazing program on the history of Negro League Baseball and the integration of major league baseball when the Brooklyn Dodgers signed Jackie Robinson in 1947. I made the arrangements to bring Buck to Colorado Springs, and I have never met a more vibrant and energetic man of any age. It was one of the best programs we had sponsored at the library, and our meeting room was packed. It was an honor to listen to his personal history with the Negro Leagues as he talked about the great ballplayers he had met, including Babe Ruth, Satchel Paige, Cool Papa Bell, and Josh Gibson.

## CLAY JENKINSON

Fans of "The Thomas Jefferson Hour" on NPR are familiar with the genius of Clay Jenkinson. During the 1990s we videotaped at least ten different performances with Clay. He was the most popular performer on the library channel during my 20 years of cablecasting. Clay Jenkinson is a bonified genius with a brilliant sense of humor. The Chautauqua performances we taped with Clay included his performances as Thomas Jefferson, Meriwether Lewis, John Wesley Powell, and Robert Oppenheimer. Having worked with Clay on many occasions, I can tell you he is a bit of a savant. He can stand in front of an audience of 500 people and portray some of the brightest minds in our nation's history, but he can't keep track of his car keys. There were many times we had to make sure he retrieved all his personal items after one of his performances.

# KRISTALLNACHT:
# THE NIGHT OF BROKEN GLASS

One of the most powerful and chilling interviews that we ever recorded at our library studios was with Adele Obodov. Adele was a witness to Kristallnacht when she was a twelve-year old Jewish girl living in Cologne, Germany. She was a credible and articulate witness to pure hate that she experienced in her birth place of Germany. An evening of terror that exploded into a murderous rampage during that horrible "Night of Broken Glass."

The original interview of Adele was the concept of Paulette Greenberg. Paulette Greenberg and her husband cardiologist Dr. David Greenberg created The Greenberg Center for Learning and Tolerance in 2003. They initiated a video history project that documented the lives of Holocaust survivors and their personal stories in their own words. The Greenberg Center for Learning and Tolerance often partnered with the Pikes Peak Library District to sponsor speakers and programs that promoted tolerance and understanding. They occasionally brought in Holocaust survivors as witnesses to some of the most horrific examples of intolerance in our world history. My friend, Sharyn Markus, who is editing this book, is currently vice-president of the GCLT and the founder of The Paperclip Campaign, now an international program to honor Holocaust victims during the annual Days of Remembrance. Paulette enlisted the help of Jane and Bob Neff. Jane and Bob were married video producers and volunteers who utilized our library studio and produced several documentaries which we aired on the library channel. They were both school teachers in Colorado Springs, and they worked hand in hand with The Greenberg Center for Learning and Tolerance (GCLT). Shooting the interview in our studio, the Neff's through the Greenberg Center history project produced "Adele Obodov: A Time of Remembrance." It is an extremely important first-hand account of what happened during Kristallnacht.

Adele Obodov moved to Colorado Springs in 1952 and was a member of Temple Shalom, the largest synagogue in Colorado Springs. Although I've produced hundreds of documentaries, none was more important than helping Jane and Bob record Adele's memories.

When Adele first walked into the studio, I immediately understood that she was a woman of great character and grace. A very intelligent woman, her detailed memory of that horrific time and place was impeccable. As she talked about her experiences, she spoke with fierce sincerity. Born in Cologne, Germany, Adele's father, Walter Brunell, owned a wholesale supply business for barbershops and beauty parlors. They sold wholesale barbershop chairs, wigs, and other beauty products. Like most Jewish businesses at that time in Cologne, the building also housed the family in an upstairs apartment.

Around 1934 Hitler started implementing his racist policies in German, isolating the Jewish population. Adele's earliest memories of this kind of intolerance was not being able to go to the ice rink she had frequented because she was Jewish. Unfortunately, things just got worse from there for the Jewish population of Cologne. On November 7, 1938, Polish Jew Hershel Grynszpan entered the German embassy in Paris and asked to see an embassy official. An embassy staff office clerk, Ernst Von Rath, left his desk to meet him; and Grynszpan fired five bullets into his body and murdered the German clerk. The murder became an international incident and an excuse for the Nazi Party to take revenge on the Jewish population living in Germany. Two days after the murder, mobs of German citizens, with the blessing and the participation of the Nazi SS, torched thousands of Jewish businesses and synagogues. Over 1,000 Jewish synagogues were burnt to the ground, and over 7,000 Jewish businesses were destroyed. This violent riot resulted in the murder of 91 Jews. Shortly after Kristallnacht, 30,000 Jews were sent to concentration camps. This was just the beginning of the Holocaust.

Like she did every school day, 12 year-old Adele said goodbye to her mother Erna Brunell, and walked with her cousin to her classes at the Jawne Jewish School operated by Dr. Erich Klibansky. Adele's school was conveniently adjacent to her synagogue. As they walked through the city, Adele and her cousin noticed that several of the Jewish businesses had shattered windows. When they arrived at the plaza, where their synagogue was located, they saw that there was broken glass everywhere, and several of the religious objects and Torahs had been thrown in the street. They immediately became fearful for their lives and ran home.

"I hadn't been home for a few minutes when the mob smashed the door of my father's store, and they went into our business and they literally smashed everything in sight. They ripped the shelves from the sides of the building, and the shelves were literally like a "V" or a tent, tipped in on each other. My mother must have been somewhat naive because she got on the phone to call the local police; and, of course, nothing happened. I don't know if they just hung up on her; but, of course, they never came. At the time I didn't think she was naïve, but she must've thought the police were there to protect her, because she had lived in Cologne all her life. Pretty soon these people started coming up the stairs. The entrance to our apartment was frosted glass; it wasn't a solid door, and we could see the mob standing outside and hear them talking . . . and for whatever reason, and to this day, nobody knows why, they decided not to come into the apartment. They left . . . and that was Kristallnacht."

Adele's chilling words made me aware of how important it was for us to record her testimony. She had been face to face with real evil. Although it was emotionally difficult for her to talk about that time, it was very important to her to share that experience so hopefully it wouldn't be repeated.

"History seems to have come to the conclusion that the fact that Kristall-nacht was allowed to happen, without any objections in the international world, that it was the start of the Holocaust. It was the start of the tremendous persecution that killed 11 million people in camps and gas chambers, six million of whom were Jews. I think it is important to remember Kristallnacht…so that if something else along those lines were to occur somewhere, that people would stop and say that this isn't right, that something ought to be done about it, before it mushrooms into such a tremendous tragedy. I just think that it's absolutely important to stand up and say what you think is right, and I have tried to live my life that way."

After Kristallnacht, her family's and the Jewish community's problems were just beginning. There were 20,000 people of Jewish faith in Cologne at that time, and only 8,000 were able to leave the country. The rest of the 12,000 Cologne Jewish population died in the Holocaust. Men, women, and children.

Even before Kristallnacht, Dr. Erich Klibansky anticipated the horrible fate for the Jews in Germany and his school. Early on in 1936, after making arrangements with the congregation of a synagogue in London, Dr, Klibansky was able to transfer 120 of his students to London, where the children lived with individual families until a Hostel could be arranged for them. Adele Obodov was one of those students, and her respect and gratitude for Dr. Klibansky has never diminished. Unfortunately, Dr. Klibansky and his family never joined his students in London. Dr. Klibansky and his family were deported in July, 1942. During their transport, they were unloaded from the train, and Dr. Klibansky and his wife and four sons were shot and killed in a forest in the region of Minsk. In an attempt to acknowledge and to accept responsibility for the horrors of their Nazi history, in 1990 a plaza in Cologne, Germany, was dedicated to the memory of Dr. Erich Klibansky and his heroic efforts.

Adele was now alone in London without her family, and the war broke out with Germany in 1939. The British moved Adele, as well as millions of British children into the English countryside. When she was 14 her British education ended, and Adele returned to London and to the hostel, along with the other girls who were in the same situation. She then found employment as a sewing machine operator in the war industry for England. Meanwhile, her parents and her older brother Karl, who were still in Germany, were desperate to leave. Her parents acquired a visa for her 17-year-old brother from a relative in America, and he escaped to the United States in August of 1939. This was just a month before England and France declared war on Germany. While in the United States, her brother was drafted in the U.S. Army and he became a naturalized United States citizen. Once he became an American citizen, he worked desperately to get his parents out of Germany. He secured a visa and passport for his parents in 1942, and they fled Cologne on a train to Lisbon, Portugal. Since it was wartime and most of the trains were used for German troop movement, it took them 72 hours to arrive in Lisbon; and the ship that they had booked passage on had already left the port when they arrived. The American Joint Distribution Committee, which helped thousands of Jews to leave Nazi Germany, secured them a place to live in Barcelona, Spain. They lived in Barcelona for a year before they were able to depart to the United States in 1943. Once they were in the United States, they worked on getting their daughter Adele's transportation to the United States from England. Adele left England on an almost empty troop ship returning to Canada in 1944. After a five-year separation, Adele and her entire immediate family were finally able to reunite in the United States. Two of Adele's aunts and her uncle and their families were able to immigrate to Argentina and America, but the rest of her extended family in Cologne perished in the Holocaust. Adele's brother Karl became a First Lieutenant in Patton's Third Army Division as a commander of a tank. In the ultimate in poetic justice, Karl ended up returning to Cologne as a combat soldier fighting Nazi Germany.

In 1950 Adele moved to Colorado and met her future husband Morris (Morey) Obodov at a Jewish Center in Denver. They married in 1952 and moved to Colorado Springs, where she has lived most of her life. Adele and Morey had three children; Judith, Joel, and Janet and all three children graduated from Palmer High School. Unfortunately, Judith (Judy) died of breast cancer at 38 years old and she is survived by her two children. Janet moved to Seattle, where Adele currently lives in order to be closer to her daughter. Their son Joel moved to Israel and lives there today with his family. Joel is a veteran of the Israel Army and has maintained dual citizenship with the United States. Adele has a total of seven grandchildren and three of her grandchildren live in Israel.

Ironically, after all the anti-Semitism she experienced in Europe, Colorado Springs was a restricted community when Adele moved to the city during the fifties. Both blacks and Jews were not allowed to stay in some of the local hotels, and they could not join certain country clubs or live in restricted neighborhoods. She personally spoke up against these policies; and, eventually, Colorado Springs became completely integrated in the 1960s.

What Adele experienced and saw with her own eyes during her life is extraordinary. She is a powerful voice for what can happen when intolerance becomes the official policy of a country.

# THE GENTLE ARCHIVIST

One of the best jobs in a large public library is to be involved in special collections or local history. Depending on the history of the community, an archivist's job can be a fascinating adventure. Discovering a photo collection or a film collection—like what Jim Bates donated to PPLD—was a great moment of joy and accomplishment. In 2001, Pat Losinki, our library director at the time, made one of the greatest hires in the history of our library. Pat hired Tim Blevins, a quiet archivist from New Mexico, who was building custom furniture at the time.

Tim had a fascinating background, and his meticulous nature made him a natural archivist. There are two types of archivists who work in public libraries. One type considers the collection their own personal possession, and they do everything possible to guard and to protect it from the public. The second type understands that the collection belongs to the public and ensures it is available to anyone who has an interest in local history. Tim, the second type of archivist, is fastidious and obsessed with keeping the collection pristine; but he understands that the community owns the collection, and he does everything possible to make it easily available and accessible to the taxpayers. Tim may still require patrons to wear white gloves, but he has great pride in the library collection and wants to share it equally with kids and adults, so that they can learn about the unique heritage of their community.

Tim, who was also very close to one of our board members Cal Otto, worked with Cal to create the Pikes Peak Regional History Symposium. Each year the library selects a theme, such as *Film and Photography on the Front Range*. The staff invites local, national, and international historians to write research papers to present at the symposium. Each year a book is published as a compilation of the various academic papers. After 12 years of these history symposia, an academically researched collection of local history of the Pikes Peak region is now part of the special collections archive.

The special collections is housed in the beautifully restored original 1905 Carnegie Library wing of the downtown Penrose Library in Colorado Springs. Tim Blevins and Pat Losinki helped oversee the restoration of the Carnegie Library, and Tim has grown and maintained this collection over the past 17 years. It is now one of the finest local history collections in Colorado. The photographic and motion picture film archive is as comprehensive a photographic record of any community in the West. Anyone visiting the Pikes Peak region *must* visit this extensive collection.

# Photo Section

---

## Family

My Grandmother, Emilia Lozano, as a terrified seventeen year-old bride.

Eugenio and Emilia Calvo in wedding photo.

My Great-Grandmother's mortar & pestle that survived the trip from Spain to Hawaii, then to San Jose, California.

Photograph of Calvo family in Spain, 1907. Eugenio Calvo tallest child in back row.

Antonuccio family at picnic near San Francisco.

Manuel, Soledad, and Victor Calvo

My mother, Soledad and her sister, Trinidad, when they were depression era farm kids.

Rita Hayworth, or could it be my mother's high school picture?

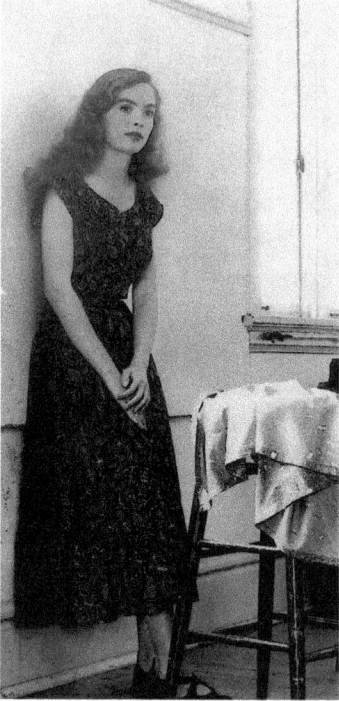

My mother as a art student at San Jose State.

My Dad (right) with friend, in Army Air Corp in Burma, India.

Oliver and Tony Antonuccio and friend in San Francisco.

Oliver and Soledad
Antonuccio

Grandparents taking us on fishing trip in Burney, California.

Mom, myself and my brother, Dave, 1959.

Posing in front of the family wagon.

Eighteen year-old Steve going to the wedding of a friend.

Myself, returning to Canar, Spain.

My daughters, Rachel and Laura Antonuccio.

Photo Section

---

Non Family

General William Jackson Palmer (Courtesy of Special Collections, Pikes Peak Library District, 005-375 Carl Mathews Collection).

Queen Palmer (Courtesy of Special Collections, Pikes Peak Library District, 001-6025 Margaretta M. Boas Photograph Collection).

Marshall Sprague (Courtesy of Special Collections, Pikes Peak Library District, 002-5909 Myron Wood Collection).

Dr. Lloyd Shaw (Courtesy of Special Collections, Pikes Peak Library District, 001-10529 Margretta M. Boas Photograph Collection).

Jim and Monica Bates (Courtesy of Special Collections, Pikes Peak Library District, 161-3319 Jim Bates Collection).

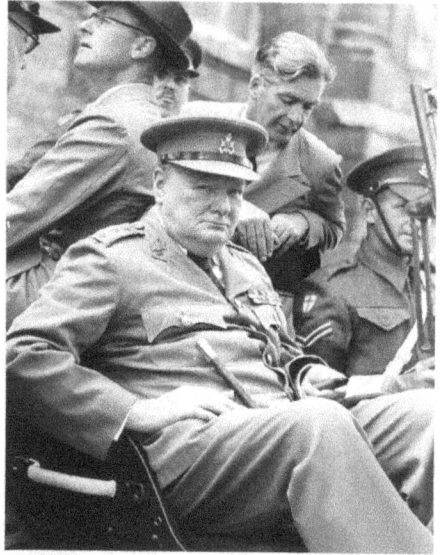

Winston Churchill (Photograph by Jim Bates, Courtesy of Special Collections, Pikes Peak Library District, 161-3312).

Lowell Thomas (Courtesy of Special Collections, Pikes Peak Library District, 001-4899 Margretta M. Boas Photograph Collection).

Alexander Film Company (Courtesy of Special Collections, Pikes Peak Library District, 056-9506 Alexander Industries Collection).

J. Don Alexander (Courtesy of Special Collections, Pikes Peak Library District, 056-9503 Alexander Industries Collection).

J. Don Alexander (Courtesy of Special Collections, Pikes Peak Library District, 056-8522 Alexander Industries Collection).

169

General Albert Clark (center) as prisoner in Stalag Luff III, (Courtesy USAFA McDermott Library).

Patrick A. Lucero
(Photograph courtesy, William Lucero)

Fannie Mae Duncan  (Photograph by Lew Tilley. Courtesy of Special Collections, Pikes Peak Library District, 099-10709).

Mabel Barbee Lee
(1902 Colorado College Yearbook,
Colorado College Special Collections).

# A DETECTIVE STORY

In 2005 Leah Davis-Witherow, a local historian who worked for the Colorado Springs Pioneers Museum, called me. She told me she had found an old 16-mm film in her collection, and she had no idea what was on it. The original label read "1928 Negro Picnic." Whenever I found a new historic film, it was like Christmas morning.

In this case, this mystery "Negro Picnic" film became a detective story for me. Over the years, I had discovered many mystery films. When Jim Bates donated his Alexander Film collection to the library, he had no idea what was on the hundred or so reels of film. In the case of the film I received from Leah, it was an easy job to find out what was on it. Over the years the Alexander Film Company, which was still in business as a film-to-DVD transfer company, worked at a reduced rate with us on transferring our film material. They kept a digital master of what we transferred. At that time Andy and Regina Hutchinson owned the company and they celebrated the company's history and loved having copies of these earlier films for their collection.

They were happy to transfer the film. When I reviewed it, I did not instantly realize the treasure we had. The film showed what looked like a wealthy white man with a black chauffeur and limousine, driving around to various African-Americans' home. It showed a picnic with African-American women and children celebrating a nondescript holiday at the original Stratton Park. They were all well dressed in their Sunday-best clothing, and both white and black people mingled at this picnic. I showed the film to Leah, and she identified the white man as Henry Sachs.

I had been in Colorado Springs for over 20 years at that time, and I had never heard of Henry Sachs. It turned out his charity and foundation were still operating in Colorado Springs as the Sachs Foundation. The foundation provided academic-based scholarships for African-American college students who lived in Colorado and who had a high school G.P.A. over 3.5. In 1932 Henry Sachs created the foundation when he was 60 years old. The mystery was about the motivation behind this wealthy Jewish man's reason to create a scholarship exclusively for African Americans.

I contacted the Sachs Foundation, and the staff provided me with more information. In fact, some of the older board members actually had known Henry Sachs, who died in 1952 at the age of 90. Henry was born in 1862 and made his fortune in Boston, where he helped finance the Gillette Safety Razor Company. In 1902 he contracted tuberculosis and moved to Colorado Springs, as many tuberculosis patients did at that time, to recover his health. Because of the dry climate and mountain air, Colorado Springs was known as an excellent place to recover from the illness. His African-American chauffeur James Jefferies and his maid Gertrude Lee dedicated their efforts to help him regain his health. He was so grateful for his two African-American employees and close friends that he decided to leave his fortune in a foundation to help African Americans acquire college scholarships. The film we found was of an integrated picnic that included local African-American children and the local Jewish Women's League. At the time that Henry Sachs created the foundation, the Klan was running the state of Colorado. Even the Colorado governor was rumored to be a member of the Ku Klux Klan. Because he was Jewish, Henry was not allowed to stay at some of the luxury hotels in Colorado Springs. He knew things needed to change, and he felt the best use of his money was to help African Americans earn college degrees and become professionals and business people who could eventually create their own wealth. The Sachs Foundation has helped over 5,000 students achieve college educations, and they have awarded close to $20,000,000 in scholarships.

I produced a short documentary on Henry Sachs which is available on YouTube. In addition to my documentary, Jane and Bob Neff, both retired teachers and volunteers for the library, produced a more comprehensive 30-minute documentary on Henry Sachs.

Colorado residents interested in applying for a scholarship, can contact the Sachs Foundation at http://www.sachsfoundation.org/.

# THE GREATER BARRIER

T*he Greater Barrier*, another film treasure shot in Colorado Springs in 1914, was discovered by Colorado film historian Dave Emrich at the Library of Congress. The Pikes Peak Film Company produced *The Greater Barrier*, considered an early independent or "orphan film," directed by Otis Thayer. A feature film shot entirely in Colorado Springs, it told the story of a Colorado College football player, Kato, who was Native American and who had a forbidden relationship with a white co-ed. Knowing that the relationship was forbidden, Kato leaves the college and returns to the reservation. Living between two worlds, he has difficulty assimilating on the reservation. He leaves to work on a local ranch owned by his former white girlfriend's uncle. When she visits her uncle, and confronts her former boyfriend, the young couple decide to get married with the uncle's blessing. When Kato's mother finds out, she travels to the ranch to confront her son with important information on who his father is. She tells him that his father is also his girlfriend's father, so they are forbidden to marry because it would be incest. Since incest is even more forbidden than mixing the two races and considered *The Greater Barrier*, they end their complicated relationship. The plot of this 1914 film is very similar to the 1996 film *Lonestar* written and directed by John Sayles.

*The Greater Barrier* features a young actress named Rosemary "Silver Dollar" Tabor. Silver Dollar Tabor was the daughter of Colorado silver magnate Horace Tabor and his wife Elizabeth "Baby Doe" Tabor. Silver Dollar, a beautiful, young brunette with big brown eyes, captivated the screen in her few scenes as the best friend of Kato's girlfriend. Her tragic life started out with her being a poor little rich girl who was heir to the Tabor silver fortune. Horace Tabor lost his fortune during the silver crash of 1893 and died of appendicitis in 1899, leaving his family penniless. Silver Dollar's acting career was not successful, and she moved to Chicago where she became addicted to alcohol and opium. She was rumored to be a Chicago gangster's mistress. At the age of 36, she died under mysterious circumstances. She was found scalded to death with boiling water in her Chicago apartment; and although no one was ever convicted, her death was thought to have been a murder.

*The Greater Barrier* was an important independent "orphan film," and its sophisticated plot was considered scandalous and innovative for its time. The film was rediscovered by Colorado film historian Joe Tarabino and was explored in depth in his documentary *The Land of Nowhere*. Joe tells the complete story behind the making of the *The Greater Barrier* and touts its significance as an important early American film. When the movie was first produced, Colorado was a popular area for early American filmmaking. This was before Hollywood was the center of the film world, and many early westerns and other silent films were shot in Colorado.

We showed *The Greater Barrier* numerous times on the Library Channel. It was a motion picture time capsule of Colorado Springs in 1914. Colorado College, the Garden of Gods, and several other Pikes Peak locations were featured in the making of this film. Colorado College football students were paid a silver dollar each to participate in a mock football game. The original nitrate print survived until 1980, when it was transferred to a safety-based film stock. The quality of the new print was remarkable, considering the original print had survived for 65 years. *The Greater Barrier* is another photographic gem that is part of the Pikes Peak Library District's special collection.

# VETERANS DAY

In 2003 I started representing the library district on the board of the Veterans Day parade in Colorado Springs. Although I was not a veteran, I always had a great respect for veterans and I had many family members who had served.

During the course of my job, including my time on the Veterans Day Committee, I produced more than 30 interviews and documentaries on a variety of veterans in the area. Since many of the cadets who graduated from the Air Force Academy returned to Colorado Springs to retire, the community was populated with distinguished veterans. The Fort Carson Army Post, NORAD, and Peterson Air Force Base also brought a large population of servicemen and women who learned to love the Pikes Peak region during their deployment in Colorado.

Each year the Veterans committee chose a grand marshal who had distinguished themselves during their service to the country. As part of my participation, I interviewed the grand marshal and produced documentaries on their military experiences.

One of the veterans I interviewed had been a B-17 pilot during World

War II and had worked as a civilian pilot for the CIA in Asia supporting various armies that the U. S. furnished clandestinely with materials and weapons. James Fore was only 18 when he became a B-17 pilot, and he was one of the youngest pilots to serve in the Eighth Airforce in England. While on his 28th mission with the Eighth Airforce, he was shot down over France and captured by the German SS. After torturing him during interrogation, they transferred him to Buchenwald as a POW. He should have been sent to one of the American prisoner-of-war camps, but Hitler wanted to make an example of some of the American pilots, since the bombing campaign over Germany resulted in so many civilians' deaths. It wasn't until Herman Goering found out that there were American pilots in Buchenwald that the German Luftwaffe commander, who believed in *esprit de corps* between pilots, intervened and transferred them to an American POW camp.

After his four months in Buchenwald, 210-pound Jim Fore weighed only 90 pounds. It was a miracle he survived! Although he was still a prisoner of war, he was relieved to be in an American POW in Stalag Luft III, where they were treated relatively well and he could regain his health. His career after the war was equally fascinating. He worked all over the world as a civilian pilot for the CIA. He was shot down a second time over Asia and was rescued. Jim loved flying, and he admitted he was a bit of an adrenalin junkie who loved the challenge of flying in a combat zone. His flying career spanned over 44 years and he flew for over 36,000 hours. He retired in Colorado Springs and wrote a book about his experiences as a combat and civilian pilot entitled *Tragedy and Triumph: a pilot's life through war and peace.*" It is an amazing book that tells the story of the son of an Arkansas sharecropper who was born to fly.

# PAY IT FORWARD

What possible connection could be made between a 19th-century Colorado hard-rock gold miner and a group of 21th-century Vietnamese school children in Chu Lai, Vietnam? Believe it or not, people can connect the dots over this very unlikely three-century- long pay-it-forward relationship.

One of the series I produced for the Pikes Peak Library District was "Colorado Springs: The Way It Was." With our enormous collection of hundreds of hours of historic films shot locally, the series featured a specific historic film and usually included an interview with someone who could expand on the history behind that film. One of the programs in the series featured the Myron Stratton Home for orphans, and it was narrated by a former resident and retired Marine Colonel John Zorack.

The Myron Stratton Home provided us with a 30-minute film shot in the late 1930s of this unique orphanage named after the father of Cripple Creek gold millionaire Winfield Scott Stratton. For John Zorack, who lived with his disabled hard-rock mining father in a shack during The Depression, being accepted at the Myron Stratton home was a monumental life-changing event. In the documentary John said, "Going to the Myron Stratton home was like being pulled out of abject poverty and moving into the home of a rich uncle who could provide you with anything you needed, while living in the luxury of a beautiful mansion."

This pay-it-forward story starts with the curious life of Winfield Scott Stratton, who was a modest carpenter and prospector living in Colorado Springs. I cannot do justice to the story of Winfield Scott Stratton in this short chapter in my book. The story of Winfield Scott Stratton is well documented in the book, *Midas of the Rockies,* by respected Colorado author Frank Waters. Stratton's life is also documented in the book, *Money Mountain*, by Colorado author Marshall Sprague.

Winfield Scott Stratton was a union carpenter in Colorado Springs for almost twenty years before he discovered his gold mine on the southwest side of Pikes Peak. In an ancient volcanic caldera, Stratton staked claim to his Independence Mine on July 4, 1891. The original Independence Mine is still an active mining area, where millions of dollars in gold are being extracted annually by the Colorado-based Newmont Mining Corporation. Before he made his mining fortune, Stratton worked as a carpenter during the winter months. For four months during the summer, he prospected around the Pikes Peak area searching for gold. In 1876 he married a woman who turned out to be pregnant before their wedding date. He left her after the birth of her son, claiming that someone else was the father of the child and that she tricked him into marriage. A loner most of his life, he lived a life of solitude before and after he made his fortune. Since he was a working man most of his life, he had an affinity for those humble people who worked with their hands in low-paying jobs. He sold the bulk of his gold mine in 1900 for $10,000,000. In today's dollars it would have equaled a fortune of $500 million and many people sought Stratton's favor because of his great wealth. He was very generous with any organization that served the working poor in the area. He bought a bicycle for every laundry woman in Colorado Springs to make their jobs easier. He purchased and built the trolley system so that the working poor could travel around the entire city with ease. When he died of cirrhosis of the liver in 1902, he left his fortune to The Myron Stratton Home, which he named after his father. Still operating today, The

Myron Stratton Home is a facility for the aged, the poor, the needy, and the orphaned children of Teller and El Paso counties. Thirty years after the home was opened, John Zorack became a resident and one of their greatest success stories. Another notable resident was Floyd K. Lindstrom, who was awarded the Medal of Honor posthumously after being killed in Enzio, Italy during World War II.

John Zorack was a retired Marine colonel and lawyer who was a successful lobbyist for the Federal Express Corporation when the company wanted to start a private mail service business in 1971. He worked closely with fellow Marine and Federal Express founder Fred Smith, helping him create his successful mail delivery company. Zorack, who was always grateful for the life-saving opportunity the Myron Stratton Home provided him, decided to "pay it forward' to a 13-year-old fatherless child in Vietnam. The story of John's generosity is told in the PBS documentary, "Vietnam Passage: Journey from War to Peace." John met Binh when he was a 13-year-old translator for the Marines. John wanted to help Binh and his family, so he gave him a bicycle. He also helped Binh's widowed mother buy a home. John's generosity to Binh continued after he returned to his home in Virginia. John invited Binh to travel to the United States and to stay at his home as an exchange high school student. Binh graduated from high school in Virginia and moved back to Vietnam in 1971 to marry his high school sweetheart. He continued to work as a translator until the fall of South Vietnam in 1975, when Binh and his pregnant wife barely escaped the country and fled to a refugee camp in California. Binh's son was born at Camp Pendleton, and he named his first born "John" after his kind benefactor. Once again, John Zorack and his family stepped in to help Binh; and they secured him a job at Federal Express. After taking advantage of this opportunity at Federal Express and working very hard, Binh eventually was offered a management position and created a great life for himself and his growing family in America. His mother was still in Vietnam, and he was homesick for his birth country.

In 1989 he returned to Vietnam and brought his mother back with him to America. When he was in Vietnam, he saw that the country was moving toward a free-market environment, and he dreamed of the day he could set up a Federal Express office in Vietnam. Only a month after the U.S. lifted the trade embargo against Vietnam in 1994, Binh opened the first Federal Express office in his former country. It was Binh's chance to pay it forward for his home country. In 1999 Binh convinced Federal Express to open a school in Chu Lai. It was an extremely poor community, and the school offered the children of his home town an opportunity to improve their lives. It was the ultimate pay-it-forward gift that originally started with Winfield Scott Stratton. From Winfield Scott Stratton directly to Marine Colonel John Zorack, and then to Binh Nyugen and his family, and finally to the children of Chu Lai, the original goodwill gesture continues to live on. This true story is an example of a most remarkable pay-it-forward generosity that has spanned several generations and started with a humble gold prospector in Colorado.

# THE FAIRY GODMOTHER OF THE ARTS

S hortly after I started at the Pikes Peak Library District in 1988, Mary Mashburn started volunteering for the library. However, we had met while I was with the cable company when I taped a program she had sponsored at The Fine Arts Center. It was a stage production of the *Velveteen Rabbit* which was part of The Imagination Celebration, a successful program that introduced the arts to young people and was sponsored by the Kennedy Center in Washington, D.C.

After the Fine Arts Center stopped sponsoring The Imagination Celebration, Mary Mashburn brought the program to the Pikes Peak Library District. The Imagination Celebration was a perfect marriage for our cable channel. Hundreds of arts-related dance, musical, and literary programs were part of The Imagination Celebration, and we taped them or showed them live on our channel. Mary Mashburn and The Imagination Celebration was a gold mine for original programming, and she kept us so busy with multiple projects that sometimes we hid when we saw her striding down the hall towards the studio. Because of her love of the arts and for young people, she was known locally as *the Fairy Godmother of the Arts*.

*Funky Fairy Tales*, was one special program that was a big part of the Imagi-nation Celebration that affected me personally. *Funky Fairy Tales* was a traveling group comprised of library employees who performed children's books as plays for local schools. They took non-traditional fairy tales, such as *The True Story of the Three Little Pigs* by Jon Scieszka and created travel-ing theatre. (Just a side note, I met the parents of Jon Scieszka while riding on a train to California. They were delighted to know I was familiar with their son's books and that we had turned them into children's plays and performed them as *Funky Fairy Tales*.)

Since most of the fairy tales required male roles for the prince, the king, and other characters, the director was always looking for male staff who could volunteer to be a member of the six-person cast. For ten years I vol-unteered to be part of this group, and I experienced immeasurable staff camaraderie and joy performing in *Funky Fairy Tales*.

The library normally assembled three teams, and we scheduled perfor-mances during the two weeks of Imagination Celebration in the Spring. We literally performed in every elementary school in Colorado Springs. We had several costume changes during our routine, so we carried a simple traveling stage. The props, the stage, and the actors fit into a six-passenger van that we drove to the different schools. We spent at least a month rehearsing and memorizing the 45-minute skits that included at least three short books converted to plays. We usually scheduled three shows per day on the stage in a school gym for sometimes 500 kids at a time. Connecting with an audi-ence of children and hearing their laughter is one of the most rewarding experiences I have ever had. We acted in front of kids who grew up watch-ing television and had never seen a stage show in their lives. They were delighted to be introduced to live theater and to see adults in silly costumes acting like fools for their entertainment. I had the privilege of performing for my own two daughters at their elementary schools. Fortunately, they were too young to be embarrassed and enjoyed watching their father act silly in front of their classmates.

We reached approximately 25,000 elementary school students during those two weeks, and we always ended our programs promoting reading and getting a library card. Since the Pikes Peak Library District is a large library district with 20 branches, we assembled our cast from all locations and job types in the district. The library district generously allowed us to receive our normal pay while performing in Funky Fairy Tales. We had shelvers, finance staff, public service, and technical service employees, branch managers, and anyone who worked for the library could volunteer to be part of the cast. It was a great morale boost for staff, and we worked with people we normally didn't see during the course of our regular jobs. Stacy Smith, the children's librarian who was the director for most of the years we performed our tales, held an end-of-the- year mock academy award party for the entire crew of 15 performers. For the two months we rehearsed and performed our plays, we really became close as staff through sharing this wonderful experience.

Each year of The Imagination Celebration, Mary Mashburn persuaded celebrated children's book illustrator Michael Hague to produce an original poster as a fundraiser. Area resident Michael Hague, with his long hair, looks like a wizard or mystical character who could walk into one of his famous illustrations. He was one the most gracious people I have ever met. I helped work on a documentary and interview with him in the 1990s. Whenever he participated in a poster or a book signing, his fans created a line that snaked all around the library. Michael signed books for hours with original illustrations by his signature. He never complained and refused to leave until the last book was signed. He spent an average of five minutes per book creating an original drawing for his fans.

One year, Mary Mashburn brought famous actress, dancer, and chore-ographer Debbie Allen to Colorado Springs to produce a children's musical, *Pepito's Story,* based on the children's book by Eugene Fern. It was sponsored by the Kennedy Center in Washington, D.C. and took a monumental effort of hundreds of talented people to succeed. It was an incredible produc-tion that involved local young people as the dancers; and they cast a local 18-year-old girl as the female lead along with a professional male dancer from Los Angeles. They had six free performances at The Pikes Peak Center in Colorado Springs and filled the 1,200-seat theater each time. I also pro-duced a documentary on *the Making of Pepito's Story* that won several cable awards. Debbie Allen, a consummate professional, worked incredibly hard to ensure a successful performance.

An off shoot of The Imagination Celebration was The Pikes Peak Writers

Conference, which is still going strong after 24 years. The conference was founded in 1993 by retired Lieutenant Colonel Jimmie Butler, who was a graduate of the Air Force Academy. Colonel Butler was an experienced author who had written several fiction books based on his time in the Air Force, including his time as a pilot in Vietnam. His book *A Certain Brotherhood* is a work of fiction that was based on his experience as a Forward Air Controller (FAC) during the Vietnam war. The conference brought in some of the biggest names in fiction and honored a contemporary author each year with the prestigious Frank Waters award. The Pikes Peak Writers Conference had a competition each year for amateur authors. Additionally, the staff worked with the local school districts and sponsored a writing competition for young people. They also partnered potential authors with publishers; and it was a great conference for budding authors to attend. The Library Channel videotaped the annual conference for the last 15 years I worked for PPLD. It made for some excellent programing, and we videotaped and archived an extensive series of author interviews and presentations.

Mary Mashburn has worked as a volunteer promoting The Imagination Celebration for almost 30 years. Her contribution to the arts in the Pikes Peak region is invaluable. Out of her generous spirit, hundreds of thousands of children were introduced to the value of the arts by *the Fairy Godmother of the Arts.*

# THE SHIVERS FOUNDATION

Clarence Shivers, who trained as a Tuskegee Airman, was another distinguished veteran I interviewed as programming for the PPLD channel. Clarence and his wife, Peggy, returned to Colorado Springs after he spent 25 years in the Air Force. In addition to being an Air Force pilot, Clarence was a gifted painter and a sculptor. Peggy was a classically trained singer. Clarence and Peggy supported the arts, and they graciously created the Shivers Foundation to promote African-American culture and literature through the Pikes Peak Library District. Clarence had created the life-sized sculpture of a Tuskegee Airman that is on the grounds of the Air Force Academy.

Clarence, who was in his eighties when I met him, was born and raised in St. Louis, Missouri, and went to a segregated high school. One of his classmates and friends was the music legend Chuck Berry. His first love was art; but when he discovered in 1944 that he had a chance to become a Tuskegee Airman, he embraced the opportunity. Through high school he had worked with his father as an auto mechanic, and he had an intuitive intelligence on how engines worked and how to repair mechanical devices.

Because of that knowledge, he tested extremely well as a potential pilot and was accepted, with a select few African-American candidates, to be a part of the Tuskegee Airmen. He faced prejudice and discrimination throughout his Air Force career. What I soon learned about Clarence, was that he was the type of person who became more determined when he faced any resistance. World War II ended before Clarence could be sent overseas to fly his P51 with the other Tuskegee airmen in Italy. In a curious connection, my uncle Victor was flying his B-24 at the same time the Tuskegee airmen escorted his bomber into battle over Germany. The Tuskegee P51 fighter escorts had a distinguished flying record, and they never lost a B-24 they escorted. After the war, Clarence became an instructor and flew almost all of the fighters that the Air Force used, until he retired in 1969 as a Lieutenant Colonel. Clarence decided to pursue his artistic career and moved to Spain with his wife Peggy for ten years to paint after his Air Force career.

They returned to the United States in the early 1980s and decided to make Colorado Springs their home and create The Shivers Foundation. Peggy had a gifted singing voice; and through their foundation, she brought in African-American opera singers and musicians to the Pikes Peak region. It really was a music education for me. I taped dozens of performances of some of the country's best musicians and singers, including world-renowned jazz vocalist Dianne Reeves. Just like Mary Mashburn and The Imagination Celebration, the Shivers Foundation provided the library with hundreds of hours of quality arts programming to air on the channel.

I became very close to Peggy and Clarence during the time I knew them. Unfortunately, Clarence's health started to fail in 2007. A week before he died, I visited him in his hospice room. We were alone together; at this point in the dying process, he wasn't conscious. He was breathing as heavily as possible, and it was torturous to see this proud man fight for every breath. When I left his room, I thought that he wouldn't last another hour. I was wrong. This tough Tuskegee airman, who fought prejudice and hate his whole life, clung to life for another five days. He might be the toughest man I ever met. A Renaissance man who was tough in spirit and kind and generous to the people whom he loved and respected.

Clarence was buried on the Air Force Academy grounds. At his funeral, the African-American cadets comforted his wife Peggy and showed their respect and admiration for this Tuskegee Airman who paved the way to become pilots themselves. They honored him with the missing-man formation with authentic P51s. What a privilege it was to befriend a man like Lieutenant Colonel Clarence Shivers. If you ever pass through Colorado Springs, you need to visit the Air Force Academy. While you are walking the Academy grounds, seek out the Clarence Shivers' sculpture of a Tuskegee airman. It is a sculpture of a proud African-American pilot in full-flying gear that bears more than a slight resemblance to Clarence.

"What I felt in terms of pride, I wanted to put in that sculpture. Not only pride, but confidence. Because when I finished the Tuskegee program, that's how I felt. I knew I could do any Damn thing I wanted to do, if I set my mind to it." Clarence proudly explained in a video program we taped at the Pikes Peak Library District back in 2005.

# CAL OTTO

I always said to my staff, when I ran a cable channel and produced video portraits at the Pikes Peak Library District, that we worked in the candy store. We had the best jobs in the world and I realized our funding was analyzed very carefully during budget time. We were, what you would call, non-essential employees in the library. I always jokingly told my staff that the primary responsibility of a good bureaucrat is to make sure you are in the budget for the next year. For the 20 years I was at the Pikes Peak Library District, I made sure we were in the budget for the next year; but I firmly believe we were in the budget because of our hard work and productivity.

The library director in a public library is not the ultimate authority. The library director has to answer to a board of directors. As Bob Dylan said in his song, everyone has "Gotta serve somebody." When I found out that a new board member, Cal Otto, at the Pikes Peak Library District had taken a personal interest in our facility I was happy, but I also knew it was probably going to be more work for myself and our staff.

When I first met Cal Otto, I was impressed by his eclectic background. He had first passed through Colorado in the 1950s as a young man in the

Army at Fort Carson during the Korean War. After he left the Army he stayed in Colorado and married a teacher he had met in Colorado Springs. After getting his degree in business through the G.I. Bill, he eventually started his own paper manufacturing and distribution business on the east coast and built his own successful company. After he sold his business for a small fortune, he moved to Virginia and was involved in the humanities and was also an avid rare book collector.

At one point in our friendship, he invited me and my staff to his home to see his book collection, which was housed in the basement floor of his house and featured over 5,000 volumes of rare books. It was like his own private branch library; his affection for books was unequaled by anyone I have met before or since. Just like myself, he loved Colorado history and especially Cripple Creek history and the gold rush of 1890. Colorado's Cripple Creek gold rush created so much wealth that Colorado Springs had more millionaires than any other city at the beginning of the 20th century. The money was made in the Cripple Creek mines on the west side of Pikes Peak, but the Cripple Creek millionaires built their homes in Colorado Springs, including the most famous millionaire Winfield Scott Stratton.

Cal had done some cable access shows in Virginia relating to rare books and ephemera, the hobby of collecting printed material. We quickly became friends with our common interest in Colorado history. Working with Tim Blevins, the head of local history, Cal started the annual Pikes Peak Regional History Symposium. Cal was also instrumental in starting the very successful All Pikes Peak Reads annual program.

Cal immediately began to line up interviews for me to do in the studio. With his contacts in town and with the military, we produced interviews on several World War II veterans. One of our interviews was with General Albert Patton Clark, who was a former Air Force Academy superintendent. General Clark was shot down as a combat pilot, early in World War II. He spent several years In Stalag Luft III, the prisoner of war camp that was made famous from the book and film *The Great Escape*.

Cal also interviewed Hal Leith, who was an Army Special Forces soldier who jumped into Formosa, right after the war ended in the pacific, to rescue General Wainwright from a Japanese POW camp. General Wainwright was the general who stayed in the Philippines after Macarthur had left the island. General Wainwright endured incredible brutality as a prisoner in a Japanese POW camp. After the war, General Wainwright was awarded the Medal of Honor for his bravery and service to our country. Hal Lieth wrote about this mission in detail in his book *POW's of Japanese Rescued!*

When I retired from the Pikes Peak Library District in 2008 I said good-bye to Cal and we stayed in touch and remained friends. In 2009 he visited me at the Barkman branch library in Pueblo and we went to lunch and talked about working on some new projects after his scheduled heart surgery. Cal never made it out of surgery. He died on the operating table at 79 years old. He is another good friend that is no longer with us. As a board member for the Pikes Peak Library District he was an unselfish volunteer who loved books and loved libraries and was a dedicated member of the "Book People." The annual Pikes Peak History Symposium is a living tribute to his contributions to the Pikes Peak Library District.

# LIEUTENANT GENERAL ALBERT PATTON CLARK

"I came to realize that our group was unique. We were survivors of a series of screening and selection processes that were most unusual. First, we had volunteered to go to war as aviators. We had been found qualified after a demanding selection process, had graduated from a dangerous flight training program with a high attrition rate, had gone off to war, entered combat, and then survived a traumatic disaster in the air. There was no other way to join this group. We were different. Our experience had left a mark on us that would remain for the rest or our lives."

—From the Preface of Lt. General Albert P. Clark's book:
*33 Months As A POW In Stalag Luft lll*

As a young person, I loved the 1963 action movie *The Great Escape* starring Steve McQueen. The movie was based on the 1950 book by Australian writer Paul Brickhill, who was a POW during the planning and execution of *The Great Escape* from Stalag Luft III. In 2005, the Pikes Peak Library District board president Cal Otto asked if I wanted to help him produce a documentary on Lt. General Albert Patton Clark and his participation in the planning of *The Great Escape*. Albert Clark was a retired Air Force general who ended his career as the Superintendent of the Air Force Academy from 1970 to 1974, but it was his 33 months as a POW in Stalag Luft III that became the focus of our interview. The first time I met General Clark he was 90 years old and was still as sharp as he was when he was a young man. You could tell when you first meet him that he was already three steps ahead of you with his gifted mind. A ginger red head, who still had a full head of hair, he was tall in stature and was in great physical shape for his age. When I saw pictures of him as a young man he always had an engaging smile and could have been a doppelganger for the Dallas Cowboy coach Jason Garret. General Clark had recently published his book *33 Months as a POW in Stalag Luft III* when we scheduled the interview.

General Clark was a 1936 graduate of West Point and after graduation he immediately went to flight training school to become a fighter pilot. With the war in Europe on the horizon, the United States Army Air Corps was growing rapidly and preparing for the important role of air power in combat. Four days after Pearl Harbor, Germany declared war on the United States, and the United States immediately went to the aid of their close ally in the United Kingdom. England was barely holding on to their Island and welcomed the American pilots with open arms. In June of 1942 General Clark boarded a ship to England to begin his combat career as a fighter pilot as a lieutenant colonel with the 31st fighter group. The American pilots trained with the British Spitfire fighters, and after a few weeks of training, Clark was sent on his first major mission to shoot down German fighters as they took off from France. Unfortunately, General Clark was shot down in his inaugural mission and he had to ditch his plane on the French coast. He was immediately captured and was one of the first Americans to be shot down in the European theater, where he spent the next 33 months as a POW.

As a POW he was immediately recruited to help the British with their escape efforts. Although not a requirement for American prisoners, the standing order for the British soldier was to always try to escape if they were captured. Once they were moved to Stalag Luft III in August of 1942 they started their tunneling efforts in this new camp. As more American and British pilots and crewmen were shot down during the intense air campaign over Germany, the pool of qualified candidates to plan and participate in The Great Escape grew. As General Clark said in his foreword to his book, the POWs in Stalag Luft III were the best and the brightest of the war effort. Mostly college educated, they had a pool of 2,000 highly skilled prisoners to recruit for their escape effort. They kept a file of the POW skills, which included construction, artistic talent for forgery, and sewing skills for civilian clothing manufacturing. General Clark was in charge of security and hiding these clandestine factories and their products from the prison guards. The forging factories were disguised as architecture classes; their desks would change over in a few moments and they looked like they were working on architecture plans rather than documents that were being forged. They had to acquire most everything they needed for the escape through trades with prison guards with chocolate, cigarettes, and coffee. Because of the Geneva convention and the efforts of the International Red Cross, the POW's would receive care packages with canned food and other desirable items. These were items that the German soldiers could not get in town and they were willing to trade almost anything with the prisoners. They also were able to secure clandestine cameras through their mail deliveries. The cameras were sent in secretly marked packages, that the prisoners were able to steal before the German guards could rifle through them.

Of the many men that General Clark admired that were his fellow POW's in Stalag Luft III, one man stood out above the rest for his cunning and bravery and that was Squadron Leader Roger Bushell. Roger Bushell was born in South Africa to British parents. He had become a pilot for the RAF back in the early 1930s. He was shot down and imprisoned in 1940, and by the time General Clark met him, Roger had already participated in two escapes. The last one was the most successful and he was able to make it to Czechoslovakia where he lived with a Czech family for over a year. When high ranking Nazi Reinhard Heydrich was assassinated by the Czech underground, the ensuing massive Nazi round up led to Bushell's arrest. The SS executed the Czech couple who had hidden Bushell and their son was sent to a concentration camp. Roger Bushell was subsequently interrogated and tortured by the gestapo and told the next time he tried to escape he would be killed. At first Roger Bushell wanted nothing to do with The Great Escape. He knew first-hand what could happen to innocent civilians that might help him escape, and he didn't want a repeat of the events in Czechoslovakia. After a great deal of personal reflection, he agreed to help with the escape and became a major player in the planning. His brilliant mind, cunning, courage, and organizational skills were the main reason why the escape was successful.

Digging tunnels, sewing civilian clothing, and forging documents under the intense scrutiny of the German guards almost made it an impossible task. The ferrets were a group of German enlisted men whose job was to watch the prisoners and catch them in their tunnel digging and escape planning. The leader of the ferrets was a German Master-Sergeant by the name of Hermann Glemnitz. Sergeant Glemnitz was a real-life Sergeant Schultz from Hogan's Heroes, except he was much sharper than the fictional character. A veteran pilot from World War I, he had an almost paternal relationship with the American and British POW's. General Clark was one of his favorite adversarial prisoners and he kept a close eye on General Clark, since he knew General Clark was the most dangerous prisoner in Stalag Luft III and would certainly be involved in any escape plans. For a time, Sergeant Glemnitz assigned a ferret to just watch the activities of General Clark. They would position their ferrets outside the gates hidden behind the trees with a telescope, so they could follow the prisoners they most feared clandestinely. It was an almost a friendly cat and mouse game between the prisoners and Sergeant Glemnitz. His ferrets would eventually uncover 100 tunnels during his time at Stalag Luft III. Only three of the tunnels were undetected and the "Harry" tunnel in the British barracks was used for The Great Escape. If prisoners were caught digging, he would promptly send the guilty party to spend time in solitary confinement in the cooler for a few weeks. He would scold the prisoners and ask them not to try and escape from the camp. He sincerely believed it was for their own good.

The camp commandant, Col. Freidrich Wilhelm Von Lindeimer, an older officer and a World War I decorated hero, also was more of a paternal figure for the prisoners and did everything he could to keep the prisoners occupied with a variety of activities. He encouraged their artistic activities like painting, woodworking, theater and musical programs and he even let the prisoners build a 500 seat auditorium for their plays and musical concerts. The most attractive male POWs would dress as females, since they needed them to portray women's roles for their theater and musical productions. Colonel Von Lindeiner reasoned that if the prisoners were involved in other activities, they wouldn't have as much time to plan escapes. Instead the POW's took advantage of his generosity and used the artistic activities to procure supplies for their escape plans. He pleaded with the prisoners not to try to escape, because it would just bring the SS to his prison, and a much harsher commandant would take his place. Unfortunately, he was right. After The Great Escape, Colonel Von Lindeiner was imprisoned and court martialed and then sent to the Russian front. The new camp commandant was a much harsher disciplinarian and was quick to shoot anyone who tried to escape.

The final escape attempt plan was to build three tunnels, Tom, Dick, and Harry. The POW's assumed the Germans would find at least one of their tunnels. When the Germans did discover one of their tunnels the prisoners acted deflated and defeated, but secretly they focused on the other two remaining tunnels. Since the Germans had seismic instruments to listen for digging, the tunnels had to be dug 30 feet down in the soft dirt. They used pieces of their bed slates to shore up the final escape tunnel, which was over 100 yards when completed. A giant Bellow was created and was pumped continuously by a prisoner to bring fresh air in their tunnel. A rail track was put down in the bottom of the tunnel to pull a cart on wheels to transport POW's and the dirt they needed to be remove from the tunnel. The most difficult thing was hiding the dirt they dug out. They created an outdoor sports field whose surface matched the light-colored dirt that was removed from the tunnels, and they would carry sacks of dirt under their uniforms, releasing the dirt through the pant legs of their trousers and cover their shoes as they mixed it with the dirt in their sports field. It was an ingenious operation and even more remarkable when you consider how well watched they were by Sergeant Glemnitz and his highly skilled ferrets.

The great escape was an extremely ambitious plan and over 200 POWs in civilian clothing with passports and German money were originally ready to make the escape. Because of General Clark's participation, he had earned the right to be one of the 200 men to make the escape. Unfortunately, before it happened, they moved all the Americans to another building at Stalag Luft III, to separate the American and British, since they suspected they were working together to plan an escape. It was only British, British colonials, and Canadian prisoners that actually made the escape. In the late afternoon on March 24th, 1944, Roger Bushell asked to speak to General Clark through the wire that separated the Americans and the British. He told General Clark they were going that night and asked him not to do anything with his men that was unusual or could cause suspicion.

As they dug up through the final few feet to the top of the escape route they immediately discovered the tunnel was too short, and it ended before it reached the forest. With the guards looking inside the camp, they decided to time their escape, one prisoner would go at a time, as they dashed into the forest. A total of 76 men made the escape before the tunnel was discovered by a German guard who had been walking security outside the fence. Then all hell broke out in Stalag Luft III. The men were forced to stand in the snow all day and night as the guards ransacked their barracks and uncovered the remaining items that the prisoners had planned to use for the escape. Hitler was furious, since the effort to capture these 76 men scattered about the German countryside, drew much needed soldiers and resources from the war effort. Of the 76 men that escaped, only three made it to safety. 73 were recaptured and Hitler ordered 50 of those men to be shot. Included in those 50 was Squadron Leader Roger Bushell. His character in the film *The Great Escape* was played by the great actor Sir Richard Attenborough.

After the Great Escape it almost became impossible to try any other attempts. The new commandant clamped down on all suspicious activity and the men knew that any escape attempt would result in their death. The British army was able to sneak in a message and let the remaining POWs know that it was no longer a requirement for British prisoners to try to escape. General Clark spent the rest of the war creating scrapbooks and archiving their life in the camps. He realized the historical importance of keeping notes, photographs, and diaries of what went on in Stalag Luft III, so he could honor the memory of people like Roger Bushell and the 50 men who were shot for trying to escape. As the Russians got closer to their camp and they could hear the sounds of artillery, they knew it was only a matter of days before they were either shot or moved to another camp. They prepared their clothing and food supplies for what they hoped would be a winter march.

General Clark approached the camp carpenter and asked if he could figure out a way to transport the camp archives that he had so carefully preserved. He told the officer he would buy him a case of whiskey, once they were liberated. The carpenter accepted the challenge and built a sled they used for dragging the scrapbooks and all their back packs. When the time came to leave the camp, they were well prepared to make the long journey. They loaded the scrapbooks and archives on the sled and they put all their food and back packs on top of it to hide this precious historical cargo, including two dozen rolls of undeveloped film that was shot with their clandestine cameras. After three days and nights of marching and train travel they finally arrived at their new destination in Bavaria. Over 100,000 American and British prisoners crammed into this vastly over-crowded prison called Stammlager VIIA in Moosburg, Germany. It was February 5$^{th}$, 1945 and all the POWs were just hoping and praying they would survive until the end of the war.

On the morning of April 29$^{th}$ all the prisoners knew they would be liberated that day. Before General Patton entered the camp, General Clark made sure his best photographers among the prisoners were ready to capture the moment. They had their clandestine cameras ready and photographed the historic moment of Patton entering the camp. After 33 months as a prisoner, General Clark was more than ready to go home to his wife and three kids.

I admired General Clark for many reasons, but his understanding of the importance of archiving history as it was happening appealed to my librarian instincts. Whenever I produced a documentary, I always scrambled to get the best visuals to help illustrate the story. Like working on a Ken Burns documentary, I relied on compelling photographs to help tell the story. When I taped the interview, I worried about the quality of visuals we could find that were available in the environment of a secure prisoner of war camp. I was pleasantly surprised when General Clark showed me the clandestine photos they had shot while prisoners. It was a photographic bounty he secured from the two dozen rolls of film he smuggled to safety at the risk to his life, if he was discovered.

As an archivist myself, I have gone through great lengths to uncover priceless historic photographs and films, but I never had to risk my life. After General Clark retired from the Air Force Academy he got very involved with the Academy library and eventually became the president of the Friends of the Air Force Academy Library. Working closely with Air Force Academy archivists Duane Reed and Dr. Mary Elizabeth Ruwell, he created a collection from the materials he saved on a sled from Stalag Luft III.

In 1977 he also went back to Germany to do an oral history with his old friend and adversary Sergeant Glimnitz as part of the archives. Sergeant Glimnitz was able to reunite with his family after the end of the war and escape to west Berlin. Sergeant Glimnitz was invited to all of the Stalag Luft III reunions and was a popular attendee with his former prisoners. The Albert P Clark collection is housed in the Air Force Academy library (McDermott Cadet Library) and is available to anyone doing historic research on the psychology and the challenging life of a prisoner of war. It is a living memorial and tribute to the 50 men who gave their lives in The Great Escape.

I recently watched the documentary on General Clark I produced with Cal Otto and thoroughly enjoyed the interview as if I was watching it for the first time. It was good to hear the voice of my old friend Cal Otto. Cal Otto died in 2009 at the age of 79 and General Clark died in 2010 at the age of 96. While watching the documentary there were a few moments when you could hear children laughing and shouting in the background. Our studio was next to the story room and there were many times we had to deal with the sounds of children through the walls in the background. You could barely hear it and it didn't take away from the interview we did in 2005, but I thought about how the kids in the background were now probably in their late teens and early twenties. Since we did the interview in Colorado Springs, which is the home of numerous military families, I'm sure many of these kids are now serving their country and some could even be cadets at the Air Force Academy. Since General Clark spent most of his retirement supporting and creating an archive in the Air Force Academy McDermott library, I'm certain he didn't mind having the happy voices of kids enjoying a library program in the background of his documentary.

# THE PHOTORAPHERS

My favorite programs and documentaries were on photographers or filmmakers. I always looked for a visual element to make the program more interesting. Two highly skilled photographers I worked with during my time at PPLD were Lew Tilley and Paul Idleman.

Paul Idleman had been a photographer and historian for most of his career. He lived on the west side of Colorado Springs and worked as a photographer and archivist for the Old Colorado City History Center. Colorado City was the original town built in the shadow of Pikes Peak and was founded in 1859, 12 years before General Palmer founded Colorado Springs. It was a wild western town with many drinking establishments and also allowed legal prostitution. When Palmer created his pristine Colorado Springs, he envisioned his town as "Little London" with no alcohol sold or consumed. The sinners in Colorado Springs would walk or ride their horse the short two miles to Colorado City to satisfy all their vices. The history of Colorado City is well documented in Irving Howbert's book *Memories of a Lifetime in the Pikes Peak Region*. Irving Howbert arrived in the Pikes Peak region with his father in 1860 when he was only 14 years old. His book is an entertaining and historical look at the early days of El Paso County. It is possibly the most important first-hand account of the history of the Pikes Peak region. Irving Howbert was the clerk and recorder for El Paso County from 1869 to 1879. Colorado City was eventually incorporated into Colorado Springs and the historic neighborhood is now known as Old Colorado City. Many of the original buildings still exist and it has become the arts district on the west side of Colorado Springs.

The Old Colorado History Center was the vision of west point graduate and proud west-sider David Hughes. Dave Hughes was born in 1928 and was an Army Colonel and a Korean War veteran who has lived an amazing life. At 90 years old, it is hard to find anyone else his age with the same drive and energy. Dave hired Paul Idleman to help him create his vision of the Old Colorado City History Center, which is located in a former west side church.

I got to know Paul Idleman when he approached me to help him produce a documentary on 19th century photographer William Edward Hook. Paul had discovered many of the original glass plates photographed by William Edward Hook, and he made it his life passion to document the life of this talented photographer.

Paul and I spent almost a year on this documentary entitled: *Kind Nature's Scenery to Portray*. Hook arrived in Colorado in 1885 and photographed the Native Americans who lived in the region as well as the early days of Manitou Springs, the west side resort city that was incorporated in 1888. He also photographed the early days of the Cripple Creek Gold Rush. The visuals that Hook shot are stunning and the documentary was one of the most aesthetic stories I had the pleasure to tell. Paul and I became good friends over the course of producing this documentary. He donated many of his Hook photos to the Pikes Peak Library District.

As I said before, one person led to another in terms of a new project, and Paul introduced me to Ira Current and his extensive film and photography collection. Ira Current was born in 1910 and bought a 16mm camera in 1928 when he was 18 years old. Growing up on west side, Ira Current produced a series of *"little rascal"* type films of the neighborhood kids doing soap box derby races and other activities he called the *Current Review*. In 1928 he filmed a train ride to Cripple Creek on the Midland Railroad. It was an amazing little film that is featured with an interview with Ira in a video seg-ment I produced entitled *Take a Ride on the Midland*. This train ride on the historic Midland is available to watch on Youtube. Ira Current graduated from the University of Colorado in 1934 with a degree in chemistry. He spent his career as a chemist for Agfa Films in New York. Ira died in 2009 at the age of 98, he donated his extensive film and photography collection to the University of Colorado.

Paul Idelman moved back to his hometown of Champaign, Illinois to run the Champaign County Historical Museum. Shortly after he moved back to Champaign he was diagnosed with throat cancer. He died in 2007 at the age of 57. During his 57 years he lived the life of an artist and his own personal work as a photographer is his fitting legacy.

Lew Tilley was another artist and photographer I had the privilege of working with. I met Lew when he went to the Alexander Film company to transfer to video of some of his early work. He had shot a 1958 film of the Colorado Springs Library and it was a cinematic time capsule of the original Carnegie Library. It showed a family visiting the library who were enjoying all of the resources of this modern library at the time. It was beautifully shot and I could tell that Lew was an artist by the quality of his cinematography. Lew grew up in Georgia and came of age in the early 1950's and lived the lifestyle of a beatnik artist. He lived as an artist in Mexico for a few years and taught filmmaking and art at the Colorado Springs Fine Arts Center, Colorado College, and Colorado State University.

Lew was constantly creating art in all formats, including oil paint-ing, photography, and filmmaking. When I first met Lew he was in his early eighties and he was like a hyperactive child who spent every waking moment creating new art. When I was visiting his home he shared with me some photographs he shot in 1955 of Fannie Mae Duncan. It was a pho-tographic treasure that captured Fannie Mae Duncan in her prime when her businesses and Cotton Club were thriving. The photographs were part of an article that a writer friend of Lew had hoped they could sell to Life magazine at the time. The article never happened, but the photography he shot was as artistic as any documentary photos I have seen. The photo of Fannie Mae Duncan in this book was photographed by Lew Tilley inside the Cotton Club. Most of his photographs of Fannie Mae are featured in her autobiography called *Everybody Welcome: A Memoir of Fannie Mae Duncan and the Cotton Club* and co-written by Kathleen Esmiol. Lew Tilley donated many of his photographs and films to the Pikes Peak Library District.

Lew Tilley died in 2005 at the age of 84 years old. His daughter Eve has spent most of her career in the arts and was the President of the Pikes Peak Arts Council for over a decade.

I did an interview in our studio with Lew Tilley and it can be viewed on youtube as well as "Kind Nature's Scenery to Portray" by Paul Idelman.

# FALLING IN LOVE WITH MABEL BARBEE LEE

"Beautiful Mabel Barbee was one of the few teachers who could always hold our attention. She had a gift for storytelling, and then we just liked to look at her."
—Written by Lowell Thomas in the foreword for the book, *Cripple Creek Days,* by Mabel Barbee Lee.

In Ray Bradbury's *Dandelion Wine*, there is a chapter about a 30-year-old reporter who falls in love with a 90-year-old woman by seeing a picture of her when she was young. He didn't know who she was when he saw her picture in the newspaper about a charity event she was sponsoring. As she admits later, it was almost a joke; but for this annual charity event, the newspaper always ran this picture of her when she was in her 20s. The reporter, not knowing she was actually 90 years old, attends the party in hopes of meeting who he thought was this beautiful young woman in the picture. When he meets her at the event, he confesses his intent; and they laugh about his confusion. They develop a social friendship; and despite the age difference, they realize they enjoy each other's company. Both of them had never been married, because they had never met their soulmates during their lives. They realize that if they had met when they both were young at the same time, they probably would have been lovers.

Almost the same thing happened to me with Mabel Barbee Lee. I had always been interested in the history of the Cripple Creek gold rush. Through my own company, I produced for the city of Cripple Creek three

60-minute documentaries on the great gold rush of the late 19$^{th}$ century in Colorado. Many local authors wrote books about the gold rush, including *Midas of the Rockies* by Frank Waters, one of the most respected authors to come out of the Pikes Peak region. *Money Mountain* is another excellent book on the Cripple Creek gold rush by local historian Marshall Sprague. My favorite of all the Cripple Creek history books, *Cripple Creek Days,* was written by Mabel Barbee Lee's on her experiences as a little girl growing up in this famous gold camp. Her father, Honest John Barbee Lee, was a southerner and a Civil War veteran, who moved to Cripple Creek to make his fortune as a gold miner. He had moderate success as a gold miner, and his beautiful daughter was witness to this historic era, in what was then, the modern city of Cripple Creek. Mabel Barbee Lee parents' died while she was a student at Colorado College. It was a devastating blow to Mabel at the time. She didn't have the finances to finish college until the hard-rock miners, who had known her mother and father, raised a scholarship fund to let her continue her education. After graduation, she returned to Cripple Creek with her teaching degree and taught grade school in Victor. One of her students was the son of a Victor physician who worked for the gold-mining company. His name was Lowell Thomas, and he eventually became one of the premier journalists of the 20$^{th}$ century.

Mabel was a beautiful young woman, with reddish brown hair and a full figure. Mabel married a mining engineer; and, unfortunately, he succumbed to the flu epidemic in 1918 that took the lives of millions of Americans. At 32, Mable was a widow and needed to find a way to support herself and her young daughter. She accepted a position as a teacher and administrator at Colorado College and spent the next 30 years as an administrator in higher education. She never remarried. After she retired, and in her seventies, she wrote a book about her Cripple Creek experiences. *Cripple Creek Days* is a fascinating book that was published by her former student and admirer, Lowell Thomas. In the forward written by Lowell Thomas, he admitted to having a school-boy crush on his teacher. They remained good friends until her death.

When I produced my first documentary on Cripple Creek, I had film footage of Mabel Barbee Lee, as an older woman, shot at the Imperial Hotel in the 1960s. Mabel Barbee Lee died in 1978 at the age of 94, so I never had a chance to meet her.

When I first saw her photo in her book, I was speechless. She is one of the most stunning woman I had ever seen, and I found myself falling in love with her. My marriage was in trouble at the time, and I suppose it was safer for me to fall in love with a woman who had been dead for twenty years. But, it was genuine love; and it wasn't just that she was beautiful. I loved her words in her biography, and she spoke to me as if she were still alive. Her freshman photograph at Colorado College in 1902 is the photo of her I fell in love with. The photo reveals a subtle Mona Lisa smile. Her beautiful face still makes my heart skip a beat when I look at the photo. Our mutual love for Cripple Creek history seduced me as much as her beauty did. I fantasied about meeting her in the early 1920s when she was a lonely widow in her mid-30s. Thankfully, she was a safe mistress in my life; but just like the school boy Lowell Thomas, I fell deeply in love with this wonderful and extraordinarily exquisite woman. If I had a time machine, there is no doubt about the time and the place I would want to go back to: Cripple Creek at the beginning of the 20<sup>th</sup> century and spend a day with the stunning and intelligent Mabel Barbee Lee.

# HER FURIOUS ANGELS

Music always has been an important part of my life. The soundtrack of my youth included Led Zeppelin, Joni Mitchell, Bob Dylan, The Who, Sly and the Family Stone, The Rolling Stones, and Pink Floyd. When Bob Dylan turned 30 on May 24, 1971, my friends and I celebrated his birthday. At that time, he was still living a quiet life after his motorcycle accident and declined our invitation to his birthday party. We still decided to celebrate his birthday among ourselves. I always had a great affection for the talents of the singer-songwriters like Bob Dylan and Joni Mitchell. I fell in love with Joni Mitchell when I heard her *Blue* album. I saw her twice live in concert in Boulder and in Denver, and she sang directly to my teen angst. I knew all of her songs by heart, and I thought she was the most talented and beautiful musical artist on the planet.

I have a history of obsessing about certain musical artists during my life. It wasn't until I was in my forties that I discovered one of the most amazing American singer-songwriters in Christopher Becker Whitley. Chris was born in Houston, Texas, and was influenced by such artists and guitarists as Jimi Hendrix and fellow Texan Johnny Winter. I was listening to a college radio station when I first heard his song *Big Sky Country* from his debut album, *Living with the Law*, released in 1992. Every song on his *Living with the Law* album is a masterpiece, with not a single weak song on his debut album. Chris is a master guitarist with the soul of a western music artist. The best way to describe his music is as if Jimi Hendrix and Hank Williams, Sr. had a child. He has the soul and the voice of a lonesome cowboy, and the musical skills of some of the finest electric guitarists who have ever picked up an instrument. He is similar to fellow Texan Stevie Ray Vaughan in his guitar-playing ability, but he has the lyrical poetry and song-writing skills of a Bob Dylan in his prime.

When I found out that Chris was giving a concert at the Fox Theater in Boulder in 2001, I contacted his manager. It was his tour to promote his new *Rocket House* CD which was produced by his biggest fan and fellow musician, Dave Mathews. Dave loved Chris Whitley's music and recognized the brilliance of his musical genius. Chris Whitley's career had been stalling after he released his second album, *Din of Ecstasy,* which had alienated his fans. Although a brilliant album, it was more of a grunge album; and *Living with the Law* had more of a country rock and blues feel. After contacting his manager, I offered to videotape the concert with four cameras and to finance the video myself. If by chance they liked the results of the concert video, I planned to work out a deal to sell it.

During my life, I have had the opportunity to meet two of my greatest heroes: Ray Bradbury at the ALA conference in Chicago in 1992 and Chris Whitley in Boulder in 2001. Chris' manager met me five hours before the concert to set up our equipment. We taped the concert with a digital recorder through their house system, and we used four independent cameras. I worked the hand-held camera in front of the stage. While we were setting up, the manager introduced me to Chris. He was like a musical Huck Finn! He was more of a street musician who was barefoot on stage, so he could work his various distortion pedals with his toes and feet. He wore a simple t-shirt and bell-bottom pants and didn't appear to be too particular about his dress or appearance on stage. He looked diminutive in person; but when I shook his hands, I felt the incredible strength in his wrists and forearms from years of working the neck of a guitar. He always had a cigarette lit and placed it between his guitar frets when he started to play. And when he played, the music was hypnotizing. I could not believe that this one musician could get so much music out of a 1928 National Guitar. When I first heard his *Live at Martyrs* CD, I could not believe that he was playing alone on stage. It was like he was playing rhythm and lead guitars simultaneously. His instrument of choice was a classic blues guitar, the National Triolian. Chris nicknamed his favorite guitar "Mustard" which was electrified and emitted some of the most amazing sounds in his highly skilled hands. Chris had a very quiet demeanor and on stage rarely spoke to the audience, but he was a master poet in his ability to write lyrics for his songs. His musical library includes at least one hundred songs that are stand-alone poems based solely on their lyrics. When I consider his musicianship and guitar skills, he is the finest musical artist I have ever heard.

We taped the two-hour concert, and I was such a fan boy standing three feet away from him, videotaping this magnificent artist in his prime. I purposely chose to run the hand-held camera at the foot of the stage to watch him up close. His acoustic version of his song "Shadowland" and "Phone Call from Leavenworth" are proof that God sometimes speaks through mortal man. It was a great concert, and I uploaded the concert on YouTube.

Unfortunately, nothing ever came of the concert video. Like many great artists, he had a substance- abuse problem, and his career self-destructed. He released a few more albums after that concert, and his 2004 CD *War Crime Blues* features one of his finest compositions in *Her Furious Angels*. At the fourth annual Independent music awards, *Her Furious Angels* won best Blues/R&B Song. It is one of the finest love songs ever written. His *Dirt Floor* album is an acoustic masterpiece which was recorded in 1997 with a single stereo ribbon microphone. On November 20, 2004 at the age of 44, he died of lung cancer—a result from his life of chain smoking cigarettes. However, for a brief and shining moment, I met him in person and listened to him play up close in his prime. His daughter, Trixie Whitely, is a brilliant artist herself who has the same songwriting gifts as her father, but an even more magnificent voice.

Another musician whose music I love was a friend of Chris Whitley, slide guitarist and songwriter, Kelly Joe Phelps. Both men's music has fallen under the radar, but few musical artists compare to their talent. Listen to Kelly Joe's *Frankenstein: Party of Three* from the album *Beggars Oil* or listen to his spiritual album, *Brother Sinner and the Whale*. I can't imagine going through my life without discovering both the talents of Christopher Becker Whitley and Kelly Joe Phelps. Although listeners won't hear either of them on mainstream radio, they both represent musicianship at its finest. If you are listening to this book on digital audio, and you also own Amazon Echo, I will make it easy for you. "Alexa, play the music of Chris Whitley."

# THE IMPORTANCE OF VOLUNTEERS

During the span of my years working in public libraries, we have depended on volunteers to make our library more successful. Our volunteers come from all walks of life and different backgrounds. You cannot run a library without an active volunteer pool. You need teen volunteers to help with your Summer Reading program. You always need adult volunteers to help with weeding your collection and your shelving needs. Wherever I worked I depended on at least 40 hours a week of volunteer help. That was the equivalent to one additional employee. The board of trustees of most libraries are also important volunteers. They represent retired or working professionals who have a successful career in their community and they also have a love for libraries. I've known volunteer trustees who have treated their volunteer activity as a full-time job and have put in at least 40 hours a week. They provide important guidance and input from the community to make your library successful.

When I managed the video studio we depended on volunteers to help with our programs, especially when we needed multi cameras to shoot it. We had access to a remote video truck that was purchased through our contract with the cable company through their franchise fees. It required a minimum of six people to operate it, and my total staff was three people. In order to use it on location we needed to hire substitute employees or use volunteers. Most of our volunteers at the video studio were interns. They were broadcasting students from Pikes Peak Community College or the University of Colorado at Colorado Springs. Interns is another name for free labor. I loved having my interns and I could not have run a cable channel without them. The typical internship contract would require them to provide ten to fifteen hours a week of labor. Since they were college students, they were usually bright and eager to work hard for us. In exchange, I was always happy to be a reference or write a glowing recommendation letter.

One of my favorite interns was a petite little blonde by the name of Sarah. She was an excellent athlete and had played college women's softball. After her internship was over we continued to hire her as a substitute employee. She had a great sense of humor and my staff and I unofficially adopted her like she was our little sister. After she graduated from college she joined the Peace Corps and worked in the African Nation of Lesthoso. Lesthoso was a former British colony where English was one of the official languages. Sarah taught at one of the schools and she loved her time in Africa. As a young girl with straight blonde hair she stood out in this African nation and the kids were fascinated by her golden hair. She said she never felt threatened, but she would be walking down the street and children would run up to her and touch her hair and even pull out a few strands to make a good luck charm.

While she was in Lesotho, Prince Harry visited the country, he was involved in a local charity that his mother Princess Diana had founded. He visited her school and she went to a party where she had a chance to socialize with the prince. She said he was a little shy, but they ended up talking for a long time at the party and they were both flirting with each other. Sarah, who was clueless about the royal family, really didn't know who he was and that he was the son of Princess Diana. She knew he was a member of the royal family, but she wasn't sure how he was connected. She kept calling him by the wrong name and after a while he got a little annoyed. He finally stopped her and said, "Sarah, my name is Harry." When she told us this story after coming back to Colorado, we teased her about her lack of knowledge of the royal family. We told her she blew her chance to become a real princess, if she could only remember Prince Harry's name. Sarah went on to graduate school in education and eventually became a school counselor,

When I became a branch manager, volunteers were an extremely important part of staying on top of my collection. I used them mostly for helping with the weeding and shelving material. The best volunteers were retired. Since their schedule was open they were as reliable as my employees. They would show up on time and were happy to dedicate their volunteer hours to the library. Most of them were readers and they loved working in a library, since they lived in the library anyway. Diane was one of my most dedicated volunteers that I had the opportunity to work with.

Diane was a semi-retired pediatrician who wanted to help the Barkman Library in any way she could. The only volunteer job available was for her to work as an extremely overqualified shelver. One of the lowest- paying jobs in a library is the shelving job. However, a good shelver can make the operation of a library easier and is critical to the accuracy and the integrity of the collection. Pat Losinki, the former director of the Pikes Peak Library District once told me, "You can go a year without a library director, but you can't go a day without a shelver." He was so right. Diane's detailed nature and her ability for precision and accuracy made her an excellent shelver. She worked for three hours once a week and was more productive per hour than any of the paid 20-hour shelvers. She was an avid reader who always left with a handful of books she found on the cart. Shelving for her was like meditation. There was no difficult diagnosis she had to make as a shelver; a book had a catalog item number or letter, and that is where it went on the shelf. As far as I know, Diane is still volunteering at the Barkman library to help with the shelving.

# LEAVING COLORADO

In 2005 my father died of Parkinson's disease and unfortunately that year my mother was also diagnosed with the same illness. My Father passed away seven years after he was diagnosed. My brother, Dave, who was a psychologist for the V.A. hospital in Reno, made arrangements for my Dad to move to the hospital where he worked in November of 2004. At that point, my dad needed skilled nursing care, and he deliberately made the decision to end his suffering. He asked the doctor if he stopped taking his medication and stopped eating whether he would die in a few weeks. After the doctor answered affirmatively, my father refused any nourishment or medication and was dead in ten days. Dad never complained about his suffering during the seven years he was fighting Parkinson's. That was the type of man he was; he never complained about anything.

We moved our mother into an assisted-living facility when we moved our father to Reno. After my mother was diagnosed with Parkinson's in 2005, the disease advanced fairly quickly; and by 2007, she needed to be placed in a nursing home. It was a difficult time for all of us. Dave and his wife Yvonne, who are both psychologists, were busy raising a young son,

Joe; and they needed help with my mother and her care. I decided to take early retirement in April 2008 after 20 years with the Pikes Peak Library District. I wanted to move to Reno for a short time to help my mother in her time of need. Just before the real estate market crashed in 2008, I sold my house in Colorado Springs. Since her health was failing fast, I thought I would be in Reno for about year. I put all my belongings in storage, drove to Reno in my 2005 Honda CRV, and rented a furnished room in a historic mansion called "the White House." It was a beautiful home, and the price was right for a fully furnished room. I had access to the house, and the 70-year-old owner lived in the master bedroom. There were three other renters who lived in their own rooms, and we all lived quiet lives and kept to ourselves. Since I had divorced in 2005 and since my kids were already grown, it was an interesting adventure at the age of 53 to start over in a new city. Reno is a beautiful city and is very similar in climate and access to mountain recreation like Colorado Springs. It is only 30 minutes from Lake Tahoe, one of the most beautiful spots in the country. For the first time in my adult life, I had an extended break from working. For the initial three months, I enjoyed all the recreation the summer offered in Reno. I was in walking distance to the Truckee River, and each morning I rode my bike or jogged by the river through downtown.

Each day I visited my mother at her nursing home and helped her with her daily needs. One of the residents, who usually sat outside in her wheelchair with her oxygen tank and smoking a cigarette, greeted me every day as I entered the facility. "It is really nice that you visit your wife every day," she remarked to me on one of my visits. My jaw visibly dropped when she said that, because my mother is 28 years older than I am. I must have looked older than I thought - or my mother looked younger than her 80 years. The lady's comment amused me, and I told my mother what she said. My mother was delighted. She told me, "I didn't want to hurt your feelings, Steve, but she is not the only person that thought you were my husband." I guess it was time for me to buy a bottle of Grecian Formula.

Since I was getting a little bored from not working, I started to look for a library-related job. The first job I applied for was as a career specialist in the Galena High School Library and they hired me. The job required me to help plan Career Day, to support the students' efforts in applying for scholarships, and to perform the duties of a librarian in a school library. I had never worked in a high school library before, but I had taught several gifted- and-talented classes for junior high and high school students in video production and had worked in a college library. Working in a school library meant regular hours. I opened the library at 7 a. m., and we closed by 3 p. m. when school was out. When I got off work I drove right by a local In-N-Out Burger and couldn't resist getting a bite to eat, before I went to the nursing home and spent a few hours visiting with mom.

Galena High School was an excellent school with dedicated teachers. The school was in the middle of an affluent community with a Hispanic student population of around 30%. Reno is a city with a dichotomy of labor. The working poor are mostly Mexican-American immigrants, a mix of legal and illegal immigrants who do most of the labor in the hotel casinos as maids, kitchen workers, and janitorial staff. They lived in apartment complexes close to downtown, but their children were still in the Galena High School district boundary. The primarily white population was children of the professionals in the area and they were mostly affluent.

One of the Hispanic students, Antonio, who lived with his immigrant family, was touched by God with mathematical ability. I helped him with his scholarship applications, although all I did was make him aware of the scholarships he was eligible to apply for. He did the rest of the work and was meticulous and thorough on filling out each application. Antonio ended up getting a full ride to MIT. That was ten years ago, and I'm sure he is now employed with a top engineering firm and is on his way to a very successful career. In my life, I've only met a select few people like Antonio. After talking to these gifted people for only a short period of time, you can tell that they have complete focus and God-given intelligence; and nothing can get in the way of their success. What makes them different from most intelligent people is that they have this incredible personal drive. These are special people from every walk of life. Whatever they put their mind to, they will achieve.

I enjoyed my time working in a high school library. I have incredible respect for public school teachers after working with them for those nine months. Even though they get summers off from teaching, they work extremely hard during the school year. My job ended at 3 p.m., but most of the teachers worked 12-hour days with extra-curricular activities, grading homework, and preparing lesson plans.

After spending the school year working at Galena and visiting my mom (or should I say my wife) on a daily basis, I needed a break and wanted to go back to Colorado for the summer. I had dated a woman off and on in Colorado Springs, and we had a long-distance relationship while I was in Reno. She had visited me for a week; and I was hopeful we could be together again in Colorado. It was one of those hot-and-cold relationships where we broke up once a month. It was a rollercoaster ride; but I had fallen in love with her, and I credit her for saving my life. When I met her, I was in a deep depression after my divorce and I was just going through the motions in my life. I was a dead man walking. I had lost any joy for life. Our relationship changed everything for me, and she brought me back to being a real person.

Moving back home was a decision that my heart made. When I first arrived in Colorado, I applied for a library job, hoping I could return to Colorado permanently and could rekindle my relationship. While I knew it would be difficult for my mother for me to leave, I planned to fly to Reno at least once every two months for a long weekend. I was fortunate to be hired as a manager for the Barkman Library in Pueblo. I jumped at the opportunity and made arrangements to move to Pueblo. The job was a success, and I was manager of the Barkman Branch for the next five years.

Unfortunately, my relationship didn't last a month after I moved to Pueblo. I kept my promise to my mother and flew back every two months for an extended visit. Mother was tougher than anybody would have thought. She had an incredible will to live; and although Parkinson's affected her body, her brilliant mind was with her to the end. Even though she never weighed more than 110 pounds during her time in the nursing home, she loved her spicy Spanish food. The bland nursing home food was difficult for her to enjoy, so I always brought her a meal from El Pollo Loco, a Mexican food chain on the west coast. I was very fortunate to have that time with my Mother. She told me stories about her youth and her family struggles and her rich family history growing up in Mountain View, California.

She lovingly nagged me about my weight. "Steve, you would be so handsome, if you just lost a few pounds." I wish my mom could see me today. After struggling with my weight my entire adult life, I've recently lost 40 pounds; and I am now very close to my normal weight range. She died in 2013 after eight years of being in a nursing home. It is amazing, after 63 years on this planet, and four years after her death, how I still seek her approval and want to make my mom proud of me.

# FALLING IN LOVE WITH PUEBLO

The Pikes Peak Library District had a video in our collection that was taped by a local television station of Lowell Thomas returning to Colorado Springs to give one of his final presentations. It was taped in the Palmer High School theater two weeks before his death in August of 1981. It was a fascinating program by this respected 20th century journalist, who was very sharp and funny as he reflected on his active 89 years. We aired the program several times on our channel and it was always well received. Lowell Thomas had been all over the world as a journalist and radio broadcaster. He was a world traveler and adventurer, long before commercial air travel made the world a much smaller place. He told the audience that he was always asked the same question wherever he was asked to speak and the following quote by Lowell is from that presentation.

"Lowell, you have been all over the world and have met kings and great world leaders as a global journalist. Is there a place on the planet you never visited? And I would have to admit to them, that I have never been to Pueblo, Colorado."

The packed theater at Palmer High School erupted in laughter. Pueblo is a little bit of a joke to the elite citizens of Colorado Springs and the rest of the state of Colorado. Even *South Park* had an episode making fun of Pueblo. Because of that lack of respect, the citizens of Pueblo have a collective chip on their shoulders that is stacked as high as the steel mill smokestacks that greet new visitors when they drive through the city. It has always been a blue-collar town where General Palmer built his steel mill to support his railroad. The reason why he built his steel mill in Pueblo was because General Palmer didn't want to have any smokestack industries in Colorado Springs. He was worried that a steel mill would pollute the skies of his pristine "Little London."

After I left Colorado to help my mother in her nursing home, I had no intention of living or working in Pueblo after 27 years of raising a family and living in Colorado Springs. But, I needed a job; and I was fortunate enough to have worked with the associate director, Kathy Knox, of the Pueblo City-County Library District. She remembered me and invited me to interview for the job of manager of the Barkman Branch Library. I had the same job title for my 20 years at the Pikes Peak Library District, and I had spent my career producing documentaries and running a library cable access channel. Although it was a manager position, and I had over 30 years of experience dealing with budgets and hiring and evaluating staff, I had never managed a public library branch. I knew I had to do a lot of learning on the job if I was to be successful. It took me approximately three months to become competent in my job; and thanks to the patience of my staff, I eventually thrived in my new position. After I moved to Pueblo in 2009, It didn't take long for me to fall in love with the city and the people of my new home. While working directly with my patrons, I learned what it meant to be a part of this city.

Colorado Springs and Pueblo are opposites in many ways. Colorado Springs is one of the most conservative cities in the country and is the headquarters of Focus on the Family as well as the home of three military installations and the Air Force Academy. As people drive through Colorado Springs, they see that the stretch of I-25 interstate that runs through El Paso County has been named the Ronald Reagan Highway. As they head south on I-25 and cross the county line of Pueblo County, the freeway changes from Ronald Reagan to the John F. Kennedy Highway. In 1963, John Kennedy visited Pueblo to dedicate the Arkansas Valley Project which created the Pueblo Reservoir, the water source for the region as well as a popular lake for summer water sports.

Pueblo has always been a solid blue-collar Democratic town and has embraced Democratic politicians like Barack Obama and Bill Clinton. During his successful presidential campaigns in 2008 and 2012, Barack Obama visited Pueblo. Both times he and Michelle visited the popular Mexican restaurant, *Jorge's*.

Pueblo also has an interesting and at times violent history since the town was founded on the banks of the Arkansas River. The Arkansas River was the original border for the Louisiana Purchase in 1802. The north side of the river was the United States, and the south side of the river was Spain. At that time Pueblo was inhabited by the nomadic Ute Indians and crusading Spaniards who lived together in the area that became Southern Colorado. In 1821 Mexico won its independence, and the area south of the Arkansas became part of Mexico. The permanent city structure was originally founded as a small trading post in 1845 where Americans, Mexicans, and Ute Indians lived peacefully and traded together at the small fort they called "El Pueblo." In 1854 the fort was raided by a band of Utes and Apaches killing 15 people at the settlement. The fort was abandoned until American citizens returned during the 1859 Colorado gold rush. The town of Pueblo was incorporated in 1870, around the same time General Palmer built his steel mill to supply his railroad. Needing labor for the very dangerous and difficult job of forging steel, poor immigrants flocked to Pueblo from Mexico, Italy, and Eastern Europe for employment. A large majority of the residents of Pueblo are the descendants of these blue-collar immigrants who worked in the steel mill.

In contrast, Colorado Springs after World War II, has always had a transient population with a large military presence. People stay for a few years and are transferred to another post. In Pueblo, the families who first immigrated to this town have rarely left the city, and it is not an exaggeration to say that half the town is related to each other. The city has some of the best ethnic restaurants in the country. Family-owned Italian and Mexican restaurants have been in operation since the early 20$^{th}$ century. The hard-working people, who escaped from the steel mills, opened their own restaurants and small businesses that still exist today. In Pueblo, things change slowly. An example of the slow change is that there is still a thriving drive-in theater in Pueblo County. *The Pueblo Chieftain*, the local newspaper, was established in 1868 and is one of the longest running newspapers in print in the West. *The Pueblo Chieftain* is owned and managed by the Rawlings family whose foundation has been a major benefactor of the Pueblo City-County Library District. The main library is named after the long-time publisher, Robert Rawlings. In 2017 Robert Rawlings died at the age of 92; his daughter Jane Rawlings took over as the publisher. Residents, including myself, still read the paper on newsprint. (The Rawlings family recently sold their paper in May of 2018.) It is the only source of comprehensive local written news, since Pueblo is so geographically isolated. Colorado Springs is 30 miles to the north, but the closest major city is hundreds of miles away. The next major city to the west is Salt Lake City which is 650 miles away. Santa Fe, New Mexico, is the next major city to the south and is 300 miles away. Wichita, Kansas, to the east is the next major city at a distance of 430 miles. There are very few towns in the continental United States that are as geographically isolated as Pueblo.

A unique historical aspect of the city is the many Medal of Honor recipients have called Pueblo home. Known as the home of heroes, Pueblo was the birthplace of four Medal of Honor recipients. These heroes include William J. Crawford – Army- WWII, Carl L. Sitter – Marines-Korea, Raymond G. "Jerry" Murphy – Marines -Korea and Drew D. Dix – Army – Vietnam. These courageous men are just an example of the character of the people who call Pueblo home.

Even though the residents are descendants of working-class men and women who started out with very little formal education, Pueblo loves and supports its libraries like no other city in Colorado. Colorado Springs also supports its libraries, but Pueblo per capita funding is greater, and the Pueblo City-County Library is part of its own district and has a separate funding source than the city. This means as the city has had to deal with some tight budgets over the years, the City Council cannot touch the library's budget, since it is funded by its own property tax mil levy. Not only do residents support their libraries, but they also use their libraries. At the Barkman branch, we had 180,000 visits a year; and at the Pueblo West Library we averaged 300,000 visits a year. In 2016 the entire library district had almost 1.5 million visits. In a town of 100,000 people, the Friends of the Libraries membership hovers around 1,000 library supporters. Those are incredible numbers when considering that the Friend's membership is almost one percent of the city population. The Friends also support a used bookstore that has generated hundreds of thousands of dollars for library capital projects.

For the past ten years the library has operated under the excellent leadership of Jon Walker. When he started, the district was going through a devastating political crisis. Although it wasn't easy, he has guided the library through a major renovation and expansion of four new branch libraries. He also coordinated the district's transition to RFID technology. One of his first hires was public relations manager Midori Clark. A former television reporter, Midori has expanded the library programming and events to an elite level. All Pueblo Reads and the Pueblo Summer Reading program are both very successful events with excellent community participation. The Pueblo City-County Library District has won many state wide and national awards and recognition. It is considered one of the finest libraries in the country.

Pueblo is also a town that embraces higher education. Colorado State University at Pueblo is a major university that calls Pueblo home. With over 5,000 students it has a significant economic and intellectual impact on the city.

The Bell game is the longest high-school football rivalry west of the Mississippi. Between Centennial High School and Central High School, the annual rivalry first began in 1892; and the winning team gets to keep the trophy "bell" for the entire year.

In 1869, before Pueblo was a city and Colorado was a state, 2,000 people attended a horse show near the banks of the Arkansas River where the city is today. That tradition evolved into the Colorado State Fair in 1876, and the state fair has been an annual event in Pueblo for almost 150 years.

In 2007 Pueblo became the headquarters for the Professional Bull Riders Association. Their offices are located on the downtown Pueblo river walk.

Pueblo is a great town with a low cost of living and recreational opportunities. People can still buy a decent small home for under $100,000. Residents and visitors can enjoy an afternoon at the downtown river walk where restaurants and brew pubs line the river. They can fly fish in the Arkansas River or enjoy water sports at the massive Pueblo Reservoir. If they explore Pueblo County, the mountain town of Beulah located on the west side of the county, is in a beautiful spot that sits among the foothills of the Wet Mountains. Pueblo County is the beginning of the Southwest, and there are families who can trace their roots to the early Spanish settlers in the 1600s or the Ute Indians who inhabited this land for over 10,000 years. The population is diverse, and over 50% of the population, including myself, claim Hispanic heritage. I've always joked about being a walking demographic of Pueblo, since I am half Hispanic, half Italian, college educated, and a senior citizen with blue collar roots on both sides of my family. My personal demographic crosses over in part with at least 99% of the people who live in Pueblo.

As much as I admire Lowell Thomas and his prestigious career as a journalist, if he were alive today, I would tell him that it is his loss that he never visited Pueblo. I actually feel sorry for Lowell Thomas, a man who traveled to nearly every city in the world, but has never had the privilege to visit the culturally rich city of Pueblo, Colorado. Pueblo is my home now, and I plan to live in this enchanting city until I take my last breath.

# THE LIBRARY NEXT DOOR

There are many excellent jobs for librarians to fit every personality type. Introverts can work in technical services and never have to deal with the public directly. Natural leaders lean toward management jobs that pay decent salaries and allow them to shape the organizations they work for. To me, the best job in a public library is working in a neighborhood branch. I have always been a little bit A.D.D. and could never sit in an office for more than a few hours at a time. The higher an employee ascends the management ladder in public libraries, the more time they spend in meetings. As a branch manager, I spent probably 15 hours per week in meetings. I spent another five hours per week at my desk working on paperwork, which included ordering materials, scheduling employees and evaluations, and writing incident reports. I scheduled at least 15 to 20 hours per week for myself working the desk and dealing directly with the public. Working with the public was the most enjoyable time I spent as a public-service librarian. A branch library is like the neighborhood bar in the television show *Cheers*, where everyone knows your name. The difference is that we served knowledge instead of alcohol.

For the most part, we had our regular patrons, a mixture of retired people, the unemployed, families bringing their children to Storytime, and young people who are using our computers for either studying or posting on social media. People who enjoy watching and observing human nature, like I have always done, should consider working in a branch library. It is the ultimate front row to the greatest show on earth of human behavior. The majority of my encounters with the public were positive and enjoyable. I always pointed out to my staff:

- We don't work for the Department of Motor Vehicles; our patrons enjoy visiting the library.

- We don't directly charge for our services.

- People who visit a branch library with their family and children are there to celebrate reading and learning.

- Patrons who come into a branch library are looking for information; and if you can solve their problem or answer their question, they are normally delighted and grateful.

The Barkman Branch is a 9,000-square foot library that was built in 1990. It was the definition of a neighborhood library with hundreds of middle-class homes within walking distance. Pueblo has a population that is over 50% Hispanic; I estimated the patrons at the Barkman Branch were over 60% Hispanic. The Belmont neighborhood was primarily built in the 50s and 60s, and is comprised of well-kept modest homes with mature landscaping and big trees. A neighborhood park is right next door to the Barkman Branch, and our customers were mostly families. Our library was a few miles from Colorado State University of Pueblo, and many of our patrons were professors, staff, or students from the university. We mostly served a working-class, blue-collar community that could afford the neighborhood homes, which cost from approximately $80,000 to $150,000.

Unlike Pueblo West, we did not get a large teen population using the library; however, we did have a number of pre-teen kids who walked or rode their bikes to the library. The fire department capped our capacity at 80 patrons, but we routinely had 200 to 250 people during our popular summer reading program. I was always hoping the fire department didn't show up for a surprise inspection during those programs.

On hot summer days in Pueblo, the temperatures exceeded 100 degrees, and the families flocked to our library for the air conditioning as well as the great summer programs. My five years as the manager of the Barkman Branch were the most enjoyable time I spent as a librarian. Since we served a low-income community, our patrons didn't just enjoy our services; they really needed our services. The kids came for our Wi-Fi and computer services, and the adults utilized our resources for job searching and employment information. What I loved more than anything was the variety of people we served. From tattooed former gang bangers who were coming into the library to help their children enjoy reading to retired college professors who loved life-long learning, we served them all.

The Barkman branch was the best example of why a community needs a public library. We were a sanctuary for many young kids and struggling adults who needed our services. Since it was a small branch, I got acquainted with almost everyone who walked through the door. I watched the babies become toddlers and watched the toddlers become grade-school students. We had our share of regulars who lined up outside to get in when we opened at 9 a.m. Serving the children of that community was the most rewarding aspect of my job. Whenever I created the first library card for a young patron, I always told them the same thing.

"Do you know what I love most about my job? It is giving a young person their first library card. I want to personally thank you for making my day."

I know there are many rewarding jobs that allow people to make a difference in a person's life. Yet, I can't think of a more rewarding occupation than being a librarian in a branch library. We look forward to going to work, and we are helping patrons, who are both our friends and our neighbors.

# THE BOOK PEOPLE

In *Fahrenheit 451,* Ray Bradbury writes about a secret community of book lovers he calls *The Book People.* Since books are illegal in this dystopian future that Bradbury has created, and all hidden books are burned by the fire department of the future, people who love books and their ideas commit their favorite books to memory. They are known as *The Book People,* and they have the important task of preserving all literature. *The Book People* are not just fiction; they do exist, and I saw them daily in the branch libraries I managed. When a new shipment of books arrives, these are the compulsive readers who go directly to the new book collection like drug addicts to their dealer. *The Book People* account for half of the monthly circulation in a public library. It is a statistical fact that *The Book People* are primarily comprised of middle-aged women of all ethnicities. These avid readers checked out an average of three to four books per week. They don't normally watch a lot of television, but they go home and generally read . . . read . . . read. They are very intelligent and know a great deal because they continue to stimulate their minds with new material and information through reading.

We had one person who put a little pencil mark on the book page that represented her age, so she would know if she had read the book and how long it had been. She happily read the book again if it had been a few years since the last time she read it. This is not the type of behavior to encourage. However, the book lovers are the core group of patrons who keep your circulation stats up and that is beneficial when trying to justify hiring another shelver. They are also very kind to librarians and always say "hello" and ask for book recommendations. They generally are the core group of branch book clubs. They are also the patrons who bring in food and bake goods on a regular basis for staff. Many of them are members of the Friends of the Library organizations and end up becoming great volunteers. They love libraries, and they understand the value of their library cards, because if they had to buy every book they read, the bill would be approximately $10,000 a year.

My Uncle Eugene Calvo is one of *The Book People*. An army veteran who was stationed in Germany in the 1950s, he attended college on the G.I. bill and graduated from Stanford University as a history major. After a career in real estate in Mountain View, he retired early and now lives a quiet life in Sunnyvale, California. At 85 years old, he walks the two-mile distance to the Sunnyvale Public Library at least twice a week. Uncle Gene has been a patron of the Sunnyvale Library for the past 40 years. Since he loves nonfiction and history, I imagine he has read every non-fiction book in that library. We talk on the phone four or five times a year, and we have lengthy discussions about our family history and the politics of the day. He is one of the most intelligent and well-read people I have ever known. My uncle is the definition of a life-long learner. Like the Burgess Meredith character in that famous *Twilight Zone* episode on the bank clerk who loves reading, all Uncle Gene wants to do is read . . . read . . . read.

However, there are exceptions to the typical book lover who comes in the library. One person was a middle-aged woman who lived on a farm in Pueblo county and drove 30 minutes to our Barkman branch once a month. She always asked to borrow a book cart and unloaded 30 books she had checked out the previous month. I helped her unload the books from the trunk of her car, and she spent an hour at the library filling up the cart with another 30 books to check out. When I asked her why she checked out so many books, she explained that they really weren't for her. She went on to tell me that the books were for her 85-year-old father who was still an active farmer and whom she lived with and helped him out on the farm. She said her father had always loved reading. When he was in high school, he was always walking and reading at the same time, and just like too many Americans do today looking at their phones and not paying attention, he would run into things while reading. I guess you could call him a distracted reader. She said her father had always lived on their family farm in eastern Pueblo County, with the exception of the three years he spent in World War II in the Army Air Corps. Her father was a crew member on a B-17 with the Eighth Air Force and was stationed in England. When he wasn't going on the incredibly dangerous daylight bombing runs, he read in his barracks. Reading about different places helped him deal with the stress of war. Reading may have saved his life. He was one of the lucky bomber crew members who made it back alive.

I never got to meet him, since he never came into the library himself. She told me he would read a book each day. Since he had minimized his work as a farmer and his wife had passed on, all he did was read . . . read . . . read on the farm. Everyone who walks into a public library has his or her own story to tell. People might go to the library to fill out a job application; they may be children who have not yet learned how to read and are coming to the library for Storytime; or one could be a loyal daughter who is helping her father pursue life-long learning by helping him read every book we had in our collection. 30 books a month, 360 a year. God bless that farmer, who is a dedicated member of *The Book People,* who just loves to read.

# MY DOG ATE MY LIBRARY BOOK

Throughout the history of public libraries, the one living creature that has been more responsible for destruction of library property has been dogs. Now, I am a dog lover, so this doesn't come from some deep-seated hatred of dogs. It is just a fact. From years of working in public libraries, I have seen their destruction. On the average of once or twice per week, anonymously returned books are put in the book drop by a patron who hoped that staff didn't notice the teeth marks on the corner of the books. I suppose it could be humans who are chewing on the book or a cat, but I am almost certain that 99% of the time that the teeth marks on a book are caused by dogs.

The typical library policy is to charge the patron for the destruction of a book. Sometimes it could be water damage. On a rare occasion we might find bed bugs (which meant we had to fumigate the collection), but most of the time the excuse was, "My dog ate my library book."

Honest patrons return a damaged book in person and sheepishly ask how much it is going to cost to replace it. In some instances, we let them buy the books themselves at a bookstore, and then charged them to process

STEVEN JOHN ANTONUCCIO

the book and to put it back in the collection. I always felt bad for the honest people who returned the book in person and sometimes I gave them a break and just discarded the book from the collection, if it wasn't a new book that was destroyed.

My favorite story of a dog destroying a book was from a frequent patron who was one of *The Book People* who visited the library on a weekly basis. She was a local RN and often visited the library in her scrubs after work. A very proper middle-aged woman, she was always polite, and we exchanged a few pleasantries each time she came in. One day she had a badly destroyed book in her hand. The book had bite marks all over it, and I could tell that a dog had used the book as a chew toy. She approached me at the desk very tentatively and apologetic.

"I'm sorry, Steve, but my dog got a hold of this book. I would be happy to pay for it, if you let me know how much it would cost to replace it."

I responded, "Don't worry; it happens all the time. Let me check and see how old the book is, and I might just discard it and not charge you anything."

Being a dog lover, since my dog is a German Shepherd and Border Collie mix, I made small talk while I looked up the cost of her book.

"What kind of dog do you have?"

She looked at me a little sheepishly, and she answered the question, knowing I would have the same response she had seen from dozens of people who had asked her the same thing.

"My dog is a Pit Bull and Chihuahua mix."

I don't care who you are. You can be the most prudish person in the world; however, when someone tells you that their dog is a Pit Bull and Chihuahua mix, you immediately visualize a powerful Pit Bull mounting a poor little Chihuahua. I'm sure she guessed the image that was in my head as my jaw dropped. I just had to ask the next question.

"Who was the father, the Pitbull or the Chihuahua?"

She quietly answered. "The Chihuahua was the father."

Again, the visual entered my head, but this time it was of a Chihuahua standing on a little foot stool and mounting a powerful Pit Bull that was four times its size.

We knew each other well enough that I responded by joking. "That Chihuahua must have had a great deal of self-esteem." We both erupted into laughter.

I must say I'm envious of that little Chihuahua and all his self-confidence. If someone bottled the confidence and fearlessness of that Chihuahua, they could succeed at anything in life.

Dogs provide great love for their owners. They are affectionate creatures, and my dog Max has kept me in shape during my retirement by walking "me" every day. However, dogs have destroyed more library property than any single person has done with spilled coffee, neglect, or water damage. Dogs not only have eaten many a student's homework, but they have also done their fair share of eating library books.

# TYPE 2 DIABETES

After I retired in 2016, I was diagnosed with Type 2 Diabetes. I have always struggled with my weight at 5' 11" tall, and I have seesawed in my adult life from 170 to 250 pounds. With diet and exercise, I recently dropped to under 200 pounds and have tested out of the diabetic range. It hasn't been easy to drop 40 pounds, but being retired has helped me find the time to concentrate on losing weight. It also helps that I'm miles away from the free food buffet called the public library. The dirty little secret that all public librarians understand, is that their loyal patrons are conspiring to get them fat.

On a daily basis, retired women are coming into the library with trays of sweets and snacks for the staff. These women love the library, and they love to cook; and they are constantly combining those two passions at the expense of our health. I do not want to blame my extra heft on my lack of self-discipline or my sweet tooth. However, I would rather blame it on a 95 year-old patron named Enola. Enola, who was born in 1917 and still comes into the Barkman Library at 100 years old. She also makes the most delicious chocolate chip cookies I have ever eaten. She is a retired teacher who has been a patron of the Barkman Library since it opened in 1990. Enola can't weigh more than 110 pounds and is as healthy as any 20 year-old who has walked through the library doors. Apparently, she has an eating disorder that compels her to cook a lot of food that she is unable to consume, so she takes it to the library. I wish Enola was the only person who conspired to keep me fat, but there is always some sort of food available to our staff left in our meeting rooms. Many times a group who held a meeting at our library leaves us with their left-over snacks. The box of donuts they brought in might be half full; and since we don't charge for our meeting space, they always graciously give our staff the leftovers as thanks for our help. Frequent patrons may have observed that many of the staff are a few pounds overweight. Don't blame the staff, as they work in a public library; and the patrons with platters of food are coming in constantly.

Enola was a member of our monthly book discussion group, and she enjoyed socializing with other people who also loved books. The book discussion meetings are like a Golden Corral Buffet potluck. Every member brings in a food dish, and the calories are stacked up on the free food table. As a library manager, I always had a programming budget that allowed the purchase of some snacks for the variety of library-sponsored events. To increase attendance for a public program, we would supply food for the patrons. It is an unspoken rule: the patrons grace the library staff with their platter of cookies; and, in turn, we provided snacks for library programs. Anything that isn't eaten during the library programs goes to the staff area. During our book group discussion, Enola talked about her life as a teacher; and at one meeting she told me that her father was in his late fifties when she was born. Her father was born in 1860 and was a small child during the Civil War. It was amazing to me that in only two generations she had a connection to the civil war. I would not be surprised if Enola lived to be 110 or more. When I was still manager of Barkman, she told me she had an older brother who was still alive. For Enola, the secret to living a long life is: don't eat the thousands of cookies you bring into the library. Hopefully, it is not too late for me to extend my longevity and that retiring from the buffet called the public library will add at least another ten years to my life. God bless Enola and her love for libraries, but does she have to kill us literally with her kindness and cookies?

# A CONFEDERACY OF DUNCES

Working as a librarian in a neighborhood branch library is the most rewarding job anyone can have. When the director hired me as branch manager in 2009, I replaced a supervisor who was not very popular with staff, so I was not following John Elway as the next Broncos' quarterback. But, I still had challenges. Since the staff had a very difficult relationship with their previous manager, they were nervous and skeptical at first. As soon as they realized that I was a fair manager, they started to trust me. I went out of my way to create a positive relationship with my staff, and I was more of a player's coach in terms of how I treated people with respect. Not that I didn't have some difficult moments with staff and administration! But, for the most part, I was allowed to do my job how I saw fit. I'm not a perfect person, but I tried to do everything possible to support my staff in their efforts to provide excellent customer service for our patrons. Everything begins with the front-line staff. They are working directly with the patrons every day, and it is that special one-on- one relationship that makes a library successful.

One of my favorite books of all time is *A Confederacy of Dunces* by

John Kennedy Toole. The protagonist, Ignatious J. Reilly, is a man of high intelligence who could not find his way through life without running into constant road blocks. He was a square peg in society and Ignatious was continuously frustrated by the duces who got in the way of his egotistical genius. The novel won the Pulitzer Prize for fiction in 1981. Unfortunately, the author committed suicide 12 years before the book was even published. The book was finally published because Toole's mother made it her personal quest to find a publisher for her son's brilliant masterpiece.

I first noticed Fernando when this 15-year-old kid walked into the library wearing the same hunter's hat with ear flaps as Ignatious J. Reilly. Although the hat kept him warm in winter, he never removed it after entering the building. And just like Ignatious Reilley, the duces were conspiring against Fernando at this time in his life. He was a sight to see: a tall, skinny Hispanic kid who walked to the library after school and literally lived between the book stacks of our branch. He was one of *The Book People* in training; and he couldn't get enough of libraries and he read everything he could find in Science Fiction. As I got to know Fernando better, I found out that he lived in a foster home with another teenager, Danny. The two of them were like night and day. Danny, a ginger redhead, looked like trouble, but in reality he was a pretty good kid. While Tony was reading, Danny homesteaded a computer and spent his time with social media.

Librarians should socialize and engage with their patrons only at the library; and like a parent, they should never have a favorite child; but Fernando and Danny were my favorite children. They always made me smile when they wandered in after school, because I knew they needed the library to survive. Fernando was a smart kid who was extremely polite and just wanted to read. For both Danny and Fernando, the library was their sanctuary. They were both terrified of their foster dad; and on occasion he stormed into the library and screamed at them. My heart went out to both of them, since I suspected they lived in this abusive situation at home. Librarians cannot cross the line outside of the library and get involved in things that aren't any of their business. While staff can help the patrons, it was forbidden, as it should be, to get involved in their outside lives. If you witnessed abuse in your library, you could call the police. However, anything you suspected was happening outside of the library, was not your jurisdiction, unless you had some proof.

Like most teenagers, Fernando and Danny were always hungry. It might have been because they were young, growing kids who needed to eat constantly, but I really felt they weren't getting the nourishment they needed at home. Danny and Fernando helped me from gaining a few more pounds, because I saved them some of our extra food given to us. I know people shouldn't feed stray cats, but I had a soft spot for Danny and Fernando. It got to the point that they ventured into the library every day just to see what food was available. They devoured it in a few minutes, and I always felt good about supplementing their diet.

At the time, I was divorced and didn't have a special woman in my life. Had I been married, I would have tried to adopt 15-year-old Fernando. He was already on the right path with his thirst for knowledge, and he would have been an easy son to raise. The timing wasn't right, and I couldn't cross that line. What I did do for Fernando was to encourage him and to suggest books he might enjoy. We talked almost every day, and it broke my heart when I thought about his living circumstances. I made sure to tell him how impressed I was with his intelligence and how important it was to develop his intellect by becoming an avid reader. I knew I wasn't going to become his father, but I wanted to let him know that his circumstances would get better and that he had the potential for a successful life. I was sincere in my praise, and he knew it. He needed to hear it from me, since all he heard at his foster home was anger.

Almost a year after I met them, Fernando and Danny suddenly moved to another foster home. I don't know the circumstances, but they both told me they were living with a wonderful couple who took good care of them. They still visited the library to eat whatever food and snacks they could find. When Fernando graduated from high school, he immediately joined the Air Force. He was finally in control of his life, and I knew this intelligent, young man would thrive in the military. About six months after he enlisted, he returned in his Air Force uniform. I couldn't believe this 6' 3" kid, who weighed only 120 pounds when he joined, was now a 180-pound man who was finally able to eat as much as he wanted at the military canteen. He was a medical assistant and was training to be a nurse; he wanted to make the Air Force his career. The military was willing to pay for his nursing education, and his life was on the right track.

On the other hand, Danny had gotten his girlfriend pregnant and was on his way to becoming a 19-year-old father. Danny had to grow up quickly, and he did the right thing and married his girlfriend. One day, he proudly waltzed into the library to show off his baby daughter; he had a sense of purpose and wanted to create the family he never had. Not all stories about foster children who come into the library have happy endings. Danny and Fernando, who are probably in their mid-twenties as I write this, have overcome their personal hardships to become responsible men. The many wonderful young people I met and befriended during my career often have filled my heart with hope. For a couple of years, Danny and Fernando became my unofficial adopted children, and I take genuine pride in how they turned out.

# A REVOLUTION IN PUBLIC LIBRARY
## CUSTOMER SERVICE

In 35 years of working in libraries, I always could count on any state-of-the-art technology used in libraries to change on a yearly basis. When I started at the Pikes Peak Library District in 1988, our director Ken Dowlin, had just accepted a job as a director of the San Francisco Library District. He was well known in the library field for his vision in terms of automating libraries and creating one of the first electronic catalogues. He also excelled at marketing. The computer used for automation was placed in the same spot where a retired librarian, Maggie, had worked. He named our first automated catalogue system "Maggie's Place." He also wrote a book, *The Electronic Library*, that laid out a vision for automating libraries.

The original Public Access Catalogue had changed dramatically with the birth of the internet. Patrons now can select and place their items on hold through their home computers. Searching and using a library catalogue had become a much more user-friendly experience, and e-books and other electronic material can be downloaded from home.

When I arrived as manager of the Barkman branch in August 2009, we were just installing our free Wi-Fi for our patrons. The circulation system,

SIRSI, was the state of the art at the time, and our books were tagged with barcodes. Patrons seldom used the cumbersome self-check system. Most of the material was checked both in and out by hand, with the staff doing all the work. Staff scanned the library card and then the items one at a time; and it was a very flawed operation. Since it was a manual process, there were plenty of opportunities for error. If a staff member was busy, there was a chance they would forget to check in an item. The item remained on the patron's card, and we received a number of user-claimed returned requests. This meant a staff member had to check physically to determine if the item was on the shelf. The circulation process was very labor intensive and required us to have more staff in the library just to provide this circulation service.

Many libraries have already made the leap to a Radio Frequency Identification (RFID) system with Automated Material Handler (AMH) equipment to check in materials. Most major libraries serving large populations have completed the RFID tagging. Unlike barcodes, which need to be scanned up close, an RFID tag can be scanned from a distance, and multiple items can be scanned simultaneously. RFID is frequently used for identifying and sorting a variety of materials in our society. The use of RFID tags in a public library was a revolutionary leap in the inventory process and controls of a collection. It has saved innumerable staff time. Librarians and library assistants have more time to focus on their patrons and programs rather than to control a collection that uses barcodes.

I spent almost a year at the Barkman Branch Library transitioning to RFID. It is not an easy or inexpensive task to make that change. Every item in the collection needed to be tagged with the RFID label and integrated with the computer system. Simultaneously, we needed to operate and to provide a high level of customer service during this transition. To be honest, I was not completely sold on the changes at first. Many of my staff members also resisted the changes. To find space for the AMH (Automated Material Handling) machine, we sacrificed our small meeting room. AMH machines are the equipment that automatically checks in material and sorts it in a variety of bins, depending on the genre or type of items. Our AMH machine was supplied by RFID systems based in Milwaukee, and they did a magnificent job getting it operational for us. We also needed to purchase new self-check machines to read the RFID tags, which made is simpler for patrons to check out their own materials. Skeptical staff often were concerned that they would lose their jobs and resisted the change. Our library director, Jon Walker, guided us through this dramatic change in how we provided customer service. Once everything was installed and all the bugs were worked out of the system, the new system was a small miracle in efficiency. We no longer had to check items out one at a time with a scanner. Our AMH system was set up to check in multiple items, and the mechanical sorters placed them in the appropriate bins so that the material handlers (shelvers) could easily sort these returned items. Our user- claimed returned problem was reduced to almost zero. Items were checked in and out accurately, and our customers learned how to do most of the circulation work themselves.

RFID for identification has been used at the Pueblo Library District for the past three years, and the additional free time the changes has provided for the staff has freed them to work on a variety of patron-oriented innovative projects and programs.

Like any technology there are days when the power goes out, and staff needs to reset the machines or the computers crash. It is not a frequent occurrence; but when it does happen, the entire staff is scrambling to serve the customers.

Technology is a wonderful enhancement and can make life as a librarian easier in many ways, but be prepared for the times when it all fails and becomes useless. Always keep a pad of paper and a pen in the customer service desk for those times each item has to be manually checked out and checked in.

# THE BOOKSECUTIONER

"A librarian who is good at weeding books from a library collection"

—a definition from *The Urban Dictionary*

At the top of my list of tasks I hate to do, is weeding books from the collection. Unfortunately, it turns out I am actually good at it. I detach and become ruthless and cruel when removing items from the collection, but I still hate to do it. Weeding books is not a job for a hoarder; and since I'm a bit of a minimalist, the job usually ended up in my lap. When I started at the Barkman Library, we had a collection of 75,000 items in a branch library that should have had 40,000 items at most. The librarians who preceded me ignored previous weeding lists. The first directive from Kathy Knox, the public service manager who hired me, was to start weeding the collection. Our shelves were filled to the max at that time, and the poor shelvers had no room to shelve books and other materials.

To clarify, weeding is the process of removing items that rarely circulate. Our weeding lists were usually set to one year; if an item had not been checked out in a year, it would appear on a weeding list for us to pull. In terms of the Pueblo City-County Library, we tried to repurpose the books we weeded. Most of our weeded materials ended up at the Friends of the Library bookstore and were sold to the general public at a discount. Weeded paperbacks that were worn out were discarded. Since paperbacks had a limited life and limited resale value, the library policy was to throw the badly worn paperbacks away and recycle them.

One time when I was throwing a load of worn out paperbacks into the recycling dumpster, a patron in the parking lot saw me. He approached me and asked me why I was throwing out books. I explained that we were getting rid of our older paperbacks that were falling apart. He didn't really believe me; and I had nothing left to say except that I was just following orders.

I spent almost five years as the manager of the Barkman branch, and I estimated I weeded 75,000 items from our collection. Since we added 5,000 to 10,000 new items a year to the collection, I needed to weed at least 20,000 items per year to reduce the collection to a manageable size with 35,000 remaining items in our collection on the day that I left. Although I did recruit staff and volunteers for the weeding effort, it was difficult to find any librarians who wanted to pull books and other items from the library. Every week I filled a dozen used Baker and Taylor boxes with books and sent them to our friend's bookstore. Our monthly list had 1,000 to 1,500 items and I sighed in horror every time I got a new list. Especially if we had not finished our last list the previous month and we were getting behind in weeding.

"I am become death, the conqueror of worlds" was the poem that Robert Oppenheimer quoted after witnessing the Trinity atomic blast. My quote was, "I am become literary death, the "booksecutioner" of a library collection." I take credit for inventing the word "booksecutioner." I personally submitted the word to The Urban Dictionary, and the editors accepted it. So, it is now on their website.

My advice to local authors or anyone who loves a particular book, is to check it out two or three times each year. That way you can insure your favorite book or item, does not end up on the death weeding list.

Unfortunately, the day came that I found one my favorite Bradbury books on the weeding list. It was *Fahrenheit 451* written by Ray Bradbury on a manual typewriter in the UCLA library. Although I took pride in my job at being an efficient booksecutioner with very little mercy, I trembled at the thought of weeding a book by the most significant author in my life. To make matters worse, it was a worn out used book in paperback form, which meant it would end up in the dumpster. *Fahrenheit 451* is Bradbury's masterpiece about people risking their lives to save books in a fascist future, where all books are burned. It would have been sacrilegious to trash *Fahrenheit 451* in the Barkman recycling dumpster. It was like God asking Abraham to kill his own son. I just could not bring myself to do it.

Although the statute of limitations for stealing this book has passed, I waited years before confessing to my crime. At the end of the work day, I wheeled out my weeded and worn out paperbacks on a small cart. I had learned not to throw out any books in the light of day, since I had been confronted by a patron the last time I was caught. Since we left the barcode on the books we weeded, the security gate lit up like a fireworks show as I passed through it with my pulled paperback books. It caught the eye of our security guard, and I coolly explained I was just throwing out a cart of weeded books. She had seen me do this hundreds of times before. I probably could have told the security guard almost anything, and she would have believed me since I was the branch manager.

*Fahrenheit 451* was on the top of the cart as I pushed it out the door. Once I got outside to throw out the paperbacks, I deftly palmed the treasured book in my right hand. Since the recycling dumpster was by the parking lot, I verified no was looking, and I unlocked my car and threw the book on the front seat. I felt it was my duty to honor *The Book People* in *Fahrenheit 451*. History will look back at my effort as being heroic rather than being criminal, even though I stole a book from the Pueblo City-County Library District. To this day, that paperback with the barcode and security tag torn out still sits on my bookshelf, just like a prized trophy would.

The booksecutioner blinked and pardoned one very important book.

Ray Bradbury died on June 5, 2012. When I heard the news, I was at work in the Barkman Branch Library. I withdrew to my office, closed the door, sat at my desk, and cried quietly. It was appropriate that I mourned his death in a library, because the library was Ray Bradbury's place of worship for most of his life. That summer I read his book *Dandelion Wine* for the 45th time. His wonderful book transported me back in time to Greentown, Illinois, and allowed me to spend another summer with the best friend I ever had, Douglas Spaulding, the character Ray Bradbury modeled after himself.

# DOGPATCH, COLORADO

In most towns across the country, communities which are considered on the other side of the railroad tracks, are where poor people struggle to survive. These proud people are not much different from the wealthier people who live in their towns. They love their children, their community, and – most of all – they love their country. They are represented in greater percentage in our military, and they have a history of giving their lives for their country in larger numbers, as well.

In Pueblo, the toughest barrio on the east side of town is derisively known as Dogpatch. The original Dogpatch was created by the cartoonist Al Capp and is the backwoods community where the cartoon hillbilly Li'l Abner lives. It is a primitive community that doesn't have electricity or indoor plumbing. Dogpatch, Pueblo, is similar to living in some poor communities in Mexico. Almost 100% Hispanic, Dogpatch is a neighborhood filled with the original tiny houses, before tiny houses became hip. Most of the homes are no more than 500 square feet and were built by their owners years before zoning and building standards existed in Pueblo. Many of these homes are surrounded by chain-link fences with pit bulls protecting the yard. It is a tough neighborhood to be born in and even a tougher neighborhood to leave. The residents have accepted their neighborhood label of "Dogpatch," and embrace it proudly as their heritage.

The Barkman branch was in the Bonforte neighborhood but also served the community of Dogpatch and most of the east side. We weren't actually in this east- side neighborhood, but we were the closest branch library to Dogpatch. For years there was always talk of building an east side library, but it was just a pipe dream.

Eva R. Baca Elementary School sits in the middle of Dogpatch. Eva R. Baca, a former teacher and principal in School District 60, was a well-respected educator. I loved visiting the school and giving out our annual library reading awards to their students. I was always inspired by their enthusiasm and positive energy during these awards assemblies. Looking out at a sea of young enthusiastic Hispanic faces, I always sensed that the future was in good hands.

One of the east side residents who wanted to improve his life was a young army specialist named Patrick Lucero. Patrick joined the military at a time when most young men his age did everything they could to avoid serving their country. He was a proud 18-year-old soldier who was shipped to Vietnam. Pictures of Pat Lucero while in Vietnam capture who he was with his muscular physique and broad, happy smile. He loved the Vietnamese children and engaged them with open arms. On March 16, 1968, he had volunteered to walk point during a search and destroy mission, when he was ambushed and killed in action along with four other soldiers in his platoon. Before he was killed, Pat pushed forward while facing superior fire power and called in an air strike on the enemy's position to protect his fellow soldiers. Pat was posthumously awarded the Silver Star with a cluster for valor. In an instant the promising life of this Pueblo Eastsider ended.

His older brother, Bill Lucero, was a good student who also exhibited great potential. Bill became a lawyer and is now the presiding disciplinary judge for the Colorado Supreme Court. Who knows what Pat Lucero would have achieved if he had survived the war? His brother Bill is a great example of the drive and the dedication of the Pueblo east-side Lucero family. Pat's boyhood friends, Jim Lewis and Bill Bailey, and his brother Bill, wanted to dedicate a living memorial to Pat Lucero in Vietnam. Working with Peace-Trees Vietnam in 2010, they built a library named after Pat Lucero in the province where he was killed. What better way to honor his life than to create a library in his name. The Patrick Lucero Library in Vietnam was created to heal the pain between the two countries that were once mortal enemies. Almost sixty thousand Americans were killed in the Vietnam War, and the Vietnamese lost a total of three million soldiers and civilians on both sides.

A few years after the construction of the Patrick Lucero Library in Vietnam, the Pueblo City-County Library District decided to open a much-needed east-side library. It was only natural that the pride of the east side, Pat Lucero, should have this new Pueblo library also carry his name. I always believed that the community we served at the Barkman branch really needed their own library. It wasn't a luxury but a necessity for the kids and the families who lived in our community as a sanctuary and a place for life-long learning. But even more than the Barkman branch, no other patrons in our city needed the Patrick A. Lucero Library than the east side of Pueblo. Abandoned by businesses that were afraid to exist in this community, the only supermarket shut down shortly after the Lucero Library was built. The east side of Pueblo embraced this new library with open arms. On December 13, 2014, the Patrick A. Lucero Library opened. The Patrick A. Lucero Library is the heart of this proud community. Located near the intersection of 7th Street and North Monument Avenue, it is part of a triad of facilities that serve the east side community. Across the street is Risely's School of Innovation, a charter school, whose building also houses The Boys and Girls Club. On the other corner is the St. Leander Catholic Church, which has served the spiritual needs of the east-side residents since 1925. Every afternoon when the students leave their classes at Risely, they run across the street to the library. Just like in Pueblo West, the Patrick A. Lucero Library is overwhelmed by young people from 3 P. M. until dinner time. Since the library opened, Diane Logie, a Hispanic woman and Pueblo native, has served as manager. She has a personal connection to the patrons she serves.

Like many poor communities, gangs have always been a problem on the east side. The library and the Pueblo Police Department have been aggressive about giving young people other options. Every afternoon at the Patrick A. Lucero library, former gang members counsel young people on how to avoid the influence of gangs and making poor decisions. Some of these dedicated counselors have bullet hole and scars on their bodies, as a result of their past bad decisions. They are also east siders who have credibility when it comes to sharing their anti-gang messages with these young people. The good that is done at the Patrick A. Lucero Library is equal to the goodness that was in the heart of Pat Lucero and his family and friends. In 2015, Diane Logie traveled half way across the world to visit the Patrick Lucero Library in Vietnam. She wanted a personal connection with this sister library in Vietnam.

Some people claim that libraries are no longer relevant, that the public can find almost anything they need on the internet. I tell them to visit the Patrick A. Lucero Library on the east side of Pueblo on a weekday afternoon. It is a sanctuary of goodness for the young people who visit this library. With the tremendous wealth in this United States, there should be a Patrick A. Lucero Library in every impoverished community in the country. Security and personal safety as well as information and learning should be free to those people who don't have the resources at home. The Patrick A. Lucero Library is a living monument to a 19-year-old soldier who was equally proud of his heritage, his east-side neighborhood, and his country. The Patrick A. Lucero Library is the finest notion the library-loving taxpayers of Pueblo have ever funded.

# ELIMINATE THE PRIMITIVE DEVICES

Of all the characters I have met working in a public library, the one I miss the most is Harold. I could set my clock to Harold, since he wandered into the Barkman Library once a day. It was usually a brief visit, but my staff scattered every time Harold appeared in the library. When I noticed three or four staff members hiding in our breakroom, I knew Harold was on site. I didn't mind a visit from Harold, as it was usually brief and to the point. He told me what he wanted for that day and sauntered out the door. When I first met Harold, I thought he was probably a homeless person. He looked like a Viking, with his long, dirty red beard and reddish-blond hair, tattered backpack, and worn clothing. However, Harold lived with his 80-year-old parents at night. During the day he wandered through the Belmont neighborhood usually yelling at cars. Despite his behavior and appearance, Harold was harmless. He was probably more of a danger to himself as he shook his fist at cars and would sometimes frighten and angered unsuspecting motorists.

Harold's story started when he was a promising physics major at Colorado State University. He had a scientific mind and a bright future. But, like many 19- year-old, naïve kids in the 1970s, Harold and his friends liked to party. One night they drank too much and decided to go for a drive. His friend was driving. During a serious car accident, Harold flew through the front windshield and suffered a major brain injury. I knew about the accident, since Harold carried a copy of the newspaper article about the car crash. It was a very tragic lesson on why people shouldn't drink and drive.

His short-term memory was affected by the accident; and every time he ambled into the library, he repeated the same refrain about how he hated cars. He knew the staff by name and this was a typical conversation:

"Hi, Steve. How you doing today? I was thinking about a new saying that would tell everyone about the evils of cars. How about this? Eliminate the primitive devices. Car crimes kill."

I usually responded politely, "That sounds really good, Harold."

He always replied, "Please pass it on and tell your friends." He then departed the library and wandered around the neighborhood. His poor elderly parents did the best they could to look after him; and, eventually, he sauntered home for the evening.

That conversation or a very similar one happened almost every day. I never got bored with it, since I knew his story. I cared about Harold; and on those rare days when he didn't come into the library, I worried about him.

When I retired from the Barkman Branch, I was hoping I would see Harold on my last day. We were behind on our DVD shelving, so I spent my last two hours furiously shelving DVDs. The DVD collection was near the front of the library, and I occasionally looked out of the corner of my eye to check if Harold was walking through the door. Finally, I saw Harold ambling up to the library entrance. The emotion of my last day surfaced, and the tears flowed down my check.

"Hello, Steve. How are you today?" Harold asked me.

"I don't know if you know this, Harold, but this is my last day. I'm retiring." At that moment, I thought how lucky I was. I had lived a full life with a family, had a great career, and I was looking at financial security and a decent pension to live on. When I was a stupid college student, I probably drove drunk at least a dozen times; I easily could have been Harold; and if things had gone better for Harold, he could easily have lived my life. He was a bright, young man who could have had a family, a career in science, and all the wonderful and rewarding aspects life can bring. I wiped the tears from my eyes and listened to my friend for the last time.

"I have a new saying for you, Steve, and please tell me what you think…Eliminate the primitive devices…car crimes kill."

"I really like it, Harold, and I'm going to miss you."

"Pass it on to your friends."

As I watched Harold exit the library one more time on my last day, I knew everything was right in the world. My last day at Barkman was in 2014; and as of this writing, my former staff reports that Harold still visits Barkman at least once each day.

# MY KIDS ARE SMARTER THAN ME

When you marry a woman who is smarter than you and has a photographic memory, there is a very good chance your kids will be smarter than you as well. My ex-wife, like her father, had a gifted mind and she passed that on to our two daughters, Rachel and Laura. As I tell everyone, I don't know what I did wrong as a parent, but both my daughters are lawyers. It is just a joke: I'm very proud of my two daughters, esquire.

My older daughter Rachel is a public defender in Iowa City and my younger daughter Laura is a corporate lawyer in Phoenix. One works for the rich and one works for the poor. They are both good at what they do and I am very proud of them. Their mother always made sure they read as kids and they spent many hours reading and in the library. As a result of that exposure to reading, they ended up being excellent writers as well as excellent lawyers. I've been very blessed with the kids I have, they have always worked hard since they were teenagers. They both worked as servers through college and law school and they have an incredible work ethic. If anything, I'm a little concerned that they work too hard. Being a lawyer is a very stressful profession, people don't hire you unless they are in a conflict that they can't solve themselves. I admire the work they do and hopefully I will never be in a situation where I will have to hire them. I love them very much and I consider them the best things I ever helped create, and I give the vast majority of the credit for how they turned out to their Mother.

Rachel and Laura both have great men in their lives. Rachel is married to Andy Jenkins who is the head of IT at the University of Iowa graduate school. He is an avid fly fisherman and loves to visit Colorado, so he can fish the Arkansas river. Laura's significant other is Kris McKee and Kris is a manager and the head chemist at a copper mine in Globe, Arizona. Kris has a PhD in Chemistry. He also loves the outdoors and Laura and Kris met when they were at Coronado High School in Colorado Springs.

# LESS THAN A DOG'S LIFE

The oldest dog that ever lived made it to 29 years old. Even if I live as long as my mother did to 86 years old, I have about 24 years left to live, which works out to being less than a dog's life. At some point in the aging process you start reading the obituary every day. You notice those people who have died that are younger than you. When you get to the point that the majority of the people in the obituary are younger than you, (I'm not there yet) you start thinking about your mortality. Fortunately, my health is pretty good at 63 years old. Both my parents' health started to fail in their mid-seventies. Mother spent the last eight years of her life in a nursing home. If I have ten more years of good health, I will feel lucky. Most of the people I have written about are no longer with us. I realize my mortality is staring me in the face and I am grateful for the advantages I have had in my life and the people I have loved. Writing this book has been a catharsis and I am very comfortable with my mortality, but I am still clinging to one activity that is a direct link to my youth. I'm not talking about Cialis and extending my sex life: I'm talking about water skiing.

The Pueblo reservoir is a magnificent lake for water sports in Colorado.

At a lower Colorado altitude of 4,500 feet, it is one of the few reservoirs in the state that has warm water during the summer. If you are a jet skier or enjoy water skiing it a wonderful resource. I don't own my own boat, but I have an even better deal, I have a friend with a boat. My friend Rick has been coming to the Pueblo reservoir almost since he arrived in Colorado with the army in 1973. An actor, Rick has worked in local theater and television since he moved to Colorado Springs. The reservoir was open for water sports in 1975, and Rick has been water skiing at the reservoir since almost the day it opened. Rick has been coming to the lake every summer for more than the past 40 years.

My father's job as service rep for Pontiac required him to travel around the bay area to put out service related fires at the various Pontiac dealerships. For most of my youth, my Dad was on the road from Monday through Friday. He had the Willy Loman road work schedule, and we would only see him on weekends. One weekend in 1968, he got all of us kids together and told us we needed to do more things as a family. He decided he was going to buy a boat and we were all going to learn how to water ski. A friend of his had built a beautiful wooden speed boat with a six-cylinder 389 Pontiac engine and my father decided to buy it from him. I was around 12 years old at the time and we started going on weekend trips to various lakes around the bay area to water ski.

From 12 years old to 19, I did a great deal of water skiing with our family. I picked it up pretty quickly and I learned how to slalom ski and really enjoyed the time with my father and our family. Even my Dad learned how to ski, and after they moved to Texas, he would take my younger brother and sister skiing on various lakes near Dallas. My sister said my father was still water skiing when he was in his fifties.

Flash forward to 2005 and the year of my divorce, I turned 50 that year and I had not gone water skiing for 30 years. My friend Rick took me under his wing and helped me make the transition to dating again. It was like the movie *30 Year-old Virgin*, except I wasn't a virgin, but I had not really dated for 30 years. I had met my wife when I was 19 years old, and the last time I was single, disco was the rage. I was back on the singles market and I had no idea how to get going again. There was the

Cheyenne group, and the first Thursday group that got together at the Fine Art Center. I could write another book about my reintroduction to the dating world at 50 years old, but that will be for another time.

The main reason that I'm forever grateful for my friendship with Rick is that he reintroduced me to water skiing. I had snow skied most of my life, since I moved to Colorado, but water skiing I had not done since I was 19 years old. Rick invited me to join him on his boat on the Pueblo Reservoir. Trying to get up on ski's after 30 years was a real challenge. I wiped out multiple times before finding my balance and finally getting up on two skis. That was 12 years ago, and for the past ten summers I've joined Rick and his friends on his boat at least 15 times each summer water skiing, fishing, and solving all of life's problems. The boat is like a floating confessional, it is so relaxing, the people on the boat feel comfortable talking about almost anything.

Rick has owned his current boat since 1982 when he paid $2,000 to buy it. His boat has been used consistently every summer for the last 30 years. Rick is a cross between Macgyver and the Humphrey Bogart character Charlie Allnut from the African Queen. He can fix anything with a roll of duct tape and a hammer. That's the key to owning your own boat, is being able to fix it. It is a modest 16-foot boat with a 140HP outboard engine, but it one of the most utilized boats in the world. Once a week during the summer, only on a weekday so we don't have to fight with the crowds, we take the boat out on Pueblo reservoir. Rick lives in Colorado Springs, so I made my home available for him to store his boat. I live about ten minutes away from the reservoir and it is more convenient for Rick to leave his boat at my home. It works out great for me, because I don't need to own a boat, and every time he goes out on the water he usually takes me with him. Our other main boating companion is Bud who is about the same age and is the pianist at the Golden Bee bar at the Broadmoor Hotel. The Golden Bee is an English pub that features Bud, who plays a variety of rag time music and traditional sing-alongs. He is a very talented musician who has worked at the Golden Bee for over 30 years. Both Rick and Bud slalom ski and are crazy good athletes despite their undisclosed age.

Bud, Rick, and I are all men of a certain age who are trying desperately to hold on to our youth. Each year when we get on the lake in early June, it is a test of our fleeting youth to see if we can get back on water skis for another year. I probably went skiing close to 18 times this year and I realize it is the last hurrah of my youth. Who knows how long we will be able to continue to ski, I suppose we will pick up a fishing rod when our bodies finally give out. Until then, we will continue to "Geezer ski" for as long as we possibly can.

# MY TRIP TO SPAIN WITH NAIELY

When my great grandparents, Manuel and Soledad Lozano, left Spain for Hawaii in an overcrowded steamship, the only item that remains that they took to Hawaii, was a brass mortar and pestle that I now have in my possession and was given to me by my mother. Mother was given the mortar and pestle from her mother, Emilia Lozano Calvo, and she got it from her mother, Soledad Lozano.

If you saw the movie *Pulp Fiction,* Christopher Walken has a long monologue about the importance of a watch he hid in his rectum while he was a prisoner at the Hanoi Hilton. This watch was passed down for three generation and finally given to this young boy, who represented the character played by Bruce Willis. Although the mortar and pestle passed through three generations, and it does not have the same history as that watch, it is a significant heirloom that represents this humble couple and their journey to the United States. That mortar and pestle is the "Rosebud" of my family heritage.

For most of my youth, I heard stories of Spain from my grandparents, and I knew they had returned several times to visit family. My grandfather

Eugenio, whose younger brother was a soldier in Franco's army, was still in Spain and the family reunions were always great celebrations. My uncle Gene Calvo, who was in the Army during the cold war, visited the family in Spain around 1953. He talked about the family and I always made it my goal to visit Spain and see where my grandparents were from.

Mother, who would have loved to go back to Spain to visit and who was fluent in her first language Spanish, never had the opportunity to return. When my mother passed away in 2013, I decided to take some of my inheritance and take a two-week trip to Spain. The first week would be to Toledo in northern Spain, where my grandfather came from, to visit his birthplace and the small town of Sotillo De Las Palomas. The second week we would spend in the town of Cañar, the birthplace of my grandmother Emilia. Cañar was an ancient town built by the Moors in the 1500's and was high up in the Sierra Nevada's. Although I had not mastered the Spanish language after taking Spanish in high school and a little in College, I knew I would be at a disadvantage not being fluent in the language. My only option was to find a girlfriend that was bilingual and proficient in Spanish, before I made my trip.

Two years earlier I started dating the woman that would be my translator and companion for the trip. Naiely Smyer, who was the older sister of one of my employees at the Barkman branch, was of both Mexican and German descent. Her mother was born and raised in Mexico City and her father was a German-American cowboy from Texas. After the Korean war, her father Wayne decided to go to Mexico City college on the G. I. bill. It was cheaper to go to school in Mexico and he knew his money would go further, and he also was interested in a little adventure going to college in another country. He also met his future wife, Berta Gonzalez, who became Naiely's mother. Wayne Smyer is also a proud member of the book people, at 85 years old, he still reads everything he can get his hands on. During his fascinating career he has worked as a rancher and cowboy, a rough neck in the oil fields, a farmer, a soldier, a deputy sheriff in Odessa Texas, a truck driver, and finally as a psychologist for the Colorado State hospital. You can't get in any conversation with Wayne that he doesn't have some insight or knowledge to add to the discussion.

I had casually known Naiely for almost a year, since I would see her when she would come into the library to visit her sister. I finally asked her to go on a date on December 31, 2010. I was jogging at the Pueblo nature center, a beautiful preserve on the shores of the Arkansas river. She was walking her two-year old rescue dog named Maximillian. Max looked like a German Shepherd, but he was a border collie and German Shepherd mix. He didn't have the coarse hair of a German Shepherd, but he did have their regal good looks. Max was a little skittish at first, he didn't trust men for some reason. Naiely thought his former male owner may have beaten him. Naiely and I hit it off immediately and we eased into a comfortable relationship. Since we were both divorced, she never had children, we were cautious about moving in together, and kept our own homes. It was a perfect relationship and Max was the glue. He demanded that we walk him every day, and he was a healthy influence on both of us in many ways. It wasn't long before I put a picture of Max on my phone screen saver. Naiely would claim that I loved Max more than I loved her. She was probably right, but I did love them both. At one point my daughters said that I should have a picture of Naiely on my phone instead or her dog. I conceded they were right, so I asked Naiely to pose with Max for another picture of the both of them, that is on my phone today.

Naiely, whose name was Zapotec Indian from Mexico, meant "full of love." Her Zapotec Indian grandfather, who ran away from home with his brother at 12 year-old, was a commercial pilot for Mexicali airlines. His brother eventually became a general in the Mexican Army. Naiely's grandparents had a successful business in Mexico City, selling Walt Disney paraphernalia. Her grandfather would fly to Los Angeles as a commercial pilot and buy Disney paraphernalia that he would bring back to Mexico City and sell in their unofficial Disney store. Naiely and her siblings owned a home in Cuernavaca that they had inherited from her mother who died of kidney cancer in 1997. Before my trip to Spain, we both took a trip to Cuernavaca for a week. Cuernavaca is a beautiful Mexican town that is around an hour bus ride from Mexico City. It is known as the city of eternal spring since the mild weather never gets too hot or too cold. The book and movie "Under the Volcano" features this magnificent city. Again, since she spoke Spanish and knew the city, I had my own personal tour guide which enhanced my visit.

I first retired from the Pueblo City Library District in May of 2014. We flew to Dallas and then to Madrid in June and had one of the best vacations and family journeys in my life. Since I wasn't quite sure what was in store for me, I decided to rent a car for two weeks and explore the cities my family came from and lived for at least the last 500 years. We stayed the first night in a very nice hotel in Madrid. Everywhere we went the food was wonderful, at the hotel Naiely ordered a gourmet burger with carmalized onions. She asked the waiter for ketchup so she could put it on her French fries. The waiter told Naiely, in Spanish, that if she put ketchup on the hamburger it would be an abomination. She assured him she only wanted the ketchup for her French fries, and we got a little taste of the pride and arrogance of the Madrid citizens. The next day we drove to Toledo and the historic capital of Spain. Toledo is a beautiful city and historic home of my mom's favorite artist, the 15th century Renaissance painter El Greco. When we got to the hotel we decided to call my second cousin in Spain, Gloria. She was the daughter of my grandfather's brother and my mother's first cousin. Her sister Isabel and Gloria were a little older than me. Her husband Julian had been a career soldier and had retired from the Army. My Aunt Nellie had visited Spain before and at 87 years old had made the same trip and got in contact with Gloria and her sister, just two years earlier

Gloria and her husband Julian could not have been kinder to us. Gloria was a whirlwind of energy and insisted we join them for a tour of Toledo with her entire family. Her son Jorge, who was in his late thirties and was an officer in the Spanish Army, had graduated from the Spanish military academy in Toledo. It was the equivalent of West Point in the United States and as part of NATO, he had already spent several tours in Afganistan and Iraq. Jorge could speak English and was a gracious host and took us to the officer's club in Toledo for dinner. Jorge was a well-respected officer and was on the career path to become a general. He had a beautiful wife who was a pharmacist and his two sons were pre-teens who also planned a career in the military. Gloria's father had been a career enlisted man in Franco's Army. The Calvo family in Sotillo de las Palomas had spent several generations as blacksmiths. It was a profession that was handed down from father to son for at least 200 years. When Gloria father turned 18, he joined the Spanish

Republican Army and fought against Franco's army during the Spanish Civil War. He worked as a blacksmith for the Army, and took care of the many horses used by the Army to move material and men. He was captured in battle and sent to a prison near his home town in the city of Talavera de La Rena. Talavera De la Rena is known for their beautiful tiles and ceramics. While in prison, Franco's army approached him to make him a deal. They knew he was a skilled blacksmith and they needed his profession to assist them in their war efforts. They told him he could get out of the prison if he joined Franco's army. Being a 19 year-old kid, who wanted to be on the right side of history, he changed sides and remained in Franco's army for the next 30 years. It provided his family security and the military tradition continued with his son-in-law and grandson.

We spent the first day touring the ancient city and the historic churches. Toledo, Spain had been a city since the time of Christ. It was a fortified city that became the capital during the reign of queen Isabela and King Ferdinand. Toledo had once been under Arab control and also had a large Jewish population. During the Spanish Inquisition both populations were either expelled or made to convert to Catholicism. Having done a DNA test recently, my heritage showed both small traces of middle eastern and Jewish heritage. Gloria's Sister Isabel had a house near their original family home in Sotillo De Las Palomas. Their Aunt Trinidad, a very healthy woman in her early eighties, lived in the original family home that my grandfather was born in. Having seen photographs of the home that my Uncle Gene had taken in the 1950's, it looked pretty primitive in terms of how they lived. However, the home had been completely restored by Trinidad and her husband. Her husband had since passed on, but Trinidad proudly showed off the home.

The original blacksmith shop was still preserved with its stone walls and ancient tools the family had passed down for centuries. It was like walking back in time. One of the things I wanted to do was preserve this visit with my digital video camera. It was a lightweight high definition camera that allowed me to discreetly film my interaction with the family. With Naiely acting as my translator, I made a video of the tour of this magnificent home in Sotillo De Las Palomas. Trinidad's daughter. Anna Maria, had a green thumb and covered the villa in flowers. Since we were there in June the flowers were in full bloom. The Villa was pristine and maintained with great care and was a show piece of restoration. After the tour, we walked downtown to the church my grandfather was baptized in as well as several generations of my family before him. My grandfather had told me stories of throwing rocks at the church bell to make it ring. He was just seven years old, but apparently, he had a good arm and was able to get the church bells to ring. The priest would come out of the church and chase him back to his home where he would hide in his grandmother's arms. I have a family photo taken in 1908, showing my grandfather with his mother, grandmother, and aunt, and most of his siblings. My Grandfather Eugenio is the kid in the back row with the big ears. When my grandfather left Spain at 12 years old, he really believed he would come back to Spain as an adult with money to help his family. When he did return home in 1952, as a man in his fifties, his parent had already passed away. Although he embraced his United States citizenship, which were overtly displayed on his arms with American symbolic tattoos, he loved his roots in Spain and he never forgot his family. My cousins remembered my grandfather and his affection for his younger brother, a man he had never met until he returned to Spain. My grandfather had inherited part ownership to their family home in Spain. Since Trinidad's mother was a widow, the rest of the siblings in the family decided to give her the home. Her daughter Trinidad kept that home and with her husband, made it a beautiful villa that was also a museum for the rich heritage of the Calvo family.

It was an honor to represent the Calvo family in the United States and to be a link to our heritage in the United States and Spain. The young woman who would eventually inherit the home was a college student at the time who was studying to be a teacher. Trinidad's daughter Anna Maria, adopted her Spanish speaking daughter Sonia as a six year-old orphan in Peru. She was a lovely girl whose appearance showed her indigenous roots. I thought it would be fitting if Sonia would live in this beautiful home in the future and raise her own family.

The first week of our trip was an exhausting time for both Naiely and myself. Although I loved connecting with my family in Spain, their endless energy and enthusiasm for taking us everywhere left us needing a vacation from our vacation. Poor Naiely worked double time translating for my Spanish family in English to me and then repeating my conversation in Spanish back to our hosts.

When we left Sotillo De Las Palomas we were ready for our four-hour drive to southern Spain to explore the birthplace of my grandmother. We decided to take a quick tour to Granada to tour the famous Moorish mosque known as Alhambra. We stayed at the famous hotel Alhambra , which was built in 1910. At one point, all of southern Spain was controlled by the Moors and their beautiful architecture can be seen throughout the country.

Our trip to Cañar gave us the opportunity to relax. We had no known family in Cañar, since my great grandparents Manuel and Soledad Lozano, left to Hawaii with my grandmother Emilia and her oldest brother Manuel back in 1906. The Village of Cañar is right out of a Disney movie. It is a beautiful little mountain fortress built by the Moors in the 1400's, trying to escape the invading Christians during the Crusades. The Moors were allowed to live in their mountain city until the reign of Ferdinad and Isabella. Like the Jewish population, the Moors were told to convert to Catholicism or be kicked out of Spain or be killed. Since the military of Spain kicked out the Moors from Cañar, the town was virtually empty back in 1500. The government invited other Spainards from central Spain to occupy the city. That is how the Lozano family ended up in Cañar. It is a shame that the history of colonizing Spain, just like the United States, is filled with tales of kicking out the original population. My great-grandfather Manuel Lozano had ironically fought in the Spanish-American war in Cuba. He was a young 20 year-old soldier who did his duty to fight for what was left of the Spainish empire. After they lost to the United States in that war, Spain fell into a financial depression. By the time my great-grandparents left Cañar, Spain was in an economic downturn, and my grandparents did not have the option to stay, unless they wanted to continue to live in poverty. The town was crumbling and forgotten for most of the 20th century. Recognizing the opportunity for tourism in Spain, money was spent on these historic towns like Cañar, to completely restore them. When we arrived in Cañar in 2014, the town had been completely restored and was a beautiful ancient city.

The cobble stone streets and small businesses and bars were immaculate establishments. Just like Sotillo De Las Palomas, the town had a central square with the original town well and a beautiful historic Catholic church. The cobble stone streets and family homes had been completely renovated. The town has a population of 360 people, including 60 people from other countries, mostly British citizens who wanted to escape the fog and rain of England, and live in a place with lots of sunshine and a mild climate.

We decided to stay at a bed and breakfast called "El Ciello De Cañar, approximately two miles north of Cañar, up a winding one lane mountain road. It was a beautiful bed and Breakfast with approximately ten rooms, and the entire building was made of stone from a nearby quarry. The bed and breakfast was completely off the grid and was powered by solar panels. The man who built this energy efficient building had won the Spanish lottery and originally meant it to be his personal home. Unfortunately, he died tragically shortly after he built it. The new owner was a retired banker from England and lived there with his Scottish wife and their five year-old daughter. They couldn't have been better hosts. I learned about the bed and breakfast from my mother's cousins Jerry and Shirley. They made a special trip to Colorado, just to tell me about their trip to Cañar and what to expect.

As we drove up the narrow winding road to "El Cielo De Cañar," I almost panicked. I was convinced I had passed it and there was no way this narrow road led to a bed and breakfast. I was wrong, we finally reached the end of the road and there was this beautiful bed and breakfast with a stable and a vineyard.

I made the decision not to ever drive back down that one lane road until we left, but instead walk back and forth to town. My decision to walk, was in part due to all the wonderful Spanish food we were eating and my need for exercise. The Spaniards are known for their variety of cured hams and most of their food is not processed like it is in the United States. When you look at this town from a distance, it looks like the mountain town of Corleone from the Godfather. It was a mountain fortress and all the homes where painted white to make the town stand out as a white jewel in the sun.

The first thing Naiely and I did was to go to the courthouse to get the birth records of my grandmother. I thought it would be a difficult process, but since it was such a small town, that never had more than 400 residents, they produced and copied her birth certificate in less than five minutes. My cousins had told me about a couple who owned one of the two restaurants and bars in Cañar. The woman was a Lozano and a distant relative. When I walked into the restaurant, the woman in the bar looked exactly like a younger version of my Aunt Trini. Naiely and I introduced ourselves and her brother was also in the bar. The whole time we visited I had my hand-held high definition camera and recorded the introduction. Out of the footage I recorded I produced three short documentaries. One was on my experiences in my grandfather's home town of Sotillo De Las Palomos, which included a tour of his family home by his niece Trinidad. The second documentary was a short video on our time in Cañar, Spain, and the third video was on my family growing up in Mountain View entitled "Early Mountain View:" These three documentaries can be seen on Youtube.

Our time in Cañar was a very relaxing week. We would walk back and forth from the bed and breakfast to the city of Cañar every day and just explore. They had a nice little honor system bar with a paper tablet at the Bed and Breakfast. By the time we left, we filled that tablet with a couple pages of our writing, which detailed the various liquor we drank as we relaxed each evening.

When we came back to the United States I created the three documentaries on a DVD for a Lozano/Calvo family reunion in San Jose, California that fall. I brought with me the mortar and pestle that my great-grandmother had carried from Cañar to Hilo, Hawaii and then to the United States. It was amazing to see all the successful people at the reunion who were the prodigy of these two Spanish immigrants from Cañar, that never lived past their thirties and left their five children orphans. Their legacy included several successful business people and business owners, a pilot, a politician, several soldiers, two psychologists, a dentist, a district judge, a mayor of Mountain View and California assemblyman, five lawyers, a graphic designer, several teachers, two university professors, an internationally renowned anthropologist, five graduates of Stanford University, a farmer, a computer expert, and a very proud librarian, After the reunion, the family donated money to put up a plaque to honor Manuel and Soledad

Lozano in their birth place of Cañar, Spain. If you visit Cañar today, you will see this plaque at the entrance to the city.

"Homenaje a Soledad y Manuel Lozano"
**"Tribute to Soledad and Manuel Lozano"**

En 1907, Soleldad y Manuel Lozano partieron para América
**In 1907, Soledad and Manuel Lozano departed for America**

y dejaron su corazón aquí en Cáñar.
**and left their heart here in Cañar.**

Al pasar los años, regalaron a sus descendientes
**As the years passed, they gave to their descendents**

muchas memorias gratas de este pueblo hermoso
**many pleasant memories of this beautiful village.**

y por eso, siempre vuelven aquí
**and therefore, they always return here,**

con mucho orgullo y satisfacción.
**with much pride and fulfillment**

# WHY I LOVE LIBRARIES

I wanted my autobiography to be a love letter to public and academic libraries. Not only is it my chosen career, but I sincerely believe free public libraries are critical to our democracy and essential to allowing all people an opportunity to improve themselves intellectually. I have seen this with my own eyes.

Life can be very hard on some people. A young man like Fernando used the library to escape his very difficult life in a foster home. With every book he took off our shelf and read, he could escape into other people's lives, which inspired him to create a better life for himself. As an avid reader, he was able to test well when he joined the Air Force. My words of encouragement I hope contributed to building the self-esteem he needed to just survive his adolescence. Fernando needed the library, and we did everything possible to help him understand his potential.

There is no greater moment of satisfaction than giving a young person their first library card. I must have done it over 500 times during my career. It was pure joy for me. I would always joke with the young person and tell them "The next time you come into the library, you show the librarian this card and tell them you know me, and as long as your parents approve it, you can have any item you want in this library for free, just bring it back when it is due."

Probably the most important programs any library sponsors is the Summer Reading Program and weekly Storytime's. Our weekly programs during the summer were some of the best live entertainment for children. Kids who grew up on television could come into the library and see live performances by clowns, storytellers, puppeteers, musicians, and magicians. When you hear hundreds of kids laughing and applauding, there is no better sound in life. When I performed with Funky Fairy Tales at the Pikes Peak Library District, the energy you would get from making children laugh, is the greatest natural drug you can take. I don't care your financial background or your ethnicity, the pride of a young mother bringing her children into the library to take them to Storytime or teach them to read is the greatest gift they can give their family.

And then there are the life-long learners, the people who use the services of the library to pursue better jobs and improve their life. You would get the older person, who had just lost their job at the factory, and they needed help to fill out an application on line. They were terrified of computers and we could direct them to the free computer classes at the library, where they could improve their skills to apply for a job they desperately needed.

The "Tower of Babel" they called English as a Second Language, is one of the finest programs for recent immigrants that we feature at the library. These are not people who want to just stay hidden in their original culture, they want to learn how to speak and read English to survive in America. I have sat in on ESL classes that had people from African, Asia, the Middle East, Mexico, and South America all trying very hard to speak English in the same class. As an ESL instructor, you don't need to know how to speak another language: you just speak English and these eager immigrants do their best to understand and repeat the English words you are saying. You can't sit in one of those classes without feeling the love for those people who struggle and are giving their best to be part of our culture and still maintain their heritage. You will laugh and you will cry. It is one of the most heartwarming experiences you will have in your life to sit in on a library ESL class.

I live a very comfortable life now that I am retired. I am not rich, but I have access to everything I could want. Being a technology junkie, I have cable television, wireless internet, access to ebooks, audible books, Alexa, Siri, and every gadget you can dream of. That is not the case for a large population of the public. There are many working poor families in Pueblo that live under a tight budget and don't have the technology at home that they need to improve their lives. The library offers wireless internet, public computers, and a free database catalogue to many educational websites and ebooks and other materials. You don't have to be a rich person to use the library. All you need is a free library card and you have access to all the technology that I have at home. I have seen countless parents come in with their children, helping them write a paper or research an item for school. They don't have access to computers and printers at home, because they can't afford it. The library helps the working poor keep pace with the technology rich world we live in and makes it possible for their children to keep up with the other students who have access to this technology at home.

I love libraries because of the "Book People." Although the library has changed dramatically with technology, we still have a hard-core group of book lovers who come into the library to check out a real paper book. They like to physically hold a book in their hands and turn the pages as they read. They hover over the new book section, and you see their names every day on the holds shelf. They bring you fresh baked cookies and they always populate your book clubs. They donate their time and money to the friends of the library and they are your core group of volunteers. Many of them are volunteers for the library boards, and they understand the importance of a library in our democracy.

What is universal about all the people I have mentioned above is that they have one thing in common. They love their public library and they also need to have the public library in their life. I spent over 30 years working in public and academic libraries and I have had a rewarding career. I've been blessed to have met thousands of diverse and intellectually curious people in my career, and I have met them all in the democratic church of free information, we call the library.

# WHERE HAVE YOU GONE ANDREW CARNEGIE?

The steel magnate of the 18th century Andrew Carnegie, built 2,509 library buildings worldwide, including 1,689 in the United States. These public libraries were built between 1883 and 1929. After making a fortune on the backs of working people, he spent the second part of his life giving back to the common man by donating his great wealth to build free public libraries. If you have used a public library in the United States, there is a good chance you have been inside an original Carnegie Library. The Pikes Peak Library District had three Carnegie libraries in our district. The Penrose Library was added on to the original Carnegie and the original Carnegie was completely renovated and now houses the special collection. Two other original Carnegies are in the Colorado Springs area, the Carnegie library in Old Colorado City and the Manitou Springs Carnegie library. The Pueblo City County Library district had one Carnegie library that they unfortunately demolished in 1965. In the state of Colorado there are 30 Carnegie Libraries that still exist.

The only thing that Carnegie required of communities who sought his financial backing to build a library was the following list of items:

- Demonstrate the need for a public library;
- Provide the building site;
- Pay the staff to maintain the library;
- Draw from public funds to run the library—not use only private donations;
- Annually provide ten percent of the cost of the library's construction to support its operation; and,
- Provide free service to all.

Andrew Carnegie was self-taught and was a self-made man through reading almost any book who could get his hands on. Carnegie was one of the original "Book People" He believed encouraging the industrious in our country and providing them with the opportunity to improve their knowledge and intellect. He wanted that service be provided to all people for no charge.

Since World War II the United States has seen an incredible run of prosperity. Millionaires becoming billionaires and the rise of the middle class has put great wealth in the hands of many citizens. There is still a divide between what we call the information rich and the information poor. Those who have access to computers and the internet and those who struggle with writing a resume. I have seen it at the two public branch libraries I managed. Our computers at the Barkman branch were is use from the moment we opened until 9:00PM when we closed. Like most libraries, we had to install software to shut down all the computers ten minutes before we closed. At 8:50 p.m. you could hear the dozen or so people on computers curse, as their screen went blank. Although the internet had made it easier for the information rich to get answers to their questions, I can't stress enough how vital it is to the working poor, such as the many patrons I served at Barkman, who needed our services. Their kids needed our computers to complete their school assignment and the parents needed our computers to apply for jobs. No one fills out a paper application anymore; everything is done by computer and researched and filled out on the internet.

The library as place, is equally important to the collection we have on our shelves. People need a place to socialize and learn and just get together. Our meeting rooms at both the branches I worked at were constantly in use. Our literacy programs and English as a second language programs are critical for immigrants to become established Americans. Believe me, these immigrants want to learn English and become mainstream Americans. Just like my mother, whose first language was Spanish, they want to get rid of their accent and assimilate as soon as they can. And just like my immigrant grandparents, they are willing to take the toughest jobs and work long hours in order to give their children an opportunity for a better life.

There are 540 billionaires in the United states. All I need is for one or two of these billionaires to listen to my plea to become the next Andrew Carnegie. I know these billionaires have worked very hard to create jobs and build wealth. I respect the intelligence and hard work it took to build their fortunes. Great men and women like Bill Gates and his wife Melinda, and men like Warren Buffett have pledged the bulk of their wealth to charity. I am asking these billionaires to just think about using some of that wealth to fund public libraries

I would love to be involved in a foundation that was dedicated to the same principles of Andrew Carnegie with the goal of building neighborhood public libraries in communities that need a safe space for kids and families to learn and explore the world or information. Libraries that have space for community meeting rooms with the latest technology. Community rooms for book clubs and Storytime, and rooms for the Summer Reading and literacy programs. Let's recruit one of these 540 billionaires to match Andrew Carnegie and commit to building 2500 new public libraries across the country. If I had any say in it, I would call this organization the Ray Bradbury Library Foundation. It would be fitting to name it after a man who dedicated his life to promoting the value of books and libraries and who wrote his most important book about intellectual freedom, *Fahrenheit 451*, inside the UCLA Library. A man who will always be known as the leader of the "Book People."

# VIDEO LINKS

**Page 13 – A POSTER CHILD FOR ASSIMILATION**
Early Mountain View, California
https://www.youtube.com/watch?v=7vUpdzOnE-M

**Page 35 – BODYGUARD UNSEEN**
BBC documentary 14 Diaries of the Great War
https://www.youtube.com/watch?v=HqNhYHlv5Qo

**Page 47 – PARTY UNIVERSITY**
College Films, Lunchroom Supervisor
https://www.youtube.com/watch?v=R33xp1jK9B4&t=3s

Do You Want to See Gold?
https://www.youtube.com/watch?v=AHwKf85gwos

**Page 57 – THE QUAKER GENERAL**
A Conversation with Louisa Creed – The G.-Granddaughter of General Palmer.
https://www.youtube.com/watch?v=WhNRgvwecNo&t=37s

The Life and Times of General William Jackson Palmer.
https://www.youtube.com/watch?v=n_Q97l8k3Bg&t=1139s

**Page 67 – WATCHING THE DETECTIVE**
The History of the Canon City Prisons
https://www.youtube.com/watch?v=aeNpFo62t-E

The Storyteller Sculptor with Michael Garman
https://www.youtube.com/watch?v=3GRMaYcYbDU&t=26s

**Page 77 – MY OWN CHANNEL**
Bear Dance By Jim Ciletti
https://www.youtube.com/watch?v=LAHwsjXfank

De Donde Eres? Part 1
https://www.youtube.com/watch?v=8nph4APigDo

De Donde Eres? Part 2
https://www.youtube.com/watch?v=1Tbz47SUesw&t=1439s

Managing Clyde – Directed by Rick Zahradnik
https://www.youtube.com/watch?v=GiV6qp2zUwg

Colorado Springs Chamber of Commerce Film from the 50's and 60's
https://www.youtube.com/watch?v=nf_9YB_oX3l&t=875s

**Page 85 – THE STORYTELLERS OF COLORADO SPRINGS**
The Life and Good Times of Marshal Sprague – 1989
https://www.youtube.com/watch?v=UJDxnAfQpAY

Past as Prologue – Growing Up in Colorado Springs - Frank Waters 1981

**Page 87 – THE BLUEBLOODS OF THE PIKES PEAK REGION**
The Tutt Legacy Documentary 1989
Curious Colorado 1936 – Produced by Spencer Penrose
https://www.youtube.com/watch?v=ptoA6JZgl9w&list=PLZTFdlc7o4VHEogzn
hTGpxMewYuawXeHx

Magic Beneath the Clouds – Spencer Penrose on Camera – 1936
https://www.youtube.com/watch?v=4sxtr_vCRBQ&t=161s

**Page 93 – MIKE'S PEAK**
Mikes' Peak Documentary 1992
https://www.youtube.com/watch?v=wxl1o1dm-68

**Page 101 – HARVEST OF LOVE**
Harvest of Love – Documentary on Venetucci Family
https://www.youtube.com/watch?v=fqkh_UlU8Dk&t=494s

**Page 109 – SCENES OF WAR**
Scenes of War Documentary on Jim Bates 1994
https://www.youtube.com/watch?v=y4u5VM4Z2bM&t=11s

1964 Chevy Commercial on Pinnacle Rock
https://www.youtube.com/watch?v=wvKvP4r4i2o

**Page 117 – THE ALEXANDER BROTHERS**

Film and Photography on the Front Range – Steve Antonuccio
https://www.youtube.com/watch?v=AckmS1asSA8

Early 1950's Alexander Films promo
https://www.youtube.com/watch?v=Ov_z6SSXszw&t=17s

Late 1940's Alexander Films promotional video
https://www.youtube.com/watch?v=WU-A7Uoe-bo&t=6s

Alexander film Car Commercials
https://www.youtube.com/watch?v=D50yJH3ryecmercial

Alexander Film 7-up commercials
https://www.youtube.com/watch?v=sFKyqqTNM-o

Alexander Film 7-up commercials reel 2
https://www.youtube.com/watch?v=cVvB59jUaSl

The Alexander Film Company – Colorado Film Company
https://www.youtube.com/watch?v=UbMYY2PgxGE

Off Road Climb up Pikes Peak in 1957 Chevy Truck
https://www.youtube.com/watch?v=e-4A5pFbuLU&t=13s

Airforce Class of 1961
https://www.youtube.com/watch?v=t4YeYMwpkbw

The land of Sunshine
https://www.youtube.com/watch?v=yft_uoglRzM&t=109s

International Girl Scout Round Up in the Rockies in 1958
https://www.youtube.com/watch?v=BaR2YuqTkRs

1929 Air Show Colorado Springs
https://www.youtube.com/watch?v=TXuP8bLSqq8

1925 Cave of the Winds
https://www.youtube.com/watch?v=9PswYVCU4zo&t=9s

**Page 125 – EVERYBODY WELCOME: THE STORY OF FANNIE MAE DUNCAN AND THE COTTON CLUB**

https://www.youtube.com/watch?v=Sw8twY3auNE

**Page 133 – THE COWBOY WAY**

Sons of the San Joaquin

https://www.youtube.com/watch?v=Gb9R1uXnN_0

Don Edwards Yodeling

https://www.youtube.com/watch?v=N4YZd1037_E

Don Edwards – Cattle Call

https://www.youtube.com/watch?v=guXhfg4-Q-A

Gary McMahan – Clips from the Great Pikes Peak Cowboy Gathering

https://www.youtube.com/watch?v=Hlvs7WcDQrQ&t=380s

Pikes Peak Range Riders – "Ridin Round the Peak."

https://www.youtube.com/watch?v=JGN_p83l1JQ&t=627s

**Page 139 – THE MAN WHO SAVED THE BELL**

Bill Bowers: A Century Remembered

https://www.youtube.com/watch?v=R_LsFZ5Kbp8

**Page 143 – THE FINEST EDUCATOR IN COLORADO**

Cheyenne Mountain School II

https://www.youtube.com/watch?v=xMci9Ed8mwk&t=518s

**Page 147 – NAME DROPPING: SOME NOTABLE PEOPLE I WORKED WITH**

An Evening with Buck O'Neil

https://www.youtube.com/watch?v=WgxrsamGiDw

Clay Jenkinson as Thomas Jefferson videotaped at the Pikes Peak Library District

https://www.youtube.com/watch?v=_OpdolAaljk

James Irwin
A Journey to the Moon with Colonel James Irwin
https://www.youtube.com/watch?v=gLBg2LGMwEY&t=1673s

## Page 151 – KRISTALLNACHT: THE NIGHT OF BROKEN GLASS
https://www.youtube.com/watch?v=fpvXWdGnygk\

## Page 173 – A DETECTIVE STORY
The Henry Sachs Foundation
https://www.youtube.com/watch?v=uxWqU1CPWyQ&t=76s

## Page 177 – THE GREATER BARRIER
The Land of Nowhere

## Page 179 – VETERANS DAY
Triumph and Tragedy: A Pilot's Life through War and Peace: James Fore
https://www.youtube.com/watch?v=8LgkztZ8UDA&t=15s

The Phantom of Ben Het by John Lamerson (MSG)
https://www.youtube.com/watch?v=LyOQJgeZgYY&t=213s

## Page 181 – PAY IT FORWARD
The Myron Stratton Home with John Zorack.
https://www.youtube.com/watch?v=pbHCEiatahA&t=1787s

## Page 185 – THE FAIRY GODMOTHER OF THE ARTS
This is Your Life Mary Mashburn

## Page 188 – THE SHIVERS FOUNDATION
My Life as a Tuskegee Airman
https://www.youtube.com/watch?v=ge2PysShE-Y&t=608s

## Page 193 – CAL OTTO
Rescuing General Jonathan Wainwright with Hal Leith
https://www.youtube.com/watch?v=-ppBjnhb8PY&t=55s

**Page 197 – LIEUTENANT GENERAL ALBERT PATTON CLARK**
The True Story of the Great Escape
https://www.youtube.com/watch?v=a2XR5Rfkp8o

**Page 205 – THE PHOTOGRAPHERS**
Kind Nature's Scenery
https://www.youtube.com/watch?v=JMfHtRZi1g8

**Page 209 – FALLING IN LOVE WITH MABEL BARBEE LEE**
Voices of Cripple Creek
https://www.youtube.com/watch?v=Xl2fmchL7kw&t=299s
The Storytellers of Cripple Creek
https://www.youtube.com/watch?v=fjopomnCYWE

The Treasure of the Cripple Creek Mining District
https://www.youtube.com/watch?v=6co1tQnWMUo

Take a Ride on the Midland
https://www.youtube.com/watch?v=8dVMHOR_Bgl

Current Review 1931
https://www.youtube.com/watch?v=Zp17Z8v543w

The Renaissance Life of Lew Tilley
https://www.youtube.com/watch?v=2DNFfJRih54&t=2459s

The Colorado Springs Public Library 1958
https://www.youtube.com/watch?v=hqQ42EwxWlM&t=72s

**Page 227 – FALLING IN LOVE WITH PUEBLO**
Past as Prologue: Lowell Thomas in 1981

**Page 273 – MY TRIP TO SPAIN WITH  NAIELY**
Sotillo De La Palomas
https://www.youtube.com/watch?v=kyTNpiHO_yc

Canar, Spain
https://www.youtube.com/watch?v=a5WluNhzsYk&t=22s

# BIBLIOGRAPHY

Bradbury, Ray. *Dandelion Wine*. Doubleday, 1957.

Bradbury, Ray. *Fahrenheit 451*. Ballantine Books, 1953.

Clark, Albert. *33 Months as a Pow in Stalag Luft III*. Fulcrum Group. 2005.

D'Aquila, Vincenzo. *Bodyguard Unseen*. New York: Richard R. Smith, 1931.

De Cervantes, Miguel. *Don Quixote*. Francisco De Robles, 1612.

Duncan & Esmiol. *Everybody Welcome: The Story of Fannie Mae Duncan and the Cotton Club*. CHIAROSCURO Press, 2013.

Fore, James. *Triumph and Tragedy: A Pilots life through War and Peace*. Skyward Press, 1996.

Howbert, Irving. *Memories of a Lifetime in the Pike's Peak Region*. The Rio Grande Press, 1925.

Kerouac, Jack. *On The Road*. The Viking Press, 1957.

Lee, Mabel Barbee. *Cripple Creek Days*. Bison Books, 1958.

Lamerson, John. *The Phantom of Ben Het*. Lamerson Publishing, 2001.

Leith, Hal. *POWs of Japanese Rescued! General J. M Wainwright* Fulcrum Group. 2004.

Montgomery, Lucy Maud. *Anne of Green Gables*. L.C. Page & Co., 1906.

Sprague, Marshall. *Money Mountain*. Boston: Little, Brown and Company, 1953.

Toole, John Kennedy. *A Confederacy of Dunces*. Louisiana State University Press, 1980.

Venetucci, Bambi. *Dammi La Mano = Give Me Your Hand*. Friends of the Pikes Peak Library District, 1996.

Villarreal, Jose Antonio. *Pocho*. Anchor Books, 1970.

Waters, Frank. *Midas of the Rockies*. New York: Covici – Freide Publishing, 1937.

Waters, Frank. *The Man Who Killed the Deer*. Chicago: Sage Books, 1942.

Waters, Frank. *People of the Valley*. Chicago: Sage Books, 1941.

# INDEX

*33 Months as a POW in Stalag Luft III* (Clark), 198

*1928 Negro Picnic* (film), 173

**A**

*Adele Obodov: A Time of Remembrance* (film), 152

adolescents, 1–4, 16, 44, 234

African Americans

    *1928 Negro Picnic* (film), 173

    Buffalo Soldiers, 139

    Cotton Club, The, 125–129

    Negro League Baseball, 148–149

    population in Colorado Springs, 128

    Tuskegee Airmen, 189–191

Air Force Academy, 179, 189–191, 197, 203–204

Alexander, Don Miller, 117–123

Alexander, Gertrude, 122–123

Alexander, Julian Don, 117–122, 169p

Alexander Aircraft Industries, 118–120, 145

Alexander Film Company

    historic collection, 173

    Jim Bates and aerial photography, 114–115

    movie advertising and, 109–110

    photo, 169p

    Pikes Peak or Bust Rodeo, 133

    theatrical advertising, 117–122

Alhambra, 279

Alire, Dr. Camila, 63–65

All Pikes Peak Reads, 194

Allen, Debbie, 187

American Joint Distribution Committee, 155

American Library Association, 11, 64

Antonio (Hispanic student), 223

Antonuccio, David, 41–42, 221

Antonuccio, Laura, 267–268

Antonuccio, Lisa, 41–42

Antonuccio, Mark, 25, 41

Antonuccio, Oliver

    children, 41–42

    death from Parkinson's, 221

    distant relationship, 270

    distant relationship with son, 67

    early years, 29–33

    photos, 162–163p

Antonuccio, Rachel, 25–26, 165p, 267–268

Antonuccio, Steven

    book destruction, 241–243

    friendship with Harold, 263–265

    life in Reno, 222–225

    photos, 161p, 164–165p

Apollo 15, 148

Aponte, Jose, 80

archive, 158, 202–203

Arkansas River, 229, 231

Attenborough, Sir Richard, 202

Automated Material Handler (AMH), 252–253

**B**

Barkman Library

    booksecutioner, 255–257

    Dogpatch, 260–261

    learning on the job, 228

    as neighborhood branch, 234–235

    new technologies, 251–252

Steven as manager, 224
visits per year, 231
Bates, Jim
aerial photography, 114–115
combat photographer, 109–116
donated film collection, 157, 173
photos, 168p
Pikes Peak Range Riders and, 133
Bates, Katherine Lee, 94
Bates, Monica, 110, 114
Bell, Mark, 126, 130
Binh, Nyugen, 183–184
Black, Baxter, 135–137
black musicians, 128
Blevins, Tim, 157–158, 194
*Bodyguard Unseen*, 37–39
*Book People, The*, 237–239, 248, 274, 285, 288–289
Boulder, CO, 55–56
Bowers, Bill, 139–141
Bradbury, Ray
*Dandelion Wine*, 10–12, 209, 257
death of, 257
*Fahrenheit 451*, 237, 256–257
failed meeting with this author, 45
library foundation named for, 289
personal inspiration for this author, 10–12
science fiction authors, 10–12
Bragg, Frances, 126–127
Bragg, Ozena, 127–128
Broadmoor Hotel, 104, 271
Broadmoor Hotel (Colorado Springs), 87–91
Bruce, Chief Irvin "Dad," 129–130

Brunell, Erna, 152
Brunell, Walter, 152
Buffalo Soldiers, 139–140
Bushell, Roger, 199, 201–202

**C**

Caler, Sydne, 80
Calvo, Emilia Lozano, 273, 279
Calvo, Eugenio, 9–10, 14–27, 238, 273–274, 277–278
Calvo, Eugenio and Emilia, 160p
Calvo, Soledad "Sally"
death in 2013, 274
failing health, 221–222, 224–225
first grandchild, 25–26
learns English, 19–20
meets Oliver Antonuccio, 9–10, 32–33
photos, 161–162p
Calvo, Tony, 32
Cañar, 274, 279, 279–282
Carnegie, Andrew, 287–289
Carnegie Library, 158, 207, 287
Carpenter, Scott, 145
*Certain Brotherhood, A*, 188
Cheyenne Mountain School (Colorado Springs), 143–146
Cheyenne Mountain Heritage Center, 143, 146
Churchill, Winston, 168p
Ciletti, Jim and Mary, 79
Clarey, Michael, 49
Clark, Albert, 170p
Clark, General Albert, 194, 197–204
Clark, Midori, 231
Cologne, Germany, 154–155
Colorado City, 206

Colorado Department of Corrections, 71–74

Colorado School for the Deaf and Blind, 105, 143

Colorado Springs Pioneers Museum, 125, 173

*Colorado Springs: The Way It Was*, 78, 181

Colorado State Fair (Pueblo), 231

computers
    Barkman Library, 288
    "Maggie's Place," 251
    personal inspiration, 83
    public access catalog, 74
    theft, 98
    young people, 234–235

*Confederacy of Dunces, A* (Toole), 247

conservatism, 55–56

Cooking Club, The, 90

Cotton Club, The, 125–130, 207

*Cowboy Way, The*, 133–135, 137–138

Creed, Louisa, 60–61

*Cripple Creek Days*, 210

Cripple Creek gold rush
    creation of wealth, 194
    Cripple Creek history, 86
    film documentaries on, 209–210
    founding of Pueblo, 229
    William Edward Hook photographs, 206

Current, Ira, 206–207

*Current Review*, 206

**D**

*Dammi La Mano*, 108

*Dandelion Wine*, 10–12, 209, 257

Danny, 248–250

D'Aquila, Oliva, 36–37

D'Aquila, Vincenzo, 36–39

Davis-Witherow, Leah, 173–174

D-Day, 110–111

*De Donde Eres?* 80

Diane, 219

"Dogpatch," 259–260

dogs, destruction of materials by, 241–243

Doman, Dave, 136

Dowlin, Ken, 251

drive-in theater advertising, 121

Duncan, Ed, 127

Duncan, Fannie Mae, 125–131, 171p

Duncan, Renee, 130

Dylan, Bob, 10–12, 213–214

**E**

El Ciello de Cañar (bed and breakfast), 280

El Pomar Foundation, 87–91

*Electronic Library, The*, 251

Ellington, Duke, 128

Emporia State University, 6–7, 74, 82–83

Emrich, Dave, 177

English as a Second Language (ESL), 284, 288–289

Enola, 245–246

Esmiol, Kay, 131, 208

Eva R. Baca Elementary School, 260–261

*Everybody Welcome*, 130–131, 207–208

**F**

*Fahrenheit 451*, 237, 257, 289

*Fairy Godmother of the Arts*, 185, 188

Fassi, Carlo, 91

Federal Express Corporation, 183–184

Feitz, Leland, 118–122

Fernando, 248–250, 283

filmmaking, 48–49

Fine Arts Center (Colorado Springs), 139–140, 185

Fitzmorris, Bob, 79

Fore, James, 180

Frank Waters Award, 188

Frank Waters Foundation, 85

Franklin, Sylvester, 130

Friends of the Library, 238

Friends of the Pikes Peak Library District, 108

*Funky Fairy Tales*, 185–187, 284, 289

**G**

Galena High School Library, 222–224

gangs, 261–262

Garden of the Gods, 126, 178

Giordano, Ralph, 79

Glemnitz, Hermann, 200–201, 204

Glen Eyrie, 59

Goering, Herman, 180

Goetzman, Dave, 7–8

Golden Bee, 271

Gonzalez, Berta, 274

Granada, 279

*Great Escape, The*, 194, 197–202, 204

Great Pikes Peak Cowboy Poetry Gathering, The, 134, 136

*Greater Barrier, The*, 177–178

Greenberg, Dr. David Greenberg, 151

Greenberg, Paulette, 151–152

Greenberg Center for Learning and Tolerance, The, 151–152

Grynszpan, Hershel, 152

**H**

Hague, Michael, 187

Harold, 263–265

Haunted Wind Chimes, The, 138

Hawaii, 14–16, 18, 273, 279

Hayworth, Rita, 13, 32, 161p

Heller, Larry and Dorothy, 109

*Her Furious Angels* (song), 215

High Flight Foundation, 148

Hispanic, 80, 232, 234, 259–261

Hitler, Adolph, 152, 180, 202

Holocaust, 151, 154–155

Hook, William Edward, 206

Hopkins, Mike, 93–96

Hopkins, Steve, 93–95

Howbert, Irving, 205–206

Hughes, David, 206

Hutchinson, Andy and Regina, 173

**I**

Idleman, Paul, 205–207

Imagination Celebration, The, 185, 187–188

Irwin, Jim, 148

Italian-Americans, 102–103

**J**

*Jails, Institution or Death*, 73

Jenkins, Andy, 268

Jenkinson, Clay, 149

JNS Communications, 52–53

**K**

Kallaus, Don, 138

*Kind Nature's Scenery to Portray*, 206

Klibansky, Erich, 153–154

**L**

*Land of Nowhere, The*, 178
lawyers, 267–268
Lee, Honest John Barbee, 210
Lee, Mabel Barbee, 171p, 209–211
Leith, Hal, 194–195
librarians
　branch manager, 233–235, 247–248
　high school, 3–4
　occupational hazard, 245–246
　profession, 5–9, 64, 83
　technology, 251–253
　training, 5–8
libraries
　branches, 233–235, 247
　director, 193
　downtown, 91
　educational, 68
　high school, 222–223
　library science, 5–8, 74
　local history, 157–158
　property, 241–243
　as sanctuary, 282–285
　science, 82–83
　security, 97–99
　staff, 6
　technology, 251–253
　teen customers, 1–4, 248–250
　theft, 97–99
　volunteers, 217–219
　weeding, 255–257
Library Channel, The, 77–79, 149, 152, 177–178, 188
*Life and Good Times of Marshall Sprague, The*, 86
Little London, 57–61, 228

*Living with the Law*, 213
Logie, Diane, 261–262
Losinski, Pat, 157–158, 219
Lozano, Emilia Encarnation, 18–19, 160p
Lozano, Manuel and Soledad, 18–19, 273, 279
Lucero, Bill, 260
Lucero, Patrick A., 170p, 260–262

**M**
Madrid, 276
*Making of Pepito's Story, The*, 187
*Man Who Killed the Deer, The*, 85
Manitou Springs, 206, 287
Margolis, Bernie, 134, 138
Marold, Richard, 143–144
Mashburn, Mary, 185, 187–188
Mathews, Dave, 214
McKee, Chris, 268
McMahan, Gary, 135–137
*Memories of a Lifetime in the Pikes Peak Region*, 205
Mexican-Americans, 229
*Midas of the Rockies*, 85, 182, 210
*Mike's Peak*, 93, 96
Mitchell, Joni, 213
Mitchell, Waddie, 135
Mobley, Ree, 86, 126
*Money Mountain*, 86, 182
mortar and pestle, 281
Myron Stratton Home, 144, 181–183

**N**
Native Americans, 36, 79, 85, 177, 206
Neff, Jane and Bob, 152, 174

Negro League Baseball, 148–149

**O**

Obodov, Adele, 151–156
Obodov, Janet, 155
Obodov, Joel, 155
Obodov, Judith, 155
Obodov, Karl, 154–155
Obodov, Morris (Morey), 155
Old Colorado City, 205–206, 287
O'Malley, Scott, 137
O'Neil, Buck, 148
Otto, Cal, 158, 193–195, 197
*Outlaws of the New West*, 72

**P**

Palmer, General William Jackson, 57–61,
78, 105, 167p, 228–229
Palmer, Queen Mellen, 58–59, 167p
Palmer Lake, 147
Patrick A. Lucero Library, 261–262
Patton, General George, 203
Penrose, Julie (Veniers), 88–91
Penrose, Spencer, 87–91
*Penrose House Conference Center*, 89–90
Penrose Library, 158, 287
*People of the Valley, The*, 85
Phelps, Kelly Joe, 215–216
photographers, 78, 94, 110–112, 138–141
Pikes Peak, 55, 94–96
Pikes Peak Community College, 53, 56,
63–65, 67, 70, 73
Pikes Peak History Symposium, 158, 194–195
Pikes Peak Library District
    El Pomar Foundation support, 91

historic photographs and films, 77
Library Channel, The, 77
Pikes Peak History Symposium, 194–195
scholarships, 82
special collection, 178
video portraits, 11, 73–74, 193
Pikes Peak or Bust Rodeo, 133
Pikes Peak Range Riders, 133
Pikes Peak Writers Conference, The,
187–188
*POW's of Japanese Rescued!* 195
Prince Harry, Duke of Sussex, 218–219
Pro Rodeo Hall of Fame and Museum of
the American Cowboy, 133–134
Professional Bull Riders Association, 134,
231
Pueblo
    Arkansas River, 229, 232
    blue-collar town, 227–229
    Colorado gold rush, 229
    Colorado State Fair, 134, 231
    Dogpatch, 259–260
    libraries, 230–231
    Patrick A. Lucero Library, 260–262
    population, 234
    Rawlings Family, 230
    steel mill, 228–229
*Pueblo Chieftain, The*, 230
Pueblo City-County Library District
    Patrick A. Lucero Library, 260–262
    weeding, 255–257
Pueblo City-County Library District awards,
231
Pueblo Reservoir, 269–271
Pueblo West Branch Library, 1–4, 6

## R

Radio Frequency Identification (RFID), 231, 252–253
Rawlings, Jane, 230
Rawlings, Robert, 230
Redford, Robert, 48–49
Rick, 270–271
*Right Stuff, The*, 147

## S

Sachs, Henry, 174–175
Sachs Foundation, 174
Salazar, Rachel, 3
Sciezka, Jon, 186
segregation, 128
*Shape Up*, 73
Shaw, Dr. Lloyd "Pappy," 143–146, 167p
shelvers, 255
Shivers, Clarence, 189–191
Shivers, Peggy, 189–190
Shivers, Sky, 136
Shivers Foundation, 189–190
Smyer, Naiely, 274–282
Smyer, Wayne, 274
Sotillo De Las Palmas, 14, 274, 276–277, 279–281
Spain, 14–19, 229, 273–282
Spanish (language), 273–275
Spanish Civil War, 276–277
Spanish-American War, 279
Spears, John, 80
Spencer, Richard, 134–135
Sprague, Edna Jane "E.J.," 86
Sprague, Marshall, 85–86, 167p, 182, 183
Stalag Luft III

Air Force Academy Library, 204
Albert Patton Clark imprisonment, 194
*The Great Escape Movie*, 197–202
James Fore imprisonment, 180
photo, 170p
Storytime, 2–3, 284, 289
Stratton, Winfield Scott, 181–184, 194
Summer Reading Program, 284, 289

## T

Tabor, Elizabeth "Baby Doe," 178
Tabor, Horace, 178
Tabor, Rosemary "Silver," 178
*Take a Ride on the Midland*, 206
Talavera de la Rena, 276–277
Tarabino, Joe, 178
teenagers, 16, 44, 234
television advertising, 121
Thayer, Otis, 177
theatrical advertising, 117–122
Thomas, Lowell, 204, 209–211, 227, 232
*Thomas Jefferson Hour, The*, 149
Tilley, Lew, 205
Toole, John Kennedy, 247
*Tragedy and Triumph: a pilot's life through war and peace*, 180
Tuskegee Airmen, 189–191
Tutt, Charles Leaming III, 88–91
Tutt, Charles Leaming Sr., 87–91
Tutt, Russell Thayer, 88, 91
Tutt, William Thayer, 88
*Tutt Legacy, The*, 89

## U

Uncle Victor, 190

University of Colorado, 47–49

*U.S. Arizona* historic bell, 140, 207

Ute Indians, 144, 229, 232

## V

Venetucci, Bambi, 143

Venetucci, Nic and Bambi, 101–108, 131

Venetucci Farm, 101–108

video links, 291–296

video portraits, 193

*Vietnam Passage: Journey from War to Peace*, 183

Villareal, Jose Antonio, 21

Von Lindemier, Col. Freidrich, 200–201

Von Rath, Ernst, 152

## W

Wainwright, Jonathan, 194–195

Walker, Jon, 231, 253

Waters, Frank, 85–86, 182, 210

Wendelken, Ben, 89

*Western Horseman* (magazine), 134

Western Jubilee Warehouse, 137–138

Whitley, Christopher Becker, 213–216

Whitley, Trixie, 215

## Z

Zahradniik, Rick, 79

Zlochower, Sol, 67–75, 131

Zorack, John, 181–184